HOLD ON TIGHT
London Transport and the Unions

Martin Eady

Capital Transport

ACKNOWLEDGEMENTS
Thanks especially to my wife Monika Eady for her constant support and help, putting up with piles of paper and books on the kitchen table and mediating between me and the computer on innumerable occasions. Also to the following for help and encouragement:
Laurie Akehurst
Janine Booth
Sarah Boston
Mick Brooks
Chris Coates
The late Bob Crow
Rex Faulks
Bob Fryer
Sally Groves
Steve Harper
Sir Peter Hendy
Barbara Humphries
Ed Humphreys
Barry Le Jeune
Colin Kelly
David Knights – Acton Historical Society
Olly New
Adrian Nicholes
Ben Schlegel
Craig Stewart
Billy Taylor
Bill Teale
Tamara Thornhill
Caroline Warhurst
Dave Welsh
Doug Wright
The Working Class Museum Library, Salford

First published 2016

Published by Capital Transport Publishing Ltd
www.capitaltransport.com

Printed by Parksons Graphics

CONTENTS

ABBREVIATIONS

AAT(VW)	Amalgamated Association of Tram (and Vehicle Workers)
ACAS	Advisory Conciliation and Arbitration Service
AEEU	Amalgamated Electrical and Engineering Union
AEF	Amalgamated Engineering and Foundry Workers Union
AEU	Amalgamated Engineering Union
ASLE&F	Associated Society of Locomotive Engineers and Firemen
ASRS	Amalgamated Society of Railway Servants
ASTMS	Association of Scientific, Technical and Managerial Staffs
ATO	Automatic Train Operation
AUEW	Amalgamated Union of Engineering Workers
BEL	Bus Engineering Limited
BR(B)	British Railways (Board)
BTC	British Transport Commission
CLR	Central London Railway
CNC	Central Negotiating Committee
C&SLR	City and South London Railway
CGOL	Compagnie General des Omnibus de Londres
CBI	Confederation of British Industry
CSEU	Confederation of Shipbuilding and Engineering Unions
DEP	Department of Employment and Productivity
DLR	Docklands Light Railway
EC	Executive Committee
EDF	Electricite de France
EETPU	Electrical, Electronic, Telecommunications and Plumbing Union
ESI	Electrical Supply Industry
EU	European Union
GLA	Greater London Authority
GLC	Greater London Council
GRWU	General Railway Workers Union
GS	General Secretary
H&SE	Health and Safety Executive
ICI	Imperial Chemical Industries
Infraco	Infrastructure Company
JNC	Joint Negotiating Committee
LBSCR	London Brighton and South Coast Railway
LBL	London Buses Limited
LCC	London County Council
LER	London Electric Railway
LGOC	London General Omnibus Company
LPTB	London Passenger Transport Board
LPU (L&P)	London and Provincial Union of Licensed vehicle Workers
LRCC	London Road Car Company
LRT	London Regional Transport
LSWR	London and South Western Railway
LTB	London Transport Board
LTE	London Transport Executive
LUL	London Underground Limited
LUT	London United Tramways
LVT Record	Licensed Vehicle Trades Record (Union Journal)
MET	Metropolitan Electric Tramways
NBC	National Bus Company
NHS	National Health Service
NJIC	National Joint Industry Council
NPWU	National Passenger Workers Union
NUR	National Union of Railwaymen
NUVB	National Union of Vehicle Builders
NACH	Notional Accumulated Customer Hours
Opsco	Operations Company
PFI	Private Finance Initiative
PPP	Public Private Partnership
PSBR	Public Sector Borrowing Requirement
RCA	Railway Clerks Association
RMT	(National Union of) Rail Maritime and Transport Workers
RNC	Railway Negotiating Committee
SC3	Sectional Council No3
TfL	Transport for London
TUC	Trades Union Congress
TUPE	Transfer of Undertakings Protection of Employment regulations
TOT	Trains Omnibuses Trams
T/Op	Train Operator
T&GWU	Transport and General Workers Union
TWF	Transport Workers Federation
UERL	Underground Electric Railways of London company
UTS	Underground Ticketing System
UPSS	United Pointsmen's and Signalmen's Society
UVW	United Vehicle Workers Union

Left Guard gives the 'right away' at Earl's Court, car No.8222, 1935

FOREWORD by Christian Wolmar

And what about the workers? The public admiration for the London Underground and the capital's bus network often focusses on the engineering challenges that have been overcome to create one of the world's best public transport systems.

However, the system would not function at all without the workforce of tens of thousands that has kept London's transport system running. The story of the creation of the network is itself fascinating. London was a pioneer in so many ways, from having the first metro system in 1863 to the creation of the astonishingly wide ranging London Transport seventy years later, and that legacy has left the capital with a public transport system that was the envy of many other cities in the world. While political shenanigans, a lack of vision and a failure to recognise the importance of continuous investment mean that there has been a relative decline in the system's fortunes, London's transport network still betters many others in the developed world. You only have to talk to the admiring tourists who soon become practiced users of their Oyster cards to recognise that.

As this book shows, the staff, like the system itself, have often not had the recognition they deserve. Transport often attracts workers with the ideal sort of temperament – steady, efficient, prepared to carry out repetitive tasks but ever ready to deal with unexpected events. It is imperative, among most of them, to keep the show on the road, though again this spirit has been dissipated somewhat by the emphasis on a strict interpretation of health and safety rules.

As this book shows in great detail, the story of the industrial relations of London transport is a chequered one. It took a long time even for the most basic rights to be recognised – even going to a funeral of a colleague killed on duty at one point led to suspension - but thanks to their ability to bring the transport system a halt, the workers gradually acquired rights and better working conditions.

Nothing came easily. Strikes and lock outs were the frequent results of disputes and managements were often remarkably obdurate. The workers on the underground have traditionally organised more effectively than on the buses, possibly because their skills are less easy to replace quickly whereas alternative drivers and conductors could be found more easily. That did not stop several major bus strikes being successfully organised over the years.

This, then, is the detailed story of an often under appreciated workforce. This history is important and many workers on the system today understand it. Their forebears had to fight for every bit of improvement and they are loath to relinquish any of their conditions. Privatisation of the bus network has undoubtedly weakened the position of its workforce. However, as the author points out, there is little evidence that privatisation has made the system more efficient, as its supporters argue, and indeed the bus network, though highly successful and well patronised, is now more dependent on subsidy than ever before.

The notion, promulgated by the Boris Johnson administration, that there could be driverless trains – and even possibly buses – is a myth. And while there will still be the need for labour, industrial relations troubles on the Tube and the buses will continue because of continued pressure to rein back hard fought rights and conditions.

Left Horse bus driver 'cast iron Billy' in top hat and conductor in bowler, 1877

SETTING THE SCENE

The process of labour relations goes on for the most part unobtrusively with the personnel officers (now called Human Relations) and their Trade Union counterparts quietly dealing with the day to day problems that arise in any large organisation. But when big issues come up conflict can and often does find expression in industrial unrest and strikes. Most Human Relations people and Trade Union leaders regard strikes as a failure of the negotiating process, and at the end of a dispute there are usually talks leading to a negotiated settlement. So this book is not intended to be a catalogue of strikes on London Transport and its predecessors, but strikes are markers of periods of change and so inevitably they do figure quite prominently.

The late Eric Hobsbawm in his useful book Labour's Turning Point 1880-1900 notes that "The impetus of the New Unionism of the 1880's could not be maintained ... it was only the next great labour upheaval of 1910-14 which made the new Unions – railway, transport etc – into the key force which we know today".

The great reforming Liberal government of 1906 opened a period of tumultuous political and industrial struggles that continued until the defeat of the general strike in 1926. Workers in the companies that were to form London Transport were not immune from these battles which intertwined with their own particular issues as transport workers. But workers on the buses and railways adopted very different organisational forms and it is this contrast which is interesting to explore.

London Transport came into being with the formation of the London Passenger Transport Board (LPTB) in 1933, which co-ordinated all public transport in London under a common management. But from 1914 the Underground Group (known as the Combine) had come to own nearly all the bus and tram companies and underground railways, the main exceptions being the Metropolitan Railway and the various municipal tramways. With a common management, the question is posed as to why the Trade Unions on road transport and trains remained separate and in fact did not even have a co-ordinating structure. There has never been a joint negotiating body including both buses and railways, except for staff who work at Head Office (55 Broadway). They seem to have been regarded as part of the railway for negotiating purposes prior to the establishment of Transport for London (TfL) as the overall umbrella body.

The explanation must be sought in the very different histories and backgrounds of the railways and buses and how this has been reflected in negotiating structures and Trade Unions.

Due largely to their position as part of a national industrial context with powerful centralised companies the Underground workers became part of a Staff Councils scheme, which has received little attention from historians. I spend some time examining how and why this came about, the failure of the first scheme of 1907 and the success of the 1921 scheme, which ensured with few exceptions industrial peace until its abolition as late as 1993.

The history of the bus workers is very different. In horse bus days they did not really see themselves as part of the working class. With the widespread introduction of motor buses from 1910 this changed rapidly and fundamentally.

The story which unfolds shows how staff and management related to each other and how they responded to the challenges they faced. It is about the people, not one side or the other. Although I was a Trade Union representative for 35 years I have tried to take an even-handed approach to showing how labour relations developed and changed.

Several themes emerge – the contrast between the Unions on the buses and Underground and their negotiating processes, the rise to predominance and subsequent decline of the bus side, the often overlooked contribution of the municipal tram staff, the change in management style from the dictatorial railway companies via the paternalism of the Combine and LPTB to the aggressive confrontational methods brought in from the 1980's.

The terminology used in times gone by referred to workers or staff as 'men', chairperson as chairman, etc, regardless of the fact that many of the people concerned were women. This looks strange to us now, but I have left these references as they are in the original documents as they are themselves part of the history and are not intended to be offensive in any way. Prior to decimalisation in 1971 the currency was denominated as Pounds, Shillings and Pence (LSD). There were 20 shillings to a pound and 12 pence to a shilling. One pound ten shillings and sixpence would be shown as 1/10/6, or sometimes 30/6 and I have used these conventions for the period up to Feb 1971.

City & South London Railway staff with electric loco and coach, 1894

THE FORMATION OF THE COMBINE

Horse tram with staff, 1879

London's public transport did not start life as the single entity we see today but as a series of separate companies. The Metropolitan Railway was the first, opening on 10th January 1863. In its early years the Metropolitan had financial support from the Great Western and joint running arrangements with the Great Northern and Midland companies as well as the Western, although it remained an independent company right up to the formation of the LPTB in 1933. The Metropolitan was also instrumental in the formation of the Metropolitan District railway, the first section of which opened on 1st October 1868. The District remained a separate company until absorbed by Charles Tyson Yerkes' Underground Group through a complex series of financial measures starting in 1901. The first deep tube, the City and South London Railway, was an independent company from its opening in December 1890 until coming under Yerkes' control in 1912 as part of the construction of what eventually became the Northern Line. The Central London Railway too was independent from its opening on 27th June 1900 until its takeover by Yerkes' ubiquitous Underground Electric Railways of London (UERL) Company on 1st January 1913. The Bakerloo and Piccadilly tubes were built directly by the UERL in a flurry of activity between 1906 and 1907. The London Electric Railway Company (LER) as a unified concern was formed on 26th July 1910. So it is not surprising that in the early years the various companies, and the LER after 1910, were seen as no different from the main line railway companies, of which there were about 120. This did not change until the formation of the LPTB in 1933.

The London United Tramways Company had been formed in 1894 to bring together the various horse tramways in West London. It came under Yerkes' control in 1901 and was to be the pioneer of electric tramways in London. The London General Omnibus Company (LGOC) was acquired by the Underground Group in February 1912. All the other private bus companies with the exception of Tillings, with whom the LGOC had running agreements, were bought up in 1912/13. The Metropolitan Electric Tramways Company, lessee of Middlesex County Council, was acquired in November 1912.

So by the outbreak of war in 1914 almost all the buses, the Underground apart from the Metropolitan, and the tramways with the important exception of the London County Council (LCC) and other municipal operators, came under a common management. Yet there were no moves to unify labour relations either from the management or the Unions. When the Tillings buses and a few other small companies were absorbed with the formation of the LPTB in 1933 they were rapidly included in the existing structures, including the negotiating bodies. Tillings and other country area operators were merged to form the Country Bus section. The municipal and company tramways came together in the Tram and Trolleybus section, while the Central Bus Committee continued to conduct labour relations in its area. The Metropolitan was included in a unified Staff Councils scheme, yet the railways as a whole remained, and still remain, separate from the buses as a whole, with different Unions, other than the Railway Clerks Association (RCA). Although initially limited to the railways, the RCA gradually expanded to cover clerical and supervisory staff on the buses, becoming the Transport Salaried Staffs Association in 1951, but did not see its role as operating jointly over the rail/bus divide other than at Head Office as previously noted.

CHAPTER TWO

EARLY YEARS ON THE RAILWAYS

Metropolitan 'G' class loco No 95 Robert H Selbie, 0-6-4T with staff, 1916

Queens Park signal cabin, 1920

A leading railway company director said in 1893 "You might as well have trade unionism in Her Majesty's Army as have it in the railway service. The thing is totally incompatible".[1]

The need for skilled and reliable staff led to above average wages for traincrew in the early years. For example, in the 1840's engine drivers got up to 45/- per week (equivalent to £265 in 2014 money), firemen up to 35/-, signalmen 22/-, porters 18/7, while turners in Manchester got 26/- to 33/-, cotton operatives 19/- and agricultural labourers 11/6 in the North but only 8/5 in the South.

Loyalty was ensured through strict discipline enforced by fines and bonuses for good conduct. Taking part in a strike could lead to loss of a railway cottage. For instance, in May 1871 engine drivers on the London and North Western railway were evicted from company owned houses in Camden Town. John Fardon on the Stockton and Darlington was fined 5/- on January 15th 1830 "for furiously driving whilst coming down the run". Magistrates might be brought in in serious cases. Porters were fined for taking tips from passengers.

The first strike on record occurred on the Liverpool and Manchester in February 1836. A number of firemen gave notice of their intention to strike. One John Hewitt was instantly discharged and most of the other drivers and firemen struck in his support. Four of them were hauled before the magistrates who found them guilty of breach of contract and sentenced them to a month's hard labour in Kirkdale prison where they had to work the treadmill for six hours a day.

Safety
Concerned with the welfare of the travelling public (not the railway workers), the medical journal the Lancet appointed a special commission which found the main danger came from the exhaustion and fatigue of workers forced to work fifteen hours a day and undertake fresh duties without sufficient time for sleep or rest.[2] Unions began to be formed, firstly on a local basis but increasingly widely across the country. Railway Clerks began to organise as early as 1865. A conference of delegates from every important railway in England in November 1866 agreed a national programme of demands, including a ten hour day, payment for overtime, time and a half for Sundays and increases in pay. Strikes on a localised or sectional basis met with mixed success because when each grade acted separately they could be defeated piecemeal by other grades being enlisted. This lesson was learned for the next round of claims in December 1871 when an all grades union was organised – the Amalgamated Society of Railway Servants (ASRS – note the terminology used).

Taff Vale Judgement
Arising from a strike on the Taff Vale railway in 1900, this judgement in 1901 decreed that a Union could be sued for damages arising from a strike. The ASRS had to pay the company £23,000 plus costs, a total of £42,000.[3] This judgement was not reversed until the Trade Disputes Act of 1906. Between 1901 and 1906 railway rates of pay fell below those of any other industry (Board of Trade survey 1906-7). From 1886 to 1905 railway rates of pay rose 5% compared with 18% in building, 23% in cotton and 26% in engineering, yet productivity rose rapidly as larger engines could pull heavier trains but meant firemen had to shovel twice the weight of coal.[4]

Office staff at Ealing Common Depot, District Railway, 1905

All grades movement of 1906-7

An all grades programme was agreed by a series of conferences of the ASRS in Birmingham, Glasgow and Dublin. It demanded that eight hours constitute the standard day for drivers, firemen, guards, shunters, signalmen and platelayers, and that ten hours should be the maximum working day for all other classes of railwaymen. Also that no man should be called upon to book on more than once for each day's work and no man should be called out for duty with less than nine hours' rest (this last was not conceded where I worked as a Carriage Examiner on the District Line until the mid 1970's). They also asked for an overtime rate of time and a half (currently time and a quarter on London Underground), and a minimum of time and a quarter for Sundays with Xmas day and Good Friday being regarded as Sundays. Also that independent of Sundays a week's wages would be guaranteed to all men. An immediate advance of 2/- a week for all grades and a London Allowance of 3/- a week was claimed. But most important of all was the demand for Union recognition: "The time has arrived when the members of the ASRS insist on the recognition of Mr Bell (ASRS General Secretary) and other head office officials by the railway companies to negotiate on their behalf, and further that we do not enter into negotiations with any company in connection with this programme without full recognition".[5]

The context for these demands was a revival of trade and an increase in railway productivity. Railway company profits were healthy with large dividends being paid. A reputable financial journal was quoted at the 1907 Royal Commission as saying "The companies can meet the wishes of those men who are performing harder and better work than hitherto and can remove the discontent which the men feel. The cost of doing so is relatively small and the additional sum can easily be provided out of increased earnings".[6] With a frustrated membership clamouring for action the field was clear for industrial action. On 12th May 1907 an estimated 150,000 railway workers took part in processions and meetings. Support was pledged by A.G.Walkden of the Railway Clerks Association (RCA) and Tom Lowth of the General Railway Workers Union (GRWU).Yet it was not until October 1907 that a strike ballot was organised. Months were spent in fruitless appeals by ASRS officials for the railway companies to negotiate, which they steadfastly refused to do. This approach of railway union officials counterposing negotiations to industrial action instead of seeing them as complementary was to be repeated many times in the years to come; it did not begin to change in the ASRS/NUR (National Union of Railwaymen) until the election of Jimmy Knapp as General Secretary in 1982 in response to increasingly aggressive management tactics.

When the strike ballot was finally taken it resulted in 76,925 voting yes and 8,773 no out of a total ASRS membership of 97,631 (a minority of railway staff at the time). GRWU members voted 3,025 for and only 84 against. A letter from President of the Board of Trade Lloyd George inviting the Executive Committee (EC) of the ASRS, its President and General Secretary to a meeting on 6th November caused the EC to defer a decision on strike action. It is noteworthy that the Government was so concerned as to get involved at this early juncture. Bagwell notes that Lloyd George worked with the greatest energy to achieve a peaceful settlement as he was aware that the failure of Postmaster General Lord Stanley to compromise with the Postal Association and Post Office Trade Union in 1906 had led to the recognition of the Unions by the Post office in 1906 following the change of Government from Conservative to Liberal.[7] The question arises, why was this insight lost on ASRS General Secretary Richard Bell and his fellow officials? Bagwell also notes that Richard Bell confessed to Mr G.E.Askwith, assistant secretary of the Railway Department of the Board of Trade, that "he was not going to press for recognition if he obtained a satisfactory method of dealing with grievances, consideration of the programme and more opportunity for the men to deal with the condition of their lives".[8] It is never a good idea to tell the other side in negotiations what your bottom line is. This goes to the heart of the question. Recognition of the Union was the crucial demand of the campaigns in many industries at this time (for instance recognition of the National Transport Workers Federation (TWF) following the 1912 Dock strike).

Other Conciliation schemes.
The Government made proposals for the establishment of a permanent Joint Board for the Docks industry, comprising Unions and employers, with sectional boards for each separate trade, modelled on the Brookland Agreement in the Cotton industry. The TWF were seeking stable, enforceable collective bargaining agreements not industrial warfare. Their formula, as Ken Coates notes, neatly prefigures collective bargaining machinery, Whitleyism, and the future Joint Industrial Council of

the Docks industry itself. But Lord Devonport, chairman of the Port of London Authority, would have nothing to do with the officials of the TWF, describing the eminently reasonable Union proposals as a "Provocative impertinence". Even a House of Commons resolution suggesting that a meeting between the protagonists would be "expedient" was rebuffed by the employers, as was a proposal by the Bishops of London and Southwark for "some arbitrator". Tellingly, they rejected Lloyd George's "cajolery" which proved so effective with the recalcitrant railway employers. So conciliators were marginalised. The 1912 Docks strike was defeated with differences between the various unions in the Federation growing and members leaving in their thousands. In particular, the conflict between dockers (who unload ships) and stevedores (who load them, a highly skilled job), continued for generations until overtaken by containerisation. Coates notes that workers on the railways, the mines and engineering had all achieved deliberate and coherent national actions by this date. The failure of the 1912 Docks strike was put down to lack of a National programme covering all ports, not just London, and a large number of separate unions (at least seven in London and five in Liverpool for instance). Dockers leader Ben Tillett, who had called for pickets to be armed against intervention by the Army, noting the inability of Government or Parliament to prevail on the Docks employers to conform to acceptable collective bargaining norms, said "The conciliation Act was inoperative, the elaborate panels were useless, the legal contracts were ruthlessly thrown over".[9]

This puts the Railway dispute into context and goes some way to explain Union officialdom's attachment to the idea of a Conciliation scheme if only the management could be made to support one. ASRS officials clearly did not see a strike as establishing a strong negotiating position, but rather thought it would inhibit efforts to seek a partnership with the railway company directors. In light of the years spent unsuccessfully trying to get recalcitrant directors to the negotiating table this may seem a little naïve, but it would represent recognition of the officials and their status if not of their union itself.

The Conciliation scheme of 1907
The strike did not happen, but the attempt to establish the Conciliation scheme in 1907 did not proceed smoothly. A report of the British Association for the Advancement of Science in 1909 entitled "Railways and the State" says that when presented with the scheme (which had already been agreed by the representatives of the railway companies) the Union negotiators were given twenty minutes to decide whether to accept the agreement or take responsibility for rejecting it and call a general strike on the railway system. When the ASRS asked for time to consult their membership they were told the decision must be taken there and then, without even consulting their executive.[10] The Associated Society of Locomotive Engineers and Firemen (ASLE&F) had previously dissociated themselves from any possibility of a strike, which may have been a factor in the ASRS representatives accepting the scheme. When the issues are posed this starkly Union officials will usually go for talks even if they know their membership are looking for industrial action to further their interests. Although some railway company chairmen rejected it the majority were happy that they had succeeded in preventing recognition of the Unions. The Times newspaper said "The basis of the scheme agreed to is entirely in accordance with the companies'

expressed views as to the best means of dealing with their employees ie by direct representation by the men concerned (note – as opposed to through their unions) – and that being so, they can well afford to concede to the other side some minor points in the formulation of the scheme for carrying that principle into effect".[11]

It was presented as a brilliant compromise imposed on both directors and union officials by a determined and public spirited President of the Board of Trade (Lloyd George).[12] Lord Claud Hamilton, Chairman of the Railway Companies Association, claimed that "The Union, of course, is not recognised in any way". Mr Beasley, General Manager the Taff Vale Railway said "My company accepted the scheme as an alternative to recognition". Only full time employees of the companies were permitted to represent labour on the sectional and central conciliation boards, excluding Union officials. Clearly, local representatives would welcome the status and elevation this gave them, not to mention time away from their jobs. The irony was that a scheme agreed to by full time officials which their members were not too happy with actually reduced the power and involvement of those same officials. The scheme also contained a commitment from the Unions not to strike for seven years and to refrain from campaigning for recognition for the same period of time. This would prove difficult for them to deliver as it represented an impossible and disingenuous commitment to police their own members. ASRS General Secretary Richard Bell stated in Reynolds News "The machinery is not as perfect as I would wish ... but if properly used by our members a good deal can be obtained through it". Although there was considerable opposition and some resentment 76 branches wrote to the General Secretary expressing approval. The scheme may have been conciliation in name but it was anything but conciliatory in spirit. It had been designed to ensure a strike free period of seven years yet was dead and buried by the great 1911 strike.

The railway company directors had only signed on the negative grounds that it guaranteed that they would not have to recognise the Unions, and after much pressure from Lloyd George. In the ASRS General Secretary Richard Bell had been convinced of the merits of the scheme but had felt obliged to resign in 1909. His successor J.E.Williams and Assistant General Secretary J.H.Thomas did not share his enthusiasm, and neither did GRWU General Secretary T. Lowth.[13] But the scheme was given a trial and in the elections to the Sectional and Central Boards the Unions secured 233,793 votes out of a total of 341,904 votes cast.[14] This was more than their total membership (the ASRS had 97,561 members in 1907, the GRWU more than 20,000), so it was clear that many non-members had voted for Union candidates. 694 ASRS candidates were elected for the total of 860 seats on the Sectional Boards. On Lord Claud Hamilton's Great Eastern Railway the ASRS gained 17 seats and the ASLE&F 6, with 9 going to others. On the Midland Railway the ASRS gained 55 of the 60 seats, and on the London and North Western 58 of 64 seats. In England & Wales the Unions gained 93% of the votes, in Scotland 81% and in Ireland 89% (ASRS General Secretary's report 1908). Representatives disliked the Sectional Boards for the interminable delays and obfuscations the management caused. For instance, management would insist on a petition signed by a large number of staff before an item could be placed before the Conciliation Board. On the Great Eastern Railway company officials even organised a counter petition stating that the signatories are perfectly satisfied with their situation.[15]

A most unsatisfactory affair

Writing in 1948, noted historian G.D.H.Cole observed "The new conciliation boards were elected without the Union having any recognised part in their choice.... The scheme was a most unsatisfactory affair ... Officials of the Unions were totally excluded ... It was so devised as to interpose long delays in the way of getting grievances remedied"[16]

But the new Councils did provide a training ground for local representatives and a platform from which they could put forward union policy. Many of the non-Union representatives soon joined the Union.[17] Non-Union candidates were given free passes, time off and other assistance by company officials. On 25th March 1908 a letter to the Locomotive Department Sectional Board secretary on the Great Western from the Loco Superintendent Mr G.S.Churchward stated "If you and those you represent are not satisfied with the conditions in my department I shall be pleased to receive your notices". And the General Manager of the Great Eastern told a deputation on 8th Nov 1909 that "The time has come when we must put a stop to dissatisfaction and agitation, and if we find men going round the line creating dissatisfaction I shall have only one duty, a painful duty, and that is to ask him to resign". (Quoted by J.H.Thomas at the 1911 Royal Commission). In most cases no agreement was reached until an arbitrator had been appointed and by the end of 1909 it was apparent that there had been no major improvement in pay and conditions. ASRS General Secretary J.E.Williams told the Royal Commission "Taken as a whole the application of the awards had left a large number of men a great deal worse off than they were before they went to arbitration", and he did not think the Unions' £30,000 contribution to the expenses of the scheme was worth it. Even Richard Bell had to admit in his 1909 Annual Report that "It cannot be said that any of the awards contain anything approaching the full demands of the programme".[18]

Even when the arbitrators made awards the companies found ways of manipulating and delaying their implementation, to the workers' disadvantage. A favourite dodge was to regrade staff to avoid implementing an award. For instance, on the Midland, goods loaders were displaced by lower paid goods porters. Numbertakers, awarded a 54 hour week by the arbitrator, were renamed sidings porters who were required to work a 12 hour day. At Leicester in July 1910 head shunters were regraded as train receivers and their hours raised from 8 to 10 a day. At Burton on Trent 170 grain porters working a 60 hour week for 18/- were awarded a 54 hour week without loss of pay. The company called this excessive and sent the permanent men to other stations, replacing them with temporary men outside the competence of the Conciliation scheme and paid only 16/11 a week. So prevalent was this practice that ASRS General Secretary J.E.Williams believed that an arrangement had been made by the companies to act concertedly "to interpret the awards in minimal fashion and to claim the exclusive right of their interpretation". There were disputes on the North British, North Staffs, Caledonian, Great Northern, Great Eastern and Midland railways over implementation of the arbitrators' awards. For instance, an award had been made for the Midland on 1st April 1909. But not until July 1911 did the company agree to the resubmission of disputed points to the arbitrator, who then gave a decision that the company had acted contrary to the spirit of the award and that the men should now be paid the 2/- a week he had originally awarded together with two years arrears.

Yet agreements were binding for four years in most cases with no opportunity for further improvements at a time when the cost of living was rising and company profits were increasing. Dividends on the Great Western rose from 3.5% to 4%, the Midland from 4.25% to 5% and others similarly from 1910 to 1911 while the average weekly wage at the end of 1910 was 25/9 – a penny less than in 1906. This is equivalent to £132.93 in 2014 terms, when the average wage was approximately £500 per week.[19]

More powerful locomotives and larger wagons enabled the London & North Western General Manager H.A.Walker to claim increased loading of something like 33% (Royal Commission). ASRS Assistant General Secretary J.H.Thomas told the 1911 Annual General Meeting of the ASRS that as a result of such changes there were 6,000 fewer engineers and firemen than in 1901 despite a million tons more freight traffic being handled and millions more passengers being carried.[20] But the Conciliation scheme gave the workers no influence over these changes. A delegate meeting at Stratford on 8th August 1910 formed an all-grades protest committee of Great Eastern railway employees to organise propaganda meetings throughout East Anglia in favour of a radical amendment of the scheme (NB not its abolition).[21]

The ticket office at Great Portland St, 1938

The scheme runs into trouble

The EC of the ASRS unanimously passed a resolution in June 1910 which reads in part "The unrest that is so evident at the present time among railway workers ... has been created largely by the vexacious attitude of many of the railway companies towards the working of the scheme of Conciliation and Arbitration agreed in 1907 ... Unless the spirit as well as the letter of the aforementioned agreement is observed more fully in the future ... this committee will have to seriously consider the advisability of repudiating the scheme agreed to in 1907". It must have taken a literary genius to squeeze so many conditionals into a short resolution. They clearly did not envisage actually withdrawing from the scheme, however unsatisfactory its operation was. Principled opposition to the scheme existed, as we shall see, but it did not find expression on the EC of the ASRS. The General Secretary noted in his 1910 report that in none other of the 262 Conciliation schemes covering two million workers in other industries was there such resistance by management to implementing arbitration awards[22] (the dockers may have taken issue with this statement).

The 1911 strike

Inevitably this uncompromising stance by the Railway Companies evoked a response. A series of unofficial strikes in various parts of the country culminated in an official strike from 17th August 1911 by the ASRS, GRWU and United Pointsmen and Signalmens Society (UPSS), the three unions which were to join together to form the National Union of Railwaymen (NUR) in 1913, plus significantly ASLE&F. The Government offered the railway companies "every available soldier in the country", though so-called Government chief conciliator Sir George Askwith warned Conservative Prime Minister Bonar Law "The territorials cannot be trusted". The Managing Director of the Underground Electric Railway of London said "Men remaining loyal throughout will receive double pay" and the Central London Railway made a similar undertaking. Subscription lists for 'loyal' railwaymen were opened on the District and Metropolitan railways among others.[23] The London local lines were stopped in some degree. The Railway Times of 10th Feb 1912 reports that 942 men struck on the Metropolitan out of a staff of 3,300, the City and South London was paralysed and the others admitted some reductions in service. The strike was a great success due to the unity shown by the four unions concerned and refusal of members of the RCA to be recruited as strike breakers. The Government climbed down and the Union leaders called the strike off late in the evening of Saturday 19th August following round-table talks with, for the first time, spokesmen for the railway managers as a whole. They claimed, prematurely, that the principle of recognition had been granted, but a full Royal Commission was to thoroughly investigate the Conciliation scheme with a view to amending it.[24] Services were back to normal on the Monday morning everywhere except the North Eastern railway.

Sir George Gibb became General Manager of the North Eastern Railway in 1891 and "had taken a firm stand against the more conservative elements in the railway world, signifying his disdain for them by wearing a tweed suit at the office".[25] Under his influence, what is believed to be the first Conciliation Board was established and the Union recognised following a strike in March 1897.[26] His knowledge of electric trains and scientific approach to statistical analysis to secure greater efficiency recommended him and he was appointed Deputy Chairman and Managing

Director of the Underground Electric Railways of London (UERL) and Chairman and Managing Director of the District Railway from 1st January 1906 at a salary of £8,000 PA, a staggering £849,000 in 2014 money.[7]

Chairman (of the Royal Commission): "Are you prepared to say here that the ship-building trade of the Thames was driven away by the action of the Unions?" Lord Claud Hamilton MP, director of the Great Eastern Railway – "Undoubtedly. The North Eastern Railway did recognise the Union and ever since ... there has been nothing but unrest ... upon that railway". Chairman: "Has the granting of recognition on the London Underground ... resulted in chaos and disaster?" Hamilton: "I do not think recognition has been granted there". Chairman: "I think you will find that Sir George Gibb succeeded in introducing the principle of recognition in his negotiations with the Unions during his management of those lines". Hamilton: "My brother, Lord George, happens to be Chairman of the Underground and he told me Sir George Gibb tried to introduce recognition, and the Board of which he is Chairman declined to accept it" (1911 Royal Commission P 401. See Appendix 1). This is an interesting glimpse of differences between managers and nepotism at work. Interlocking directorships and complex lines of ownership obscured the controlling influences, but Barker & Robbins note that Lord George Hamilton did indeed replace Sir George Gibb as Deputy Chairman of the Underground Electric Railway of London Company (the Combine) in 1910. Sir George was Chairman of the London Electric Railway from 1910 to 1913.[28]

PP626-628 of the Enquiry report show the costs to the Union of the Conciliation scheme on the various railways. Those for the Underground are as follows:

Metropolitan District	£16
Metropolitan	£66
UERL	£7/16/9

Were the Underground companies any different?

Dr Philip Bagwell's thorough work on the history of the NUR contains few specific references to the Underground companies. The attitude of the railway companies generally was extremely anti-union and contemptuous of their staff. Were the Underground companies any different? The references in the previous paragraph to Underground companies offering bribes to staff if they worked during the strike indicates that they believed many of their staff would join the strike, and evidence submitted to the Royal Commission indicates costs for the Conciliation scheme for Underground companies including the Metropolitan. Barker & Robbins in their book 'A History of London Transport opine that "Trade Unionism among railwaymen was quiescent" although they adduce no evidence for this (it is hard to prove a negative). "Railway service usually occupied a whole lifetime and was not, as so often on the omnibuses and trams, merely incidental employment". They note the existence of the ASRS and ASLE&F.[29] The all-grades movement of 1906 did embrace the Underground as well as the main lines. The basic working week in the locomotive department of the Metropolitan Railway "was reduced from 57½ hours to 54 in 1871, though it was still 54 in the 1890s", although Sundays would be in addition to these hours. Signalmen are reported as working an eight hour day, porters and ticket collectors 9.5 or 10.[30] Yet it is also reported that signalmen worked 12 hour days on Sundays in 1891 and ticket collectors 14 or 15 hours.[31] So it seems that hours worked varied considerably but were not as extreme as those on some of the main line railways. Again, Barker & Robbins tell us "It was very unusual indeed for any employee of the District or Metropolitan railways to work more than 12 hours, but overtime was much more usual on the suburban services of the main line companies than on the Underground".[32] A driver on the Metropolitan was earning 6/- to 8/- a day in the 1890s and a fireman 3/6 to 4/6.[33] In 1896 signalmen and ticket collectors could earn 20/- to 30/- per week, guards 20/- and porters 15/- to 25/- though tips were scarce.[34] By way of comparison, Booth's 1896 survey also revealed that bus conductors could earn as much as £4 or £5 in a good week, though 35/- to £2 would be a likely guess for the average. Fuller says that at the time an unskilled worker received an average of £1 per week (£116 in 2014 terms) and a skilled worker 30/-. Although bus workers were the highest paid section of the working class the hours were extremely long, typically 15 or 16 hours a day 7 days a week.[35]

Pay and conditions
Unlike bus staff, railway staff had free uniform and free travel, enabling them to live in "the outer ring of the metropolis". Metropolitan chairman Sir Edward Watkin is quoted as claiming that low rent housing at Neasden attracted "a better class of workmen ... we gain indirectly a great benefit by practically improving the comfort of the people we employ"[36] The Metropolitan even appointed a medical officer. The Metropolitan board had always sought to treat their staff in a friendly paternal way, having set up a provident society in 1877 and a pension fund for wages staff in 1908 but "The Metropolitan paid somewhat below Underground rates".[37] Earnings of administrative and clerical staff are harder to ascertain but we are told that at the formation of the LGOC in 1855 clerks received a tidy £120 per year and bookkeepers £250.[38] The RCA initially represented junior salaried grades. Supervisors and Head Office staff were not allowed representation until 1919.

The 1912 report of the Board of Trade enquiry based on the year 1907 tells us the following:

Motorman (electric)	38/10	for 6 day week
Signalman	31/11	for 6 day week
Platelayer	28/10	for 6 day week
Lift attendants	25/5	for 6 day week
Conductors & gatemen	24/7	for 6 day week

These 6 day workers had a basic 54 hour week and received overtime for Sunday duty at flat rate.

The others did a 60 hour week. Only 60% of staff got holidays with pay. At £74 per year on average the electric railway worker was close to the national average of £71, but with the considerable advantage of job security.[39] The fact that railway staff had well organised unions behind them may not be unconnected with these relatively favourable conditions.

The equivalent in 2014 money for the Motorman is £7,685 per year, while the present day Train Operator receives £48,000 pa.

Electrification
Charles Tyson Yerkes, head of the Combine, met the General Secretaries of the ASRS and ASLE&F in October 1904 to discuss labour problems arising from electrification.[40]

Note that the American Yerkes seems to have had no problem talking to the Unions, unlike his colleagues on the main line railways. ASLE&F wanted to retain two men in the driving cab, a demand they only achieved on the Metropolitan for drivers of electric locomotives, not unit trains. The District railway wanted to pay motormen less than steam drivers. New men would come on at a lower rate but ex-steam drivers retrained as motormen would receive about the same as before. The working day was to be 10 hours with no enhancement for Sunday work (as far as we know, the Metropolitan retained a 9 hour day). A District pay sheet for the week ended 17th December 1904 has survived. It shows most steam drivers working seven days at 8/- per day.[41]

Syndicalism and workers control

Charismatic labour leader Tom Mann had become convinced that Parliamentary action was inadequate and advocated militant class struggle. Given the uncompromising attitude of the railway companies his call for revolutionary syndicalism after the French style found a ready audience among railway workers and a full-scale revolt ensued. But Tom Mann ended up serving four months hard labour for his trouble.

The ASRS Annual General meeting of 1912 adopted a resolution advocating the syndicalist objective of workers control as well as the existing policy of railway nationalisation. "This AGM declares for the workers to make themselves the complete masters of production and their own conditions".[42] These stirring words meant different things to different people, however. An NUR special conference in 1917 called for a system of workers control through representation on local and national railway management boards. The diversion of the syndicalist demand for workers control into representation on railway boards of management is noteworthy, as is General Secretary J.H.Thomas's threat to resign rather than have "the leading of a railway strike on his conscience".[43]

CHAPTER THREE

BUS ISSUES TO WORLD WAR ONE

Staff at the LGOC coach works, 1911

Starting with George Shillibeer in 1829 buses started running in competition with Hackney carriages, the forerunners of taxis. These were protected by the Hackney Act which gave them an effective monopoly. Buses, Hackney carriages and stage coaches were operated by small individual proprietors rather than large companies, though there was a trade in licences. From 5th January 1832 short stage coaches and omnibuses were permitted to stop for passengers in the central streets along the route for which they had been licensed.[1] So they were controlled by the Commissioners almost from the start. Fares were high so they were only accessible to the well off. The conductor's job was not only to collect fares but to "cajole and entice the hesitant into his vehicle".[2] Drivers would crawl or stop altogether until their vehicle was full, then race to the next stop. In 1838 an Act of Parliament obliged all conductors and drivers of Metropolitan stage carriages to take out licences and to wear a metal ticket on which was inscribed their licence number. If the driver was found guilty of obstruction or other road offence, or the conductor of abusive behaviour or sharp practice, they were liable to a fine of up to 20/- (£1). They had become employees while the proprietors formed Associations to regulate traffic on the various routes ie form a cartel, and control staff. In the late nineteenth century busworkers were still looked upon (and continued to see themselves) as semi-skilled quasi self employed workers.[3] Not surprisingly proprietors often engaged in related trades such as livery stables, coach builders and 'job masters'.[4] Despite the collusion between operators in their Associations, new operators displaced from long distance stage coaches by the spread of the railways entered the field. This competition, along with rapidly increasing demand led partly by passengers arriving at railway stations, resulted in a considerable reduction in fares.[5]

The railways had not been permitted to build lines into the heart of London. The Royal Commission on Metropolitan termini of 1846 did not allow railways from the North to penetrate beyond the New Road (Euston Road), City Road, Finsbury Square and Bishopsgate St.[6]

The cut in mileage duty (to which buses and Hackney Carriages were subject) and the increase in the size of buses, including allowing passengers to ride on the roof, also enabled fares to be reduced.[7] Mileage per vehicle increased and the proprietors again collaborated to petition for a further reduction in mileage duty. The largest company possessed only 48 vehicles of the estimated 810 horse buses running in London in 1855 when the London General Omnibus Company (LGOC) was formed.[8] Some proprietors could see the benefits of collaborating in a single company, but the main influence came from Paris where a single company was given a monopoly of road transport services with blessing and support from the Commission Municipale in 1855. With support from progressive politicians in London who were concerned about traffic congestion in particular, this French company went about establishing a similar company in London, having seen how profitable the Paris venture had been. The French company was subject to strict conditions of working, fixed fares and frequency of service. The London company (Compagnie General des Omnibus de Londres – CGOL) proceeded to buy up the London companies, not without consider-able opposition. At this time conductors' wages on the various routes seem to have been standardised at 4/- a day and drivers' at 5/6 or 6/-. Horsekeepers were paid 3/6.[9] Unlike the Railway companies, this was no ordinary British company, being largely French financed.[10] In particular, being incorporated in France the CGOL was run by

'Gerants' (Managing Directors) subject to supervision by a 'Conseil de Surveillance', which was the watchdog of the shareholders.[11] The resistance of most of the London proprietors was overcome by the offer of £510 cash for each bus – "compensation on a very generous scale".[12] 'Gerants', district managers and former proprietors were well rewarded with £400 per annum.[13] But crucially unlike the Paris company the CGOL was not granted a monopoly and profits on the Paris scale were not forthcoming.[14] The CGOL was superseded by the British LGOC (London General Omnibus Company) on 1st January 1859, albeit still with some French capital and directors.

When a rival to the LGOC, the London and District Omnibus Company, was promoted in 1880, investors included a number of conductors and drivers, indicating that their financial standing was quite high.[15] "It was an open secret that conductors kept back a proportion of their fares and shared the spoils with the drivers and horse keepers". The LGOC did not use tickets but relied on a "staff of persons travelling continually in the omnibuses who were unknown to the conductors, who make their report of the number of passengers entering and leaving the omnibuses, and this report is checked with the waybill".[16] The Road Car company was paying royalties to the Bell Punch ticket company in 1883, and the tramways had used tickets from their beginning in 1870. The LGOC decided to introduce tickets on 31st May 1891, and this led to a strike from 7 – 12th June.

"The fundamental difference between those who worked on the railways and the buses arose from the way in which fares were handled. On the railways they were paid at a booking office and whoever was collecting them was under very close supervision. Tickets and turnstiles made personal gain almost impossible. On the roads, however, fares were collected by hundreds of men on moving vehicles scattered throughout the length and breadth of the Metropolis and any check was far more difficult. Consequently, while the men who worked on the railways had to rely on their wages, plus any gratuities which might come their way, those who worked in road transport were, throughout most of the nineteenth century, to greater or lesser degree, in business on their own account, lessees of their employers' vehicles rather than mere wage earners".[17] This was undoubtedly a major factor in the differences in the ways bus staff and railway staff dealt with labour relations issues, but not the only one. The differing approaches of the employers were also significant, the bus companies having to deal with a workforce that, as Ken Fuller says, saw itself as quasi self employed.

Charles Booth, in his 'Survey of Life and Labour in London 1895', reports: "If the money received rose above a certain sum – which could vary a little according to circumstances – the conductor kept back the surplus. On the other hand, a certain amount was expected by the company and if, one time with another, it was not forthcoming, the conductor was discharged. Whether he had failed to collect enough or had helped himself too freely was not inquired into". Booth noted that conductors could earn as much as £4 or £5 in a good week. It seems probable that 35/- to £2 would be a likely estimate for the average. Such an income would put omnibus men among the highest paid sections of the working class. Fuller says (P19) that at the time an unskilled worker received an average of £1 a week and a skilled worker 30/-. The busworkers' figure becomes less attractive when it is translated into an hourly rate, for the hours were extremely long. They worked 15 or 16 hours a day, 7 days a week. During terminus breaks, usually only about 15minutes, the crews had to snatch

LGOC horse bus conductor in 1895. Note bowler hat, badge with number, ticket machine, police licence number on bus and profusion of advertisements

what refreshment they could. Despite these very long hours, "the lure of high weekly earnings never failed to produce a long queue of men eager to do omnibus work".[18] But "the spoils system had its hazards as well as its prizes. Omnibus crews were hired by the day and fired on the spot". Despite the high rate of instant dismissals "there certainly does seem to have been a larger nucleus of seasoned veterans than the high turnover rate suggests".[19]

The 1891 Strike

"In 1889, at the time of the dock strike, ... Thomas Sutherst, a barrister who had interested himself in tramway and omnibus men's conditions, organised between 2000 – 3000 tramway men and some from the omnibuses into their first Trade Union."[20] Fuller notes that "the impact of the new Union on omnibus crews was minimal", though the tram companies "gave the men better conditions ... and treated the men with more civility and altogether better than they did previous to any Union being formed".[21] The conductors looked upon the practice of pocketing some of the takings as traditional. It had been inherited from the coaching era and the company had turned a blind eye to it. Ticket machines were introduced on 31st May 1891, and drivers' wages were increased to 7/- a day, or from 42/- to 49/- a week. Conductors with more than 3 years service increased to 5/- a day, 4/6 for 1 to 3 years service, and no increase if less than 1 year service.

A mass meeting of 3000 – 4000 LGOC staff was held at Fulham Town Hall. The demands were for a 12 hour day, 1 day off every fortnight, a weeks notice for dismissal, abolition of stoppages for accidents, and 8/- a day for drivers, 6/- for conductors, and 5/- for horse keepers and washers.[22] "The strikers could hardly base their claim upon the loss of illegal earnings, although everyone knew these were the real cause of the dispute".[23] The following night a further meeting at the Great Assembly Hall, Mile End, was asked by Sutherst: "Are you determined to see that no buses leave the yard if you do strike?" Hats were flung in the air and the men cheered wildly for several minutes.[24] "Some men remained loyal to their employers but their efforts to take their omnibuses out were frustrated by the angry mobs of strikers gathered at the stable gates".[25] Crews employed by the London Road Car company (LRCC) and others came out in sympathy, although Tillings, having conceded 'Sutherst's terms', continued to run. On the second day of the strike Sutherst met the LGOC and LRCC directors. The 12 hour day was conceded along with a conductors wage rise to 4/6 a day during their first year of service, and 5/- a day thereafter, horse keepers to 4/- a day, but drivers only to 6/6 a day. The strikers held out for better terms for several days but on 13th June Sutherst agreed to the companies' offer and the dispute ended.

It is interesting that it was an outside sympathiser, Sutherst, who set up the Union and did the negotiating. Also it is significant that the strike covered all the companies in dispute and that the two largest companies agreed to negotiate jointly and directly with the Union, in stark contrast to the attitude of the railway companies. Yet Barker & Robbins in Chapter 9, especially page 288, consider the railway companies' treatment of their employees to have been positively 'enlightened' compared to the bus companies'; not an opinion which I share. "Of 1047 conductors in the LGOC's service on the day before the strike began only 670 remained 11 months later. Sutherst himself confessed that the Trade Union contained very few members at the time of the strike". The 12 hour day unfortunately did not last long. It was interpreted by the companies as an average – crews were 'permitted' to work alternate days of 9 and 15 hours. Booth in the mid 1890's found that omnibus men were working 15 hours more often than 12. An 'Amalgamated Omnibus and Tram Workers Union' appears to have been ineffective and was "completely broken up" by 1892.[26]

Interesting light is shed upon the situation on the buses in this extract from the diary of G.F.Bloxham for Monday 26th march 1906: "We talk at home this evening on the subject of motor buses. It transpires that the men who work the service from Waterloo to Chalk Farm have gone on strike under somewhat unique circumstances. Until lately the drivers, who are engineers, have been paid at the rate of 10/- a day. The Company offered a scale at so much per journey, but this the men found impractical, because one fellow spent several hours or more each day in repairing his motor after breakdowns. This being so unfair, the men have struck".[27]

It was not until the formation of the London and Provincial Union of Licensed Vehicle Operators on the eve of the First World War that London busworkers began to organise effectively, again in stark contrast to the railway workers. "Most of the other 'new unions' of the 1889 upsurge eg dockers, gasworkers, recovered from the employers counter offensive. The fact that the London busworkers did not recover for at least a decade indicates that there were special factors at work within the industry which hindered the development of a Trade Union organisation. The high earnings available (despite the conditions that made them possible) and the method by which they were earned would have encouraged an individualistic attitude in crews, and one which would have resisted attempts to organise for the pursuit of collective demands ... Ironically, the decision of the LGOC to introduce ticket machines may well have had the long term effect of proletarianising the conductors' view of themselves, thus removing one of the subjective obstacles to Trade Union organisation ... With the coming of the motor age they would achieve full aristocratic (!) status and permanent Trade Union organisation".[28]

CHAPTER FOUR

ON THE TRAMS – MUNICIPAL INFLUENCES

Tram staff outing, 1902

Horse tramways spread rapidly across London from the 1870s to the 1890s, helped by cheaper fares than the buses as the same pair of horses could pull a vehicle on rails with twice as many passengers as a bus on the road. The Board of Trade required the initial three tram companies to charge not more than 1d (old penny) per mile subject to a minimum fare of 3d, which could after three years' operation be reduced to 2d if the Board of Trade thought this was warranted. The Companies were also obliged to provide workmen's fares at not more than a halfpenny per mile with a 1d minimum. The degree of regulation by Government agencies is noteworthy. The starting times were much earlier than the buses to serve those who had to be at work between 6am and 8am. Workmen's trams on the North Metropolitan Company's lines started at 4.45am. South of the river workmen's trams ran between 5am and 7am – returning workmen could take any tram after 6pm, an instructive illustration of typical hours of work in the late nineteenth century. Normal fares soon fell to the level of the workmen's fares as the number of passengers increased rapidly.[1] The North Metropolitan carried more than 1 million passengers on its route from Bow to Whitechapel during its first six months and forecast a 12% dividend for its shareholders.[2]

The trams were not allowed to penetrate the centre of London at all, being banned from The Cities of London and Westminster and the Borough of Kensington. The Board of Trade had the power to overrule these local authorities but local business people and property owners united to prevent tramways being approved in central London.[3] They feared an influx of poorer people into their exclusive areas. In 1872 Parliament declared central London a zone prohibited to trams.

In 1889, after much social unrest and rioting, the undemocratic Metropolitan Board of Works was replaced by the directly elected London County Council (LCC), in its early years noted for its radicalism. "Its persistence in indulging in attacks upon privilege and vested interests was uncompromising, almost ruthless" say Gibbon & Bell in their 'History of the LCC 1889-1939'. The LCC saw the acquisition of tramways as an important means of social reform. The profits would add to its income for relief of rates (local property tax) and it would provide cheap travel to and from its new suburban housing schemes, allowing the clearing of slums. It would also give an example of how an enlightened employer should behave.[4] From 1891 they set about buying up the tram companies under rights granted under the 1870 Tramways Act. In the beginning, before the LCC had built up an operating infrastructure, lines were temporarily leased back to the companies, and clauses were included relating to employees' hours of labour and rates of pay, the operation of workmen's cars and fares to be charged. In 1896 the LCC was granted powers to operate the tramways itself, which the bus companies did not have.[5]

The tram companies had used tickets right from the start and because of this their conductors were paid slightly higher wages than the LGOC buses, which did not use tickets until 1891. In the 1870s pay on the North Metropolitan Tramways started at 5/- a day, rising to 6/- after six months. The drivers received the same as the conductors as tram driving was considered to be less skilled than bus driving. However, according to an account written by conductor George Lovett tickets did not entirely prevent conductors from pocketing fares. Used tickets would be issued again, or sympathetic passengers would not insist on their ticket being punched.[6] Hours of work were as long as on the buses, 16 hour days being common. The Union organised by Thomas Sutherst in 1889 had most of its membership on the trams. There is no record of any industrial action but Barker & Robbins note that the lot of men on the North Metropolitan improved a little after formation of the Union.[7] John Atkinson, a tramway man who later became a Union official, is quoted as telling the Royal Commission on Labour in 1892: "In 1889 most of the companies gave the men better conditions of labour and the inspectors … treated the men with more civility and altogether better than they did previous to any Union being formed, and furthermore the system that had been in vogue of fining the men excessive fines was practically abolished from the first agitation."[8] Three hours' rest was allowed in the middle of the day (spreadover) and the Company also put up £1,000 to start a provident society. Employees paid in 6d a week and received 2/6 a day in case of sickness, £15 in the event of death and £10 if their wife died.[9]

Charles Booth in his 1896 study 'Life and Labour in London' put tram drivers' usual pay at 5/6 a day and conductors at 4/6. Inspectors got 35/- a week and horse-keepers 24/-. No uniform was provided. In 1891 the North Metropolitan employed 1,800 men altogether; conductors were dismissed at an average rate of 5 a week and drivers at 2 a week.[10] Stan Collins, a London tram driver from 1913 to 1951, notes in 'The wheels used to talk to us', edited by Terence Cooper, that the North Metropolitan was by the 1890's a good employer for its time. "Its wages were the best of any tramway company in London and it contributed to a sports club and a sick club for its staff. Like most companies it levied fines on its staff for loss or damage. The London Tramways Company also fined its staff for misdemeanours, and all staff had to deposit £5 with the Company when they were taken on." A table of wages and conditions for various jobs on the London Tramways Co in 1898 is given:

Drivers	31/6 – 42/-	7 day week	80 hours
Conductors	31/6 – 42/-	7 day week	80 hours
Stablemen	23/- – 30/-	7 day week	77 hours
Washers	22/- – 28/-	7 day week	77 hours
Farriers	33/- – 36/-	6 day week	56.5 hours
Track cleaners	21/- – 24/6	7 day week	77 hours
Pointsmen	15/- – 20/-	7 day week	77 hours
Trace horse boys	15/- – 18/-	7 day week	77 hours
Ticket Inspectors	40/- – 42/-	7 day week	80 hours
Regulators	42/-	7 day week	80 hours
Night Inspectors	32/- – 42/-	7 day week	74 hours
Foremen	36/- – 55/-	7 day week	80 hours
Deputy Foremen	40/-	7 day week	80 hours

By 1905 wages and hours on the LCC tramways were as follows:

Drivers	28/6 – 37/6	6 day week	60 hours
Conductors	28/6 – 37/6	6 day week	60 hours
Stablemen	26/-	6 day week	60 hours
Washers	25/- – 30/-	6 day week	60 hours
Farriers	39/- – 43/6	6 day week	54 hours

Track Cleaners	25/-	6 day week	60 hours
Pointsmen	24/-	6 day week	60 hours
Trace horse boys	14/- – 18/-	6 day week	60 hours
Ticket inspectors	42/-	6 day week	60 hours
Regulators	42/-	6 day week	60 hours
Night Inspectors	42/-	6 day week	60 hours
Foremen	42/- – 64/6	6 day week	70 hours
Deputy Foremen	42/-	6 day week	70 hours[11]

By 1899 the LCC trams covered South London from Greenwich to Streatham and Tooting, carried well over 100 million passengers a year and employed 25 Foremen, 1,870 tramwaymen, and 7 senior staff, including a relatively well paid woman in charge of conductors, checkers and 17 Head Office staff.[12]

Electrification started in 1901 with the London United Tramways Company (LUT) in West London, followed rapidly by municipal operation in East Ham on 22nd June 1901, and Croydon on 26th September (municipalised in 1906). The LCC started electric operation on 15th May 1903. Outside the LCC's area of control the Metropolitan Electric Tramways company (MET) developed tramways in North and Northwest London in association with the Middlesex County Council, the first in 1904. Further Municipal electric tramways opened in Ilford, Barking and Bexley in 1903, West Ham in 1904, Erith and Walthamstow in 1905 and Leyton and Dartford in 1906, along with the company operated South Metropolitan from Penge to Sutton. The LCC was not its own street authority so was powerless to control these developments. It tried to operate horse buses to cover the hole in its operations in central London but the bus companies took the matter to court. The Court decision led to the discontinuation of LCC buses on 6th March 1902.[13] As the LCC expanded and bought up company owned horse tramways it went out of its way to improve the hard lot of tramway employees who used to work 16 hours a day and often 7 days a week. It had already concerned itself with conditions on the horse tramways which came under its control in the 1890s. It increased the wages of the lower paid and introduced a 6 day working week and moved towards a 10 hour day, at a cost of £14,000 a year. After declaring a credit balance of £53,000 on its first year's working a further £10,000 was devoted to reducing the working day on trams from 11.25 to 10 hours without loss of pay. Free uniforms were introduced.[14] The LCC also provided lower fares for the travelling public, workmen's fares at not more than 1/2d a mile, for instance, and 2d a day return on trams reaching their destinations before 8am. Night services were provided in South London. The LUT Company gave up to 3.5 miles for 1d but did not offer a 1/2d fare. The LCC claimed that their trams were about 1/2d cheaper per journey than company operated trams. Passenger numbers boomed.

	LCC trams	All trams	Buses
1906	314 million	509 million	292 million
1908	413 million	636 million	340 million
1910	505 million	764 million	377 million

The last LCC horse tram ran on 30th April 1915. But before this the surplus had turned into a loss as a result of the introduction of reliable motor buses, which of course had unrestricted access to the all-important central area. It was estimated that the cheap workmen's tickets lost the LCC £65,000 in the 1910/11 financial year. From 42 million workmen's tickets in 1910/11 the total rose to 77 million in 1913/14, which by this time were being paid for out of the rates.

However, the MET Company continued to win traffic, and just before the war started all London's trams together still carried 90 million more passengers than the buses.[17] But by 1909 the LUT Company was in serious financial trouble. Dividends on ordinary shares were down to 2% in 1907 and nothing at all in 1909, even on preference shares. The Managing Director, Sir Clifton Robinson, resigned early in 1910 before the Annual Meeting of shareholders, where it was revealed that much of the earlier profit had been at the expense of adequate repair and maintenance of permanent way and rolling stock.[18] This background to a strike in 1909 was not revealed to readers of a press hostile to the strike, nor the fact that one of the staff's complaints was the poor standard of maintenance of the Company's tramcars. The following account by John Grigg appeared in 'Labour Heritage' Autumn 2004 and is used by permission.

The 1909 Fulwell Tram Strike by John Grigg
At the beginning of the 20th century the public transport system in West London and Middlesex was the tramways of the London United Tramways Company whose trams clattered from Hammersmith to Uxbridge and Hounslow, from Hanwell to Brentford and down to Hampton. The service was reliable and cheap and the company employed 1,200 drivers and conductors who worked a 63-hour week for six shillings a day. Sometimes men worked 10 hours without a meal break and continuous duties of 20 hours were not unknown. The company employed 'spots' whose job was to spy on employees and report breaches of regulations – like eating in the cab – and many suspensions and dismissals resulted from this system. The Amalgamated Union of Tram and Vehicle Workers was not recognised by the Company and those employees who pressed for recognition were warned off or dismissed. There were plenty of jobless men waiting to take up any vacancies.

Despite the difficulties the Union began recruiting and on Saturday, April 3rd, 1909 Jack Burns, the full time secretary of the Union's West London branch, wrote to Sir Clifton Robinson, the Company Chairman, asking for a meeting to discuss the growing discontent among the employees. Sir Clifton refused to meet Mr Burns and said he would only meet employees of the company. Jack Burns wanted to discuss Union recognition, a six day week, time and a quarter for rest day working, wages, reinstatement of men discharged because of Union activity, and tramcar maintenance.

At the Fulwell depot near Hampton, when they heard that Jack Burns' request had been refused, there was talk of an immediate strike, but the men decided to approach Sir Clifton again, this time asking him to receive a deputation of 20 employees headed by Jack Burns and another Union official, Mr Watson. Sir Clifton said he would meet the 20 employees but not the officials. The drivers and conductors knew that one of the Fulwell men, who may have been the local union branch secretary, had been dismissed and they feared the consequences of a meeting with Sir Clifton.

After an angry meeting at the depot on Easter Saturday, addressed by Jack Burns, the men voted to strike immediately and pickets were despatched to the Hanwell and Chiswick depots.

The Company, however, had acted quickly and when the pickets arrived they found that men reporting for work, who of course had no knowledge of the events at Fulwell, were required to sign a declaration of loyalty to the company. Two Chiswick men who refused were dismissed. At Hanwell the men were offered an extra day's pay to man the trams normally run by the Fulwell men. The Company took on extra workers and immediately dismissed all the strikers. Jack Burns rushed over to Hanwell and Chiswick but it was too late and he persuaded only a few men to join the strike.

On Easter Sunday morning a large crowd of strikers and their families gathered outside Fulwell depot. Several local men were booed as they reported for work and the crowd grew angry when three tramcars arrived full of strikebreakers from Hanwell. As the Hanwell strikebreakers drove out of the depot some of the women in the crowd broke through the police lines and ran screaming at the drivers. The women supported the men throughout the struggle and joined in a march to Chiswick later that day, taking their children with them. In the evening there was trouble in Fulwell as returning trams had their windows smashed by stones from catapults and strikebreakers were pelted with orange peel.

On Easter Monday 2,000 people stood outside Fulwell depot, jeering and hooting and eventually just standing in disgust as their fellow workers ran the service for the company. Sir Clifton Robinson gave triumphant interviews to the local press and blamed the Union for misleading the men into a strike which caused their dismissal. There were, as he pointed out, two men waiting for every job that became vacant.

The strike failed because the Fulwell men came out before Jack Burns had sought the support of the men at Chiswick and Hanwell, and before the Union's Executive Council had considered the issue. The Fulwell strike was therefore unofficial and no strike pay was available. Some of the dismissed employees tried to sue the Union.

During the three weeks following the strike mass meetings were held, mainly in Hounslow, where the tram employees' grievances were aired. There was a march from Fulwell – that attracted much publicity as it passed through Hounslow, Brentford and Chiswick – of dismissed strikers to hand back their uniforms. The Union made some headway in recruiting members.

In May questions were asked in Parliament and Winston Churchill, President of the Board of Trade, said there were no regulations concerning the number of hours that a tram driver might work. Although nothing was done about the hours further questioning resulted in a new regulation that obliged the police to be satisfied with a man's driving ability before he could drive a tram. Until then the Company could put anyone from the street corner into the driver's cab.

Little was done to help those who had been sacked apart from meagre collections among the public and men still employed by the tram company. The determination displayed at Fulwell had been overwhelmed by the pressure of poverty which forced men to take the strikers' jobs.

The local press, particularly the Chiswick Times, attacked the Union for spoiling the public's pleasure over the bank holiday, and Sir Clifton Robinson was set up as a local hero who had triumphed against great odds. The Union was a demon that had misled innocents to their destruction.

The Chiswick Times found a 'well-known local trade unionist' who was reported as saying: "Personally, I do not believe in strikes. They are a thing of the past. The fact that during the last eight years there has been a decrease in the wages of the workers of the country as a whole proves conclusively that strikes are absolutely hopeless. Trade Unionism has lost its grip, and if the workers of the country want to bring about better conditions for themselves, they must do it through the ballot box."

The 'well known trade unionist' was in fact urging support for the newly formed Labour Party and his remarks reflected the continuing conflict in the Trade Union movement over whether industrial or political action was the best way forward.

Men and women staff at Croydon's tram depot, 1918

LUT tram No 141 at Hammersmith Metropolitan station, c.1910

The LUT came under the control of the UERL Combine and on 20th November 1912 was merged with the MET.

Meanwhile at the LCC

In October 1899 a General Tram and Bus Workers Union issued a circular appealing to the LCC Tramways to abolish the system of fines. In 1901 it again demanded the end of fines and improvements to wages up to 42/- a week for drivers and conductors. It was alleged that the Council had broken the 10 hour day/6day week agreement. The wage increases were refused and the Council denied the rostering allegations. The Chairman of the Highways Committee justified the continuation of fines on disciplinary grounds, pointing out that they only averaged 5d per man per year as against 8d under the companies. The Committee also refused to grant holidays with pay and when years later they were eventually granted they had to be taken in the winter months. The Union also asked that drivers be allowed to smoke after 8pm but this was also refused, although men on all – night cars could smoke until 6 in the

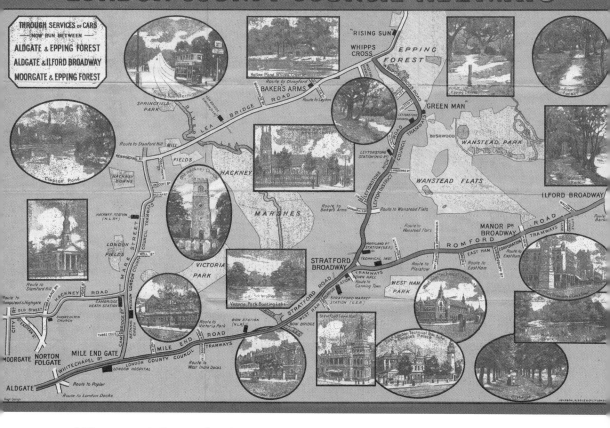

LCC tramways in East London shown on map from around 1911

morning. In 1904 it was suggested that drivers of electric cars be allowed to sit down but this was considered improper and unsafe. Horse car crews had been allowed to eat on the tram as no meal break had been given but when they changed to electric cars this was no longer allowed. Alfred Baker, Chief Officer of LCC Tramways, wrote just before he left in October 1903 that graduated pay scales for drivers and conductors were justified on the grounds that new men were more liable to accidents than long service men, and that the LCC and Glasgow Corporation were the only employers paying the same rate to conductors as to drivers. No person under 21 was allowed a police licence to work on trams and he said that LCC crews were the best paid in the country.

The TUC had backed the eight hour day as long ago as 1891, supported by social campaigner Sidney Webb, and by 1903 the ten hour day was the norm on municipal tramways. East Ham Corporation staff, for instance, worked a nine hour day and a 13 day fortnight. Apparently in Cardiff they had a 54 hour week and got time and a half for Sundays and double time for bank holidays. The LCC's 10 hour day could be spread over 18 hours with a break in the middle. Although the LCC offered improved wages and working conditions "to secure good men and an efficient service" Stan Collins says its policy "was not one of intemperate benevolence to its staff". The ideals of social advance and enlightened employment practices did not last long.

Around 1903 the General Tram and Bus Workers Union was absorbed by the Amalgamated Association of Tramway and Vehicle Workers Union (AATVW), which had originated in Salford in 1889. It offered a sick club, which was important at a time when there was no sick pay and no retirement pension. The LCC had wound up the North Metropolitan Company's sick club shortly after it took the company over, although Chief Officer Baker advocated the formation of Friendly Societies as a way of "attracting the most desirable class of men to the service". The AATVW claimed a reduction of the working day to 9 hours and reduction of the maximum spreadover to 12 hours, plus an increase of the top rate to 6/3 a day. They also asked for spare men to be paid 2/- a day when they showed up but were not given work – the Committee agreed to their being paid 1/- a day. The Union claimed one week's paid holiday per year after two years' service, to which the Committee replied that they already had one day off every week. They also claimed time and a half for working a stood-off day (rest day in today's parlance) and were granted time and a quarter. Most interestingly, in 1904/5 they requested a Board of Conciliation on the pattern soon to be tried on the railways (see chapter 2). Four years later four Boards were set up covering all tramway grades, in parallel with the first Railway conciliation scheme, and these first met in February 1910. The glacial pace of movement on the claim is extraordinary.

From January 1907 rates for drivers and conductors were increased to 30/- – 39/- (£159 - £207 in 2014 money), and in March 1910 agreement was reached through the new machinery on the other claims. Tramway staff also received a daily allowance of 30 minutes for signing on and off, preparing cars for service and stabling them, collecting tickets and cashing up. It was also agreed that leave could be taken all year round, not just in Winter. Spreadovers on Sunday were reduced to 8 hours but the claimed 12 hour spreadover for the rest of the week was not agreed. These improvements were worthwhile, but the cost of living began to rise and by 1914 the LCC tram employee was worse off than in 1907. Only one strike took place in this period, at Stamford Hill in 1912, believed to have been in sympathy with striking dockers. Stan Collins notes that the AATVW achieved little for its members in the pre-war decade, and when the L&P Union was formed in 1913 it began actively and successfully recruiting LCC Tramway staff. It was altogether more militant than the AATVW and soon approached that Union for amalgamation. But the L&P did not have the finances to take on the sick club responsibilities of the AATVW so for the time being the Unions competed for members. The AATVW had a majority of the seats on the Traffic Conciliation Board and its sick club became the only one in London when the London Bus and Tram Men's Sick Provident Society was wound up in 1914.

CHAPTER FIVE

THE FIRST WORLD WAR AND ITS AFTERMATH

Woman conductor on 'B' type bus. Note that the passengers are all women so this may have been a training session.

Immediately on outbreak of war in 1914 the Government instituted state control (though not ownership) of the railways. The cost of living rose rapidly and for the first time ever there was a national series of negotiations directly between the railway Trade Unions and representatives of the railway companies, for a war bonus. Unfortunately, youths under eighteen, workshop staff, women and the staff of the District and UERL (Underground Electric Railways of London) were excluded from this bonus. However, national wage negotiations continued after the war. The NUR, which did not admit women members until 1915, took the position that women should receive the minimum rate of pay for men employed in each grade and the same war bonus as men. Some companies were not even prepared to pay this minimum until the Union threatened to cancel the national wartime industrial truce agreement, and in August 1915 the companies, including finally the Underground, agreed. Many branches and districts of the NUR favoured a policy of equal pay for women, and the NUR argued that women were just as adversely affected by rising prices as men, but equal pay was not achieved. Managers claimed that women's labour was only three fifths as productive as that of men, particularly with ticket collectors. The NUR pointed out that by 1915 some stations, such as Maida Vale on the Bakerloo Line, were staffed entirely by women and yet all the tickets, not just three fifths of them, were successfully collected, and furthermore there was a distinct improvement in the dress and manners of men on these stations.[1] The LCC tram strike of 1915 is covered in Chapter 8.

There was a strike of London bus women in August 1918 in support of the claim for equal war bonus payments (see Chapter 7), and women employed on the LER (Underground) struck in sympathy. The NUR eventually achieved an increase in the bonus but not equality. Barbara Drake in her book 'Women in the Trade Unions, written in 1920, notes: "On the railways, in spite of repeated protests, the Union failed to secure more than a part of its demands. Broadly speaking, women received the men's minimum wage in each grade, ranging from 16/- for porters to 27/- for district examiners, but only a woman's scale of war advances amounting in November 1918 to 20/6 against 33/- received by men." The comparison with the buses is particularly interesting. The figures given above were achieved through the Conciliation machinery by Unions which had suspended all official industrial action for the duration of the war. The buses, with a militant Union willing to support industrial action, achieved war bonuses of 20/- for women and 25/- for men. However, despite the reservations of their Unions, the equal pay strike on the buses rapidly spread to the Underground.

The Daily News reported on 26.08.18: "The equal pay strike on the Tube railways which was suddenly declared on Friday night is still in progress, and a meeting of some 1500 strikers at the Ring, Blackfriars, last night, instructed their committee to make the demand for equality of wages as between men and women on a national basis. It was decided to remain out pending a report on the result of this application to be made at a further meeting tonight. Inquiries last night showed that the District, Central London and Metropolitan lines were practically unaffected, while there had been a seven minute service all day on the Piccadilly and an eleven minute service on the Bakerloo and Hampstead tubes ... Friday night's strike decision was at once put into force and the resultant disorganisation of the tube services on Saturday greatly inconvenienced the public ... The majority of the strikers were women and they

Woman gateman on the Bakerloo line at Watford Junction 1918. The term 'gateman' was used for women as well as men.

Woman lift attendant, 1919

Woman working on an engine casing, 1918

Women bus conductors, 1916

were joined on Saturday by other women and by some men employed at Paddington, Smithfield and Euston. There were unconfirmed reports of sympathetic strikes at two provincial centres ... The women demanded to be paid the same war bonus of 25/- a week received by the men instead of their present bonus of 12/6 ... In a statement issued by the Ministry of labour on Saturday it was pointed put that the stoppage of work was unauthorised, and that Mr J H Thomas with the support of the NUR executive had notified the persons concerned of his unpreparedness to negotiate for a settlement of the points at issue until work had been resumed. Mr Thomas said: 'We are neither going to be bluffed or intimidated by actions of this kind which ... will be ruinous to the country'". So much for NUR support for equal pay!

The Times 27.08.18. reported: "The tube railway workers on strike in London decided yesterday to resume work tomorrow pending the result of negotiations, and to maintain the strike committee until the principle of equal pay for equal work is settled". But there it remained; it seems that 20/6 was the most that was achieved for the women, well short of the men's rate.

Over the entire period of the war prices rose by 120-125% but railway wages only rose by 117% on average.[2]

As soon as the Armistice was signed in November 1918 industrial hostilities recommenced. A strike on the Underground started on 3rd February 1919 over meal breaks being included in the eight hour day for crews of electric trains. Train crews, like bus crews, had not previously been allocated meal breaks, taking refreshment on the train as and when possible. A national agreement had been reached giving effect to the principle of the eight hour day for electric train staff as and from 1st February 1919. Signatories were Sir Albert Stanley, President of the Board of Trade and Chairman of the Underground Group, H. Walker, acting chairman of the Railway Executive Committee, and Walter Hudson, acting General Secretary of the NUR. A similar document was signed by ASLEF General Secretary John Bromley. It is noteworthy that the Government was so involved. However, the ink on the settlement was not dry before a strike took place on the Tube railways. The motormen's conditions in the agreement with the companies were that the working day should constitute nine hours, split turns excepted, inclusive of at least 30 minutes relief for meals ... In arranging the eight hour day the officials decided to cut out the meal time, so that it would be part of the working day, which the men contended was a breach of the agreement.[3] The Lots Road power house men also withdrew their labour so that the Metropolitan District was closed as well as the Tubes. Mr Hudson, acting General Secretary of the NUR, issued the following appeal: "Regarding the regrettable unauthorised strike on the part of the London Tubes, I have to say that we are in danger of the negotiations being held up by the rash action on the part of the men ... the Electric Railway Company have handed to the men an agreement as follows: 'If the employees remain loyally at work on the question of payment for meal relief being decided by the Negotiating Committee and the railway trade unions ... on 12th Feb, Underground management agree to make such decision retrospective to 1st Feb'".[4] Clearly the Unions were committed to the Conciliation scheme but their members were not prepared to wait for the cumbersome machinery to act when management had acted immediately in a way that appeared to them to undermine a national agreement. It also illustrates that national railway agreements applied equally to the Underground even if Underground management were not usually so dictatorial and anti-Union as their main line colleagues. Alcock notes on P530 "The whole proceedings from start to finish were a bungle and something in the nature of a fiasco". However, the EC of the NUR then passed the following resolution: "This Committee are strongly of the opinion that our members who are on strike as a consequence of the violation of their conditions of service by the managements of the railways concerned are justified in the action they have taken and we decide forthwith to recognise the strike". Clearly there was bad feeling not only between management and staff, but also between the NUR's acting General Secretary and his Executive.

The strike lasted from 3rd to 8th February. The ASLE&F sent out a letter to their members on 4th Feb. stating: "Your EC are dealing with the strike on the London Underground Electric Railways and on electrified sections of certain steam railways running into London ... support our London members who are on strike and are calling out our members on the London Brighton & South Coast Railway (LBSCR) and London & South Western Railway (LSWR)." The NUR sent out a letter on 7th Feb. stating: "The conditions of service since 1912 of the men on the LUER provide for a meal relief of not less than 30 minutes, which is paid for. In consequence of the Underground Railway Company not including this meal relief allowance in the arrangements for working the eight hour day ....there is a strike of their employees".[5] The difficulty was resolved in the following document headed "Metropolitan District Railway, London Electric Railway (LER), Central London Railway, City & South London Railway" (NB not the Metropolitan) stating: "We understand that the Underground trainmen are to be booked on for eight hours work. Meal times are not included in the eight hour day but the Companies are to offer all reasonable facilities to meet the ordinary physical needs of the men ... A man should be nominated for each railway who would co-operate with the companies to assist in seeing the proper carrying out of the arrangements for securing facilities to meet the ordinary physical needs of the men".[6] NUR General Secretary J.H.Thomas, addressing a public meeting the next day, said: "Never was there a time when there was so much discontent, ill feeling and dissatisfaction ... I believe that the cause is the inevitable reaction after four years of war strain and suffering".[7] Alcock also notes "Mr Thomas, it was well known, was against what had taken place". Thomas said later "Our Union is the strongest in the country ... However strong and powerful we may be, the state is more powerful and more important. Citizenship has a stronger claim than any sectional interest".

CHAPTER SIX

THE 1919 EVENTS AND THE 1921 RAILWAYS ACT

Women staff at West Kensington (District Railway) 1919. Note semaphore signals

The year 1919 was one of widespread industrial and social unrest. Major industrial conflicts ... were postponed 'for the duration' ... Every day that year an average of 100,000 men were on strike.[1]

The NUR and ASLE&F called an all out strike which lasted from 27th September to 5th October 1919. The strike was highly successful and as it continued gained increasing public support despite opposition from the press. On 30th September Ernest Bevin of the Transport Workers Federation was confronted by demands from London bus staff, tramway workers, and dockers to be called out in support of the railwaymen. Bevin did not favour this and the NUR and ASLE&F did not request his support, again forgoing an opportunity for co-operation between bus and rail workers. The union leaders could all see that any escalation would "Challenge the power of the state" in Bevin's words.[2] A conference of Trade Union and Labour Party leaders on 1st October carried a resolution declaring that the fight was "A purely Trade Union fight for wages and conditions"[3], explicitly ruling out any challenge to state power. Nevertheless, faced with the distinct possibility of extension of the strike to other trades the Government capitulated.[4] Wages were increased significantly.

However, the NUR EC minutes for 29-30th January 1920, under the heading 'National Settlement – LER' say: "being convinced that the present financial position of this company, through not being under Government control, is such as to prevent our members benefiting from the national settlement, and whilst in no way departing from the declared policy of the NUR for nationalisation", supports their Bill to raise fares to meet the changes. And on 24-27 March 1920 they state: "In view of the fact that considerable unrest exists among our members on the Underground in consequence of the company not complying with the settlement of January last ... we shall ... take such action as will compel the company to agree".

Barker & Robbins note (Vol 2 P321) that the Metropolitan was never completely stopped although 84% of the staff were on strike. 284 'volunteers' were taken on. Some 'knew their business' but others did considerable damage. Managers and supervisory staff performed many railway jobs. Motor lorries were used in place of trains between Chorley Wood and Harrow. The Underground as a whole enrolled over 5,000 'volunteers', got Lots Road power house running and began a restricted service on Tuesday 20th September.

Employment of Women on the railways. The NUR EC minutes for 27-28 May 1920 contain this rather strange resolution: "This EC decides to take up with the companies concerned insisting on either the same rate being paid to them as men, or alternatively, their dismissal". Following the end of hostilities most women staff had already been dismissed.

National agreements on pay and conditions were granted in 1920[5] but the dispute was not continued to achieve nationalisation. Instead the Government offered two seats for the NUR and one for ASLE&F on the Railway Executive Committee. This was seen as a step in the right direction.[6] NUR President Charlie Cramp said: "We have obtained a Ministry of Transport ... as a result of our demands for full workers control. We are urging a joint board which shall control all railways. In any case the recent strike struggle will have made it easier to get the principle of joint control accepted ... We ultimately want to destroy capitalism altogether".[7] This fascinating quotation suggests that the NUR leadership had fatal illusions in the opportunities for advance under the Conciliation scheme, bordering on wilful self delusion. Anyone with any experience of the Conciliation scheme would quickly realise that it was not a route to workers control at all, much less the abolition of capitalism. Yet the late Syd Bidwell MP, in conversation with me as late as the 1980's, viewed the Conciliation scheme precisely as workers control in his experience as a guard in the 1940s and 1950s.

The NUR called for complete nationalisation of all railways with equal representation on management both national and local for the NUR.[8] The Government, realising the need for some control over the private railway companies and having seen the success of such control during the war sidestepped the demand for nationalisation by creation of the Ministry of Transport. Charlie Cramp in a speech in 1920 saw this as a necessary precondition for the advance of railway workers despite still demanding nationalisation "if possible".[9] The diversion of the syndicalist demand for workers control into representation on management boards is extraordinary. General Secretary J.H.Thomas said in 1921: "Our conception of workers sharing in management is not that they should be merely Trade Union delegates whose only interest is in the wages and conditions of the men. It means something much bigger than that; it means a genuine contribution by practical men towards the solution of the difficulty common to industry".[10] These ideas, while not shared by all, were popular in that period and gave enough of the illusion of participation to gain considerable support. They formed the basis of the Conciliation scheme. A Government White Paper of June 1920 stated: "The Government are of the opinion that the time has arrived when the workers, both official and manual workers, should have some voice in management". Joint boards were set up to deal with wages and conditions of service, and another joint board heard questions on which the first failed to agree. Not surprisingly there was little opposition to these boards as they gave the Unions a voice at the top level of management. The Unions were left with no choice but to accept the proposals while deploring the failure to nationalise. The NUR EC minutes of 27-28 May 1921 note tersely: "EC decides to accept and adopt the principle of the scheme as submitted to us".

Critics noted that the position of railway staff representatives on Boards of Directors running the railways primarily for dividends and only secondarily for public service would be untenable but the three Unions affirmed their determination to secure for railway staff a share in management and control.[11] One advance finally conceded was that Union officials would be entitled to represent members in disciplinary cases, long resisted by the companies. Another important safeguard was included protecting the rights of staff made redundant. Agreement was reached on 3rd May 1921. In Parliament it was described as "An epoch making document which is actuated by and which breathes a spirit of peace in the industrial world – a document of the most supreme importance as marking one of the greatest steps ever taken towards industrial peace".[12] Hyperbole aside, its significance cannot be overestimated. Certainly on the Underground it lasted until 1993 and the number of strikes and other industrial actions was reduced almost to zero (1926 general strike excepted). NUR General Secretary J.H.Thomas said: "The scheme has been created not only in the hope of industrial peace but also of a genuine co-operation between the railway companies and the railway employees in the provision of the most efficient transport service possible".[13]

The Act stated that "All questions relating to rates of pay or conditions of service ... shall, in default of agreement between the railway companies and the trade unions concerned, be referred to and settled by the Central Wages Board, or on appeal the National Wages board ... The Central Wages Board shall be composed of eight representatives of the railway companies and eight representatives of the employees ... 4 NUR, 2 ASLE&F and 2 RCA".[14] The RCA's claim to negotiate for clerks and supervisors had been finally recognised on 4th Feb 1919.[15]

In 1921 A.G.Walkden of the RCA had drafted a National Transport Services bill which provided for nationalisation of railways and canals, which gained the support of the Trade Union Congress (TUC).

Far from being nationalised the railways were re-privatised in 1921, the plethora of companies being grouped into four regional privately owned monopolies. The Metropolitan Railway asked to be included as it had always seen itself as a mainline company, but along with the Underground Group it remained independent until being absorbed into the LPTB in 1933. The Metropolitan paid wages 'somewhat below Underground rates' (Barker & Robbins Vol 2 P320) but had a paternalist approach to its staff. Sectional Councils similar to those on the main line companies were set up in 1922 but parity of wages with the District and Tubes was not granted.

The 1921 Act gave statutory backing to the Conciliation scheme. A strong reason for the NUR to abandon its pre-war principled opposition to 'class collaborationism' was that the Act also gave statutory recognition to the railway unions -NUR, ASLE&F and RCA, something that the private companies still would not concede. This in turn had the effect of excluding the other Unions, in particular Bevin's emerging Transport & General Workers Union (T&GWU) which he was building as a united transport union following the previous attempts to build the Transport Workers Federation, and which became hegemonic on the buses. Some NUR branches wanted to join this but the leadership were suspicious of being drawn into sympathetic strikes and did not want to surrender their autonomy. Permission for any affiliation was refused.[17] NUR EC minute of 27-28 May 1920 decides not to discuss fusion with the Transport Workers Federation. In the workshops, which were not covered by the Conciliation scheme, the traditional craft Unions organised skilled workers but the NUR, not the T&GWU, organised the semi-skilled and unskilled. Until 1912 ASRS policy had been to leave recruitment of workshop staff entirely to the craft Unions. But the GRWU, which merged with the ASRS in 1913 to form the NUR, had significant numbers of unskilled workshop staff in its membership (10,000 in 1911).[18] Workshop staff who had not served an apprenticeship were not eligible to join the Amalgamated Society of Engineers or other craft Unions.[19] Until 1912 only 20% of workshop staff were members of craft Unions. By 1916 over 50,000 non-craftsmen had joined the NUR.

So, from a total refusal by the companies to even talk to the Unions in 1907 to statutory recognition in 1921. Great progress, but at the price of severely circumscribing the Unions' ability to take industrial action (not a bad thing in the view of some), and many illusions in the value of joint management or workers participation. Separate but similar schemes were drawn up for the Metropolitan and Underground companies. The NUR EC minutes for 5-6 October 1921 record: "Underground Railways Scheme for dealing with questions of wages, hours, conditions of service and other matters affecting the staff. Every employee shall in the first instance address his case to the official immediately over him or through him to the official or officer authorised to deal with it. Failing a satisfactory settlement the undermentioned scheme will apply. Sectional committees shall be established to deal with: a. local interpretation and administration of the agreements covering employment. b. questions relating to conditions of employment ie working hours, reliefs, timekeeping, holidays, rosters, seniority, suggestions and welfare ie everything except wages. c. questions of mutual interest affecting the efficiency or economy of operation." There were initially twelve of these sectional committees covering the District and Tubes plus five departmental councils and an overall Railway Council (see NUR EC minutes 2 November 1921). These minutes also note under the heading 'Withdrawal of Labour' : "In connection with matters covered by this scheme, no withdrawal of labour or interference with efficient operation shall take place until the cause of dispute has been dealt with under these proposals, and a settlement has not been reached within 28 days after reference to the Negotiating Committee". Similar arrangements were agreed for the independent Metropolitan Railway, but when a new unified staff council scheme was set up on the formation of the LPTB in 1933 it was noted that the Metropolitan had worse conditions than the Underground group, whose conditions should be applicable to the Metropolitan. (NUR EC minutes).

Right up to the abolition of the scheme in 1993 the approach of Union officials was that industrial action was to be avoided at all costs. Now, as a Union representative for 35 years including two years on the EC of the NUR I understand fully the need to negotiate and avoid strikes if possible, but this does depend on management adopting the same approach. If they do not, which increasingly became the case after the abandonment of the paternalist style in 1988, it sometimes becomes necessary to use the threat and the actuality of industrial action to concentrate minds and bring management to the negotiating table. If management insist on imposing their own ideas without consultation, while issues of importance for the members are endlessly shuttled back and forth at various levels of the machinery in a way which would have been familiar to Richard Bell in 1907, the Conciliation scheme loses its validity. It can also become a comfortable refuge for Union officials and a protection for them against their own members who may become more independent by recognition and establishment of a shop stewards system. That said, the scheme did empower local representatives to an extent never envisaged by officialdom and delivered significant advances for the Unions. That it lasted so long indicates that it was able to deliver a degree of stability and protection, and some modest advances for railway workers. By requiring nearly all management decisions to be consulted upon it allowed the Unions to delay undesirable changes, and sometimes modify them. Think of One Person Operation on the Underground, originally proposed in 1966 and not finally implemented until 1985 (though see chapter 18 on the 1989 unofficial strikes). In some cases the management actually came to rely on the Unions to help, particularly with rosters, leave and staff welfare where the unions became almost indispensable. Many would now argue that this was an unhealthy situation. Especially after nationalisation in 1948 management became much more willing to work in partnership with the Unions and industrial action became virtually unknown for many years. The comparison with the situation on the buses will be explored in later chapters.

The various theories of workers participation and joint committees have a long and discreditable history, being based on false visions of what is possible in the real world. The attempts by the 1966-70 Labour Government to incorporate Trade Union leaders in the management of industry fall into this category, and conveniently ignore the fact that the Railway Conciliation scheme, despite many benefits, never pretended to involve workers in management, indeed management always insisted on their 'right to manage'.

Workshop staff were not accepted as part of the agreement due to the dispute between the NUR and the craft unions. NUR EC minutes for 6-7 May 1920 note under the heading 'Railway Shopmen' "Machinery for the purpose of discussing and settling all questions between representatives of the Ministry of Transport, railway companies and representatives of the NUR. Shop stewards – Departmental Committees- General works committees – Line committees – National shops committee . Accepted." And on 18-21 May 1920: "Working arrangement with United Vehicle Workers sought (noted they had not replied to a request for a meeting)". The NUR EC minutes for 12-15th January 1921 record : "The Amalgamated Engineering Union (AEU) have definitely declined to negotiate jointly with us and the craft unions. The G.S. To write to the EC of the AEU inviting them to a conference with a view to a frank discussion of the whole position". At a meeting in November 1919 to discuss a claim for an advance of 15/- a week the craft union representatives walked out as soon as the NUR delegation entered the room.[20] The craft unions believed workshop staff should be paid the district rate while the NUR favoured a national industrial pay scale. Eventually the issue was referred to a court of arbitration which on 8th July 1922 vindicated the NUR position.[21] But it was not until 15th August 1927 that agreement was reached for setting up works and departmental committees for workshop staff and a procedure for settling disputes was established separate from the conciliation boards for operating staff, who henceforth came to be known as conciliation staff.[22]

MORE COMPETITION FOR ALREADY OVERCROWDED 'BUSES: A SCENE AT THE ELEPHANT AND CASTLE.

LONG ODDS AGAINST GETTING A PLACE : ANOTHER TYPICAL MOTOR-'BUS QUEUE IN LONDON.

Scenes at Elephant & Castle and 'a West End tube station' during the 1919 Underground strike

CONFLICTING PLACARDS : THE ELEPHANT AND CASTLE TUBE STATION CLOSED AND IN CHARGE OF POLICE.

UNDERGROUND TO NOWHERE : POSTERS REFUTE ADVERTISEMENTS AT A WEST END TUBE STATION.

CHAPTER SEVEN

ALL CHANGE ON THE BUSES

The canteen at Cricklewood bus garage, 1911

With the exception of the 1891 Ticket Machine strike industrial relations on the buses up to 1913 continued very much on an individual level. Bus staff could earn considerably more than the working class norm if they could survive the long hours and this ensured that no serious disputes arose. "When we want six conductors we probably have 60 or 80 candidates" said the LGOC General Manager in 1877.[1] Staff turnover was very high; although a claim that three quarters of the company's conductors left within a year was denied, it was not far off the mark.[2] LGOC profits and dividends were high until they started to face serious competition from two directions. The opening of the City and South London Railway (C&SLR) in 1890, the first deep tube, although only a short line, had shown the potential for electric traction. The Central London Railway (CLR), opened in 1900, traversed the length of Oxford St and linked important Western suburbs like Shepherds Bush to the City. Barker & Robbins note on P123 of Vol 2 that the number of horse buses running along Oxford St was reduced for a time by about one sixth.

Then the explosion of Yerkes tubes in 1906/7– the central parts of what are now the Bakerloo, Piccadilly and Northern lines – suddenly made the LGOC's horse buses seem very slow and old fashioned. The effect of the proliferation of horse tramways from 1870 on the LGOC was limited by the fact that the City of London Corporation and Westminster and Kensington Councils refused to allow trams into their areas. This created a hole in the centre of London giving buses and taxis a monopoly of surface transport but encouraging the development of underground railways. The lessons learned from electric operation of the deep tubes were rapidly applied to surface transport. The first electric trams in the UK had been introduced as early as 1885 in Blackpool and this form of transport was taking the USA by storm by the turn of the century. Good profits from horse traction led the LGOC and the tram companies to adopt a cautious stance. But electrification spread, starting with the London United Tramways Co. in West London in 1901 and East Ham and Croydon Councils in 1903. The London County Council, initially in South London but soon throughout its large area, bought up the horse tramway companies, electrified their lines and extended them out to rapidly growing suburbs. Other municipalities soon followed. Speeds, averaging 10 mph, were slow by modern standards but this was more than double what could be achieved with horse traction. By 1908 there were 636 million tram passengers and 340 million bus passengers.[3]

The LGOC decided not to enter the tramway field. In 1900 they had 1372 horse buses while in 1901 the London Road Car company (LRCC) had 455.[4] In 1904/5 Tillings were in the forefront of experiments with petrol buses. Motor buses gradually became more reliable. Their higher capacity came into play when the regulations were relaxed to allow a weight of 5 tons instead of 3 tons and a maximum width of 7' 2" instead of 6' 6". Longer operating hours saw the introduction of shift working for crews.[5] There were three shifts – early (10.5 – 12.5 hours), late (11 – 13 hours), and spreadover (15 – 16 hours with a break in the middle to cover both peaks). Drivers had one Sunday in three off.[6] However, profits turned into losses in 1908/9 and the LGOC decided that as the motor buses they had bought were unreliable they should manufacture their own. Borrowing heavily from the French de Dion bus, considered the state of the art at the time, and after some experimentation the famous 'B' type emerged from the works at Walthamstow in 1910. The LGOC was still running 343 horse buses but within a year all had gone, the last one running on 25th October 1911.

Total omnibuses licensed in Greater London (not just LGOC):

1907	2557 horse	1205 motor	3762 total
1910	1103 horse	1200 motor	2951 total
1912	376 horse	2908 motor	3284 total

The widespread introduction of motor buses coincided with a slight drop in the total number of buses but an increase in total capacity due to the great increase in speed and size of vehicles.

It also led to the first issue of a uniform. On the horse buses crews had been required to supply their own workwear, a dark suit, and a top hat for drivers and a bowler hat for conductors. They now received a double breasted coat at 13/6, a cloth cap at 1/5, waterproof covers, and brass badges at 2d each. Motor bus drivers also received two summer dust coats, cap cover and badge, at a cost of 17/-, half of which was borne by the staff. The company undertook to pay for the washing of the coats at 3d per week. An increase in pay was granted to reflect the greater skill required to drive a motor bus.[7]

The Underground (UERL) Combine bought up the LGOC in 1912. Competition from the new motor buses increased the pressure on the hitherto independent C&SLR and it was bought up by the Combine in 1912, followed by the CLR on 1st January 1913.

With the change to motor vehicles, buses were no longer middle class vehicles charging middle class fares and starting their journeys when most of the working class were already at work. They were now carrying passengers of all classes at profitable rates. The LCC trams as part of the Council's progressive social policies went on issuing cheap workmen's tickets at a loss.[8]

Black bus driver with 1905 Straker-Büssing bus No. F82, 1908

Not many drivers of the old horse buses survived the transition to motor buses. In 1913 only 1908 out of a total of 4346 staff in the service of the LGOC had been employed by the company for more than three years; of these only 502 had driven horse buses. This was a more skilled workforce with greater self esteem and greater bargaining power.[9] They began to see themselves as something of an elite group within the working class, comparing themselves with skilled trades like engineers, and feeling the need for a Union to defend their interests. The Amalgamated Association of Tramway and Vehicle Workers (AATVW) had been organising tram workers in London for some time but never had much success in recruiting bus workers. In 1913 the London Cab Drivers Trade Union absorbed the London Bus, Tram and Motor Workers Union, renamed itself the London and Provincial Union of Licensed Vehicle Workers (LPU) and rapidly recruited 9000 of the 12000 bus workers.[10] Unlike the railway Unions, the LPU did affiliate to Bevin's Transport Workers Federation (TWF) in 1916. As in the railway Unions, syndicalism had a powerful influence, but a completely different outcome. The Manchester based AATVW had not been able to achieve uniform or consistent increases covering the various tram employers. For instance, their 1914 Report notes that improved conditions on East London tramways achieved 4/- per week to men only at West Ham, 3/3 at Leyton, 3/- at East Ham, 2/6 at Walthamstow and a lowly 2/- at Ilford. Busworkers, with one dominant employer (the LGOC), wanted London–wide wages and conditions, and by 1915 the LPU had come to represent half the tram workers as well as most bus workers.[11] A tram strike took place in 1915 – see Chapter 8.

Known as the 'Red Button' Union, the LPU's first confrontation was with Tillings. In September 1913 a dozen staff were suspended for refusing to remove the Union's red button from their uniforms. The company refused to receive an LPU deputation and by the third week of September the strike had spread to the LGOC. 600 buses were off the road but the LPU leadership intervened to restrict the dispute to Tillings. Albert Stanley, Managing Director of the UERL Combine, stated that the recently acquired LGOC had no objection to its staff joining a Trade Union.[12] After arbitration both companies granted recognition to the LPU although the Union was prohibited from involving itself in questions of discipline and management. The Union gained 2700 members during the dispute.

By 1918 the LPU had 20,000 members organised in 40 garage based branches, some 90% of all London busworkers. Full time officials were elected every two years and each route had a steward to deal with grievances.[13] The comparison with the railway staff, whose Unions had declared an industrial truce in the interest of winning the war, and whose negotiators were locked into the cumbersome staff councils scheme is, well, striking. The bus workers retained a highly combative stance during the war although there were few strikes. In fact, the LPU was one of the very few Unions which opposed the 'Imperialist' war on the principled basis of the need for international working class unity.[14] Officials were elected and mostly carried out the wishes of their members. The movement of many buses and their crews to the battlefields of Belgium and Northern France showed that their opposition to the war had nothing to do with cowardice or pacifism, but it did increase the bargaining power of those who remained behind. The anti-war position of the LPU got stronger as the war dragged on. A member serving in the forces wrote from France in September 1917: "The boys out here are just thirsting for a revolution in dear old Blighty. We out here don't intend to come back to the old conditions of life." 'Hendonian' wrote in April 1917: "I am a man who has seen active service in France and therefore no milk and water pacifist" (a reference to the reformist Fabian socialists) ... ." There is one answer, revolution, then lasting peace". A report from Germany in the Licensed Vehicle Trades Record noted that "The German Union of transport workers endeavoured to steer clear of all chauvinist and bellicose machinations, to which unfortunately so many sister Unions appear to have fallen victim".[15] Fuller opines on P53 "By the end of the war there had been established within the 'Red Button' Union a political culture which was quite firmly anti–capitalist. To a certain extent this would have been due to the developments within the working class movement ... and to the small tightly organised nature of the Union ... To a large extent industrial militancy and political radicalism would have fed off each other, especially during the war ... The combination of these two characteristics would provide many a headache for Trade Union leaders during the following two decades".

Wages and conditions 1914-1918.
In 1914 the LPU signed the first ever written agreement with the LGOC and Tillings (subsequently, with the exception of 1916, the two companies always negotiated common agreements with the LPU and its successors, although Tillings were noto-rious for straying from their provisions). For the first time staff were provided with a free uniform and the agreement stated that: "No contributions to the accident club by drivers and conductors shall be enforced after 1st July 1914 and therefore no cash stoppages shall be made in consequence of any accident". Each member of staff received a travel pass. All new schedules were to be sent to the Union's schedules steward three days in advance of being posted and if the schedule was not to the staff's liking the Union representative could within seven days request a meeting with the company.[16] These great advances for the Union in limiting management's ability to unilaterally impose their will, and considerable advances in conditions, were achieved without having a Government enquiry and without having to accept a scheme of conciliation machinery. The companies had recognised that they could no longer impose conditions on their workforce, but that these would have to be negotiated with the Union. The fact that all operating staff were in the one Union immeasurably increased their negotiating power. Compare this to the railways, where most drivers, with their ability to stop services at a stroke, were (and remain) in a separate Union which sees the interests of drivers as mostly separate from their fellow railway workers.

Further grievances arose from the intensification of labour due to wartime condi-tions. Without recourse to industrial action a further agreement was reached with the LGOC in 1916, though Tillings were reluctant to agree and went to arbitration. The busworkers had discovered that "The frontier of job control was actually at the garage level and the crucial problems of scheduling and discipline had to be dealt with on the spot if the workers' collective power was not to be totally undermined".[17] The advances gained were not considered anywhere near sufficient by the members of the LPU, however, in particular as hours were still excessively long and insuf-ficient progress had been achieved on the demand for a 9 hour day. A 'vigilance committee' was formed, a form of rank and file organisation within the Union that was to persist for many years.

Women during the war

Labour shortage caused by men going off to war and increased wartime arms production led the LGOC and UERL to introduce women workers. The LPU Annual Report
for 1916 records: "The question of female labour in the Trade caused a certain
amount of uneasiness among our membership and a resolution was received from the
Telford Avenue branch requesting us to oppose it".[18] A highly contradictory position
was reached. The Union wrote to the Home Secretary and the Commissioner on 25th
October 1915: "While protesting at the employment of women, because it was not a
fit occupation for them, we were, however, if it was proved that a real shortage of
labour existed, prepared to agree to their employment, subject to them doing exactly
the same work, and at the same remuneration, and that their employment should be
terminated at the conclusion of the war".[19] On 18th January 1916 the LGOC 'resorted'
to female labour for bus washers and eventually met the Union's demand for women
workers to receive the male rate of pay. However, a London District meeting of
the TWF unanimously decided to "support the agitation against the employment
of women drivers and coloured labour being introduced (sic) ... if members of the
respective Unions involved are alive, we should win outright against any further
dilution of our trade".[20] The objection to 'coloured labour' is particularly offensive
as by then many 'coloured' (terminology regarded at the time as polite) soldiers from
various parts of the Empire were bravely fighting in the British Army on the battlefields of Europe. The Home Secretary agreed to issue driving licences to women. A
mass meeting with 2000 present at the Euston theatre on 8th February 1917 carried
a resolution stating "We view with the greatest alarm the recent decision of the
Home Secretary to give permission to the Commissioner of Police to grant licences
to women to drive public carriages, and we hereby pledge ourselves to resist their
employment at all costs, both in the interests of licensed vehicle workers themselves
and to public safety." So much for women doing 'exactly the same work'. No women
drivers were employed.

On 14th February 1917 the LVT (Licenced Vehicle Trades) Record reports: "We
agreed to the introduction of women conductors, and they have to the extent of more
than 75% replaced male conductors called to the colours" (male conscription was
introduced in 1916). Barker & Robbins note in Vol 2 PP 197/8 : "Of the 1702 women who
joined the LGOC as conductors by the end of 1916, 43% gave their previous employment as 'domestic servant'. Over 3500 women in total were engaged by the LGOC.
LGOC women conductors wore relatively short skirts and leather leggings although
Tillings women had to wear ankle length skirts". The Daily Express reported on 4th
January 1917: "'The women conductors are proving capable, considerate and cour-
teous' added the LGOC Operating Manager. 'We employ 1800 of them and engage
about 100 new women every week ... They must be robust girls with some knowledge
of arithmetic (!) ... Far from resenting that women should be paid at the same rate
as themselves the men have from the first insisted on it." The women conductors
proved to be just as willing as the men to defend the terms negotiated by the Union,
and the Union in turn proved just as willing to defend them.[21] A dispute at Palmers
Green garage involving suspension of 6 men and 4 women became entangled with a
claim for a ten shilling war bonus; then the LGOC and Tillings withdrew recognition
because the Union had voted to terminate the clause forbidding sympathy strikes.

The whole fleet came out on strike, in violation of wartime regulations. On 17th May 1917 the Board of Trade got involved and the members at Palmers Green were reinstated, but the Union was obliged to back down over sympathy strikes. The Committee on Production in less than a month awarded a war bonus of 5/- to bus and tram workers, but to men only. In July 1918 a similar award was made, again excluding women. The women struck. Barker & Robbins note in their Vol 2 P315 that "most trams and buses were affected". As recounted in Chapter 4, the strike spread to the Underground. In her book 'Women workers in the first world war' Gail Braybon notes on PP 80/1: "In the August 1918 strike the women were supported by the London & Provincial Union and opposed by the Association of Tramway & Vehicle workers ... Unfortunately both Unions had opposed the use of women as drivers and also spoke out strongly against their continued presence in the transport industry".[22] By the time the Union leadership was forced into recognising the strike it had spread to Bath, Bournemouth, Brighton, Bristol, Folkestone and Hastings, and women working on the Underground were out too.[23] At least the bus women had the support of one of their Unions. 'The Common Cause' reported on 18th May 1917: "By an agreement between the Railway Executive Committee, NUR, ASLE&F and workshop delegates war bonus of 5/- is to be paid to men but only 2/6 to women". As a result of the strike, bus women were included in the Committee's awards.[24] Barker & Robbins Vol 2 P315 says that the principle was still not conceded, although contemporary newspaper reports suggest otherwise. Atheneum September 1918 states: "It is true that the actual strike was not very wide. From the trams and buses owned by the Combine it spread to some extent to the tube railways but the LCC trams remained almost unaffected". As stated in 'Women in the Trade Unions' by Barbara Drake[25] "The LCC paid women men's full rates of wages plus men's full war advances subject to twelve months' probation". See chapter 8. But the effect of the victory was widely felt and had a national impact.

The Star on 26th August said: "There were many prophesies in the days when we were all disputing about Women Suffrage of the effects which would follow the enfranchisement of women. Few predicted as immediate a triumph as that which the women bus conductors won last week ... The women were fighting a cause that unites women, trade unionists and soldiers ... The remedy lies in the amalgamation of Unions on industrial lines and the throwing open of the skilled Union to semi skilled and unskilled workers on absolutely equal terms". An interesting opinion from a national newspaper. The Engineering Union did not open up to semi skilled and unskilled workers until the 1980s, by which time it was a bit too late.

Management usually keep the reasoning behind their decisions a closely guarded secret so information on this is not often available to the researcher. The minutes are generally a masterpiece of obfuscation and opacity designed to record positions while giving as little away as possible. So the letter from William C. Burton, resident director of the LGOC and UERL to the Times of 27th August 1918 is of particular interest:

"Before any women were employed the matter was fully discussed between the omnibus company and the London & Provincial Union of Licensed Vehicle Workers, which represents the employees and which the women have joined. The following are the relevant sections of the understanding arrived at at a meeting on June 31st 1916:-

That as soon as practicable after the termination of the war, the women will be replaced by men; the rate of pay for women shall be the minimum rate for the men they replace; that no war bonus will be paid to women.

"In spite of the agreement that women should receive no war bonus ... the women since March 1918 have received £1 a week war bonus, the same as paid to men. After a further hearing the Committee on Production decided that the bonus to men should be increased to 25/- and that the bonus to women should remain unaltered at 20/- ... At the time they struck their average earnings for a 6 day week were 63/- (43/- wages and 20/- bonus)." -£189 in 2014 money. If true, the statement that the L&P Union agreed to no war bonus at all being paid to women is hard to square with the Union's stated position.

A proliferation of newspaper articles following the strike clearly led to much debate on the principle of equal pay for women in all industries, and there were strikes in many areas. The Times 30th August 1918: "The award of the Committee on Production on the questions arising out of the recent strike of motor omnibus and tramway workers was issued last night and is as follows:

"1. The parties to this reference are: The Municipal Tramways Association; the Tramways and Light Railways Association; the London United Tramways company; the Metropolitan Electric Tramways company; the South Metropolitan Electric Tramways company; The LGOC; the London omnibus section of Thomas Tillings; the National Steam Car company; the Croydon Corporation; the British Automobile Traction company; and the National Transport Workers Federation ...

2. That equal total payments be made to women as to men for equal work in the tramway and omnibus undertakings ...

3. That any future changes of payments should take place conjointly with those of the men."

Women certainly played their part in the Unions. The LVT Record notes of the Seven Kings garage branch: "Our meetings are continually on the increase, more so with the ladies, who are taking a great interest in the work and doings of our organisation".[26] 'Women Worker' in its October 1918 edition notes: "The Gold Badge of the Women's Trade Union League was presented to Mrs Fountain (Vehicle Workers Union) for the magnificent work she had done in connection with the 'bus girls' strike."

After the war
At the end of the war, in a period of great industrial unrest throughout the country, a further improvement in wages and conditions was achieved without recourse to industrial action. In particular, the 1919 agreement abolished the hated mileage system of payment, to the great advantage of bus crews who now got paid by the 48 hour week but actually operated their bus for considerably fewer hours than this. In 1906 bus drivers had been the second highest paid group of semi-skilled workers, earning £93 (£10,190 in 2014 money) per annum compared to the £72 average. By 1924 London bus and tram drivers were still second highest at £190 pa (£10,021 in 2014 money) compared to the £150 pa average (£7,911 in 2014 money). But while in the early period this had been achieved by extremely long hours, after the 1919 agreement to end payment by mileage, hours were greatly reduced. An achievement which the management set about rowing back in 1921. This was the short interval to which Ken Fuller's claim of aristocratic status for busworkers refers.

CHAPTER EIGHT

THE WAR AND THE 1924 TRAM STRIKE

Woman tram conductor with LCC tram No 211, 1916/7

In the six months from July 1914 prices rose by 10-15% and demands placed on LCC staff increased with munitions production rising and fewer buses being on the streets. There were complaints that trams serving the Woolwich Arsenal were grossly over-loaded, sometimes by more than 50%. Drivers were criticised for late running during blackouts. The L&P Union complained that an over-zealous night foreman at New Cross depot spent his off-duty mornings looking for dirty trams while the workload of car washers had been increased by 50%, and they received less protective clothing than their 'under the capitalist' colleagues on the LGOC buses. From Clapham depot came complaints that drivers of trams towing the first trailer cars in December 1914 received no extra money. Because staff were joining the Forces there was a sudden influx of new conductors, and regular men training them were held liable for any cash or tickets the trainees lost. This catalogue of what Stan Collins terms 'niggles' was added to by a new sick leave scheme introduced early in 1915 whereby employees pronounced fit by the Company Doctor were handed a form headed "Application for re-employment". Then the L&P voiced its concern at the employment of women tram conductors in Edinburgh, soon to be replicated elsewhere, especially if they received a lower wage than men.

Both Unions had agreed in June 1914 to freeze wages and conditions on the LCC Trams for one year, but in February 1915 the AATVW asked for an all round 15% pay increase. The LCC offered a war bonus of 3/- for all staff earning less than 30/- a week, which would only cover 12% of all staff. Then in April 1915 new schedules were introduced which increased the proportion of spreadovers by reducing the number of cars in service at slack times. The L&P Union denounced what it called 'shameful exploitation by a public body' and in May 1915 issued a 'Call to arms of the Tramwaymen of London' demanding shorter spreadovers, proper overtime payments and a substantial war bonus. Stan Collins estimates that the L&P by this time repre-sented around half of the employees and was still recruiting.

At 11.30pm on Thursday 13th May 1915 a meeting was held at the Gaiety Theatre in Brixton. One of the 530 L&P members at New Cross depot wrote in the L&P Journal 'The Record': "We have had the screws put on us for a long while ... Walking home from Brixton ... we decided to call out the men, and at 3 o'clock we started. In an hour over 100 men were out with us, and by 7 o'clock the pavement was blocked with strikers." LCC Tramways Chief Officer Mr Fell visited New Cross and attempted unsuccessfully to halt the strike, but he would not negotiate unless the men returned to work. By nightfall 2,000 LCC Tramways employees were on strike. On the following day the whole of South London was tramless but North London appeared normal. A second mass meeting was held at the Euston Theatre of Varieties where a resolution was passed giving notice that unless the AATVW demand for a 15% increase be conceded the following day 'it is our intention to withhold our labour from the tramway service'. So on Monday 17th May 6,500 LCC staff and 3,000 MET staff failed to report for duty and over 2,000 London trams remained in their depots.

The LCC posted dismissal notices in all the depots and advertised for new recruits, while the London Commissioner of Police relaxed the stringent tram driving test procedure, new training schools were opened and 'a good class of intelligent men' came forward. Only those over military age were accepted. Although the strike was solid some cars were operated by LCC officials. The press, of course, were unfriendly towards the strikers, although the London Evening News published some actual timesheets with shockingly long spreadovers. Munitions, of course, were a particularly sensitive issue in wartime, with workers at Woolwich Arsenal and Enfield Lock especially dependent on trams and it was considered by many to be unpatriotic to withdraw labour in time of war. At one stage the joint strike committee agreed to run a special service for workers at the Woolwich Arsenal. The L&P recognised the strike as official and began paying strike pay right from the start, but the AATVW members had to wait a fortnight before they received any money from their Union.

From Wednesday 19th May men began to return to work, especially on the North side where the AATVW was strongest. On Saturday 22nd May Fell ordered the following notice to be posted in depots: "All men on strike who are eligible for military or naval service are instructed to return their uniforms and badges to the tramway depots". No man eligible for the Forces was allowed to return to work and Fell, who Collins states "handled the whole issue with ruthless insensitivity", clearly played the patriotism card and agreed that strikers who enlisted would receive favourable consideration for reinstatement after the war. By Wednesday 2nd June the Times reported that return tickets were again being issued although some L&P men were still on strike. The next day the AATVW notified Fell that it was withdrawing from the joint strike committee. Shortly after the strike finished all LCC Tramway traffic staff received a war bonus of 3/- a week. The lesson of the strike for many was the need for a single Union. Many members of the AATVW were disgusted by the actions of their non-elected Executive, and membership of the L&P continued to rise. LCC Tramway staff continued to complain of their conditions, including allegations that Belgian refugees were employed to spy on staff, that money was being held back from conductors' wages to make up for short paying in, and that the only way to get a day off was to be caught ostentatiously smoking and be suspended.

The L&P compared LCC management negatively with the LGOC and there was no love lost between Mr Fell and the Union. The Conciliation Boards continued to meet during the war. The Traffic Board had two AATVW representatives, two L&P and two miscellaneous rep's but demands for improved wages and conditions were referred to arbitration. In 1916 the L&P sought to abolish the Boards, claiming that the AATVW and miscellaneous rep's often voted with management against the L&P, and in 1918 all the staff representatives resigned from the Traffic Board. A year earlier, the Whitley Committee, noting growing wartime demands for workers' control, had proposed National Councils, including one for the tramways industry, composed of nominees of Unions and employers. The National Joint Industry Council for tramways (NJIC) was constituted in 1919, and conceded a 48 hour week for all platform staff. From this time on the LCC ceased direct negotiations with its staff on matters not peculiar to London and accepted the wages and conditions negotiated by the Metropolitan District Council of the NJIC, on which it was represented, an interesting parallel with the Railway Conciliation scheme.

Stan Collins notes: "The overwhelming evidence is that by 1919 London tramway staff had fallen far behind the bus staff in the matter of wages, although ten years earlier a rough parity had existed. It was not until the 1930's, after the formation of London Transport, that they began to catch up with their rubber-shod colleagues. In one respect only – albeit an important one – were LCC staff better off than Combine employees, and that was their guaranteed week. On the crudest comparison of the jobs of bus and tram crews, throughout the 1920's the LCC consistently underpaid its staff by around 15% ... The LCC was also the rate setter for the Combine's tram staff, whilst its rates were below those which suburban municipal operators paid ... The LCC employee was worse off than the LGOC busmen when both were amalgamated into London Transport in 1933 ... The popular image of the LCC Tramways as a benign and considerate employer is a false one, and the London tramwaymen had everything to gain from amalgamation."[1] Stan could find no evidence that the LCC ever recognised the T&GWU.

Women on the trams

In October 1915 the Metropolitan Police agreed to grant licences to women conductors, and on 30th November the first of them began work on single deck tramcars. From there they progressed at the end of August 1916 to double deck trailer cars. On 31st March 1918 LCC Tramways employed 1,521 women conductors, roughly one for every three male employees, but on 29th October 1919 the service of the last of them was terminated. Stan Collins says they received their first war bonus in May 1917 and in March 1918 67% of women conductors received full war bonus of £1 per week. In August 1918 came the Equal Pay strike described in chapter 7. Many LUT staff were involved in the strike but only 5% of LCC staff due to the LCC policy of equal war bonus for women, albeit only after one year's service. Collins also notes that the women stimulated the organised social life of tram staff. From 1916 concert parties were held in several depots, to which wounded military personnel were transported in free special cars.[2]

Miss E. Claydon, a conductor of Stamford Hill depot, was run down and killed by a lorry on 8th September 1917 after changing points in the blackout. In a classic example of what Stan Collins describes as thoughtlessness at Chief Office three of her colleagues who went to her funeral in Suffolk were suspended. The L&P Union recommended the LCC to learn something of man (and woman?) management from the capitalist LGOC.[3]

The AATVW merged with the L&P in 1920 to become the United Vehicle Workers Union (UVW). A Whitley Council scheme for London busworkers had been proposed and rejected by L&P members in a ballot in 1918. The Executive Committee (EC) of the L&P amended the scheme and forced it through a delegate meeting. A Rank and File committee was formed and took their EC to court, following which the London bus workers were excluded from the scheme.[4] By March 1921 the UVW had voted to become part of the new Transport and General Workers Union, (T&GWU), with Ernest Bevin as its General Secretary. In the discussion that preceded the merger the National Organising Secretary of the Omnibus Section of the UVW George Sanders wrote in The Record (UVW Journal) of November 1922: "I want to state quite frankly that I should have been much more enamoured of the scheme that is now in front of the members had the NUR and ASLE&F been included in the list of Unions for the proposed amalgamation. Whether they have been approached or not I am unable to state, but at any rate if at all possible to get them in it ought to be done without delay. It appears to me that an amalgamation of transport Unions is not complete without these two bodies, and instead of rushing the present scheme every effort should be made to persuade these two Unions to come into the scheme, or if they have refused, it ought to be made quite clear to members of the constituent Unions who are asked to support the new scheme". (Fuller P 65).

He was right, of course. A single Union across the road – rail divide would have given more power to the workers' hand, but the differences were too deep and the personalities of Bevin and the NUR's Jimmy Thomas were too powerful to co-exist in one organisation. The NUR and ASLE&F were by now deeply attached to the Conciliation scheme, which by giving them, along with the RCA, statutory recognition, kept the T&GWU off the railways altogether, a situation that continues to this day. As we saw in Chapter 6, despite some interest in Bevin's Transport Workers Federation from the rank and file, the NUR leadership, afraid of sympathy strikes and loss of control over their members, opposed any amalgamation, though whether they informed Bevin of this is not recorded. But when Bevin asked for support from the rail Unions for the 1924 tram strike the fact that they were separate organisations did not prevent the rail Unions offering their assistance.

In 1921 the Tram NJIC, responding to a falling cost of living, agreed that wage rates should be adjusted at three monthly intervals according to a national index. A Court of Enquiry in 1921 had recommended the standardisation of wage rates on London's trams but nothing had been done. Between October 1922 and October 1923 wage cuts totalling 5/- per week were imposed. Then in June 1923 the three Combine tram companies, though not the LCC, announced a further reduction in wages, arguing that this was necessitated by losses incurred by competition from motor buses of the LGOC and other companies.[5] For the T&GWU Bevin pointed out that the three tram companies and the LGOC were all part of the same Combine under Lord Ashfield's control so this argument was nonsense, although the so-called pirate companies did cause a problem and declined to observe Trade Union agreements.[6] The Union again demanded a single traffic authority for London as had been recommended by a Parliamentary Select Committee in 1919 and a Royal Commission as long ago as 1905. In August 1923 the tramworkers asked the District Joint Industrial Council to consider the wages question, the need for legislation to control passenger transport

Tramway pointsman, 1939

in London, and to progress the standardisation of wage rates. The companies were demanding wage cuts but the T&GWU claimed a rise of 8/- a week, emphasising the wide disparity in wages between the top rate of a bus driver after six months service of 86/6 (£214.44 in 2014 money) while a tram driver after two years' service got only 67/- a week (£166.10 in 2014 money). The claim covered the LCC as well as the private company tramways.

In February 1924 a mass meeting of tramworkers instructed their committee to call a strike on 15th March if agreement had not been reached. In an impressive display of unity the bus workers authorised their committee to strike in sympathy. Harry Gosling, President of the T&GWU and Minister of Transport in the first ever Labour Government, which had just been elected, requested that the strike be delayed for six days. On 20th March 1924 both sides met at the Ministry of Labour. The 'pirate' companies offered to go to arbitration while the LCC put 5/- on the table. Despite the fact that a Court of Enquiry was ordered the strike went ahead at midnight. London's 16,000 tramworkers and the LGOC's 23,000 busworkers were out solid. Underground trains and the 300 pirate buses were heavily laden. On 24th March the Court of Enquiry reported that the merits of the Union case could not be faulted and that "the present crisis has, in the main, arisen through the tramway undertakings in the Metropolitan area being unable to earn sufficient to meet the claim." However, they offered no solution to the dispute.[7]

The Government brought in the 1924 London Traffic Act which introduced regulation of the number of buses and their routes. This gave the LGOC the green light to buy up the 'pirate' companies, and helped the position of the tramways. Most of the Companies came in line with the LCC's offer of a 5/- increase and a proposal that the rest of the claim should go to arbitration. The T&GWU rejected this and Bevin asked the Rail Unions for support. The NUR organised mass meetings which agreed to strike in sympathy while ASLE&F instructed its members to strike from 28th March. The Labour Government then threatened to invoke the Emergency Powers Act, which led to a joint resolution from the TUC General Council and the National Executive Committee of the Labour Party deploring the Government's measures and urging it to take control of London's transport and pay the wage increase by means of a subsidy. The employers finally agreed to pay an increase of 6/- per week. The proposed Underground strike was called off and the tramworkers accepted the offer in a ballot on 29th March despite still not achieving parity with the busworkers. Right up until the last tram ran in 1952 they never did achieve parity. The Union faced criticism for supporting a strike while a Labour Government was in office but responded that "a strong industrial base is the best support a Labour Government can have". Bevin's reputation as a tough and successful negotiator was sealed and recruitment to the Union shot up in response to its strong display of unity.[8]

Between 1924 and 1933 the LCC, the three companies, and West Ham Corporation paid drivers and conductors 73/- a week, but the other councils paid from 71/- down to a mere 65/- a week at Erith. The question arose whether the cheap fares which helped poorer sections of the community were paid for at the expense of tramway employees. These rates were significantly less than busworkers received despite the fact that trams could each carry up to 50% more passengers than a bus. By comparison, despite wage cuts in 1932, in 1933 an Underground Motorman received 93/- a week and a guard 69/- a week (after six years' service).[9]

THE END OF THE POST WAR BOOM AND TECHNOLOGICAL PROGRESS

LUT Feltham tram No.358 at Hanwell Depot when new, 1931

Late in 1920 the short post war boom broke. Unemployment rose and prices and wages generally began to fall. LCC tram fares were reduced in 1921 and the Company owned tramways and buses followed suit. Passenger numbers on the trams held broadly steady in the 1920s at about 1,000 million, while figures for the buses grew significantly from 936 million in 1920 to 994 million in 1922, 1,214 million in 1923, 1,822 million in 1927 and 1,958 million in 1930.[2] Technical development of buses moved ahead rapidly, allowing faster speeds and higher capacity, from the 34 seat 'B' Type of 1909 to the 54 seat 'S' Type of 1920, without any increase in running costs.[3] By 1927 the Police finally permitted larger buses with top covers and pneumatic tyres and in 1928 allowed the maximum speed of buses to increase from 12mph to 20mph. In 1929 the Police allowed the maximum width of buses to be increased to 7' 6" and windscreens to be fitted, all of which stimulated the increase in passenger numbers.[4]

Barker & Robbins note that the Combine's rates of pay were mostly equal to and often considerably above comparable rates outside. Mess rooms, sports associations, benevolent funds and retirement grants improved conditions and were examples of the paternalist style of management which the Combine adopted.

In 1927/8 61,000 men applied to the LGOC for drivers jobs. Of the 3,936 selected for testing, 44% failed the medical examination and eventually only 1,023 were selected as drivers. Frank Pick said in 1929: "The labour market being as it is, we can pick and choose our drivers with some care, and with some very strict regard to a standard". (Evidence to House of Lords Select Committee on Road Vehicles Regulation Bill). T&GWU Assistant General Secretary John Cliff believed that Lord Ashfield would never risk a dispute leading to a public enquiry into the Underground group's finances because this would reveal the very high profits on the buses, on which the busmen could then have based substantial pay claims. The bus profits were used to cross subsidise the tram companies and Underground railways.[5]

The advantageous terms of the 1919 wage agreement on the buses were replaced in April 1922 with a consolidated rate of one shilling nine and seven eighths pence for drivers and one shilling one and one eighth pence per hour for conductors.[6] By February 1921 unemployment had already passed the 1 million mark. The mine owners demanded a wage cut of 20% on the 1914 level. The Triple Alliance of Miners, Railway workers and Transport workers declared a strike for which London busworkers built support by establishing, along with workers from other industries, the South East District Vigilance Committee, which planned picketing. But the strike was called off by the Triple Alliance and the miners were betrayed. A deputation of busworkers occupied the UVW Union Head Office in protest and locked out the officials. It was in this fraught climate that the LGOC and Tillings tried to impose a pay cut of 3/- per week from October 1921. Following negotiations these cuts were withdrawn but concessions in other areas had to be made. What Ken Fuller describes as 'The Jewel in the Crown', the 10 hour maximum spreadover, was replaced by a 25% spreadover for all duties with a new maximum of 12 hours, albeit with an allowance of 12/6 for all duties with a spreadover of more than 10 hours. After 4th April 1922 wages would be cut by 1/4d an hour for drivers and 1/8d an hour for conductors for every 5 point fall below 135 in the Government's cost of living index. If the index fell below 85 both grades would lose 1/4d an hour for each subsequent fall of 5 points until the index reached 70. However, holidays were actually increased from 6 days to 8, and the disciplinary system was redrawn to give staff well-defined rights.

The UVW asked that all new entrants should join the Union. George Shave, the LGOC Chief Engineer, said: "We cannot put it in an agreement. We have done that, and Lord Ashfield has told you that it is being carried out, but I do not want to put it in the Agreement. There is no need to emphasise it". The eventual agreement permitted the Union to have collectors "within the shelter of the garages" provided they were employees of the companies and that "the privilege is not abused". Ken Fuller notes that the fact that the agreement contained improvements at a time when employers all over the country were tearing up collective agreements can only be seen as a testimony to the strength of London bus workers. UVW General Secretary Stanley Hirst wrote: "By the strength of organisation we were able to maintain most of what had previously been won, and in comparison with employees in other trades our members generally are favourably situated". But many London bus workers still saw it as a betrayal,[7] laying the basis for their support for the tramway staff in the 1924 strike described in Chapter 8, and further struggles. Fuller notes that even though the Agreement stated that "there shall not be any systematic overtime" the LGOC was forcing the men to work a 7 day week. At a special conference of garage delegates on 13th December 1921 Lloyd of Palmers Green garage complained that when route 20 was opened up 22 of his members had been sent to Chalk Farm to work their rest days and there had in fact been no rest days that year. Adams of Battersea garage pointed out that when summer schedules were being operated the Company, by forcing crews to work their rest days could put on 200 extra buses without employing a single extra man. The LGOC had also instructed staff to carry 5 standing passengers on the new 'S' and 'N' type buses without reference to the Union.[8]

Following the support of bus workers for the tram workers in the 1924 strike T&GWU General Secretary Ernest Bevin refused to lead the bus workers into any further struggles to improve their own wages and conditions. The Bus Committee demanded the practical abolition of spreadovers, that membership of the T&GWU should be a condition of employment, the abolition of voluntary rest day working and regular rotation of rest days, and an equal rate of 92/- a week for drivers and conductors, which amounted to an increase of 5/6 for drivers and 12/6 for conductors. Bevin dismissed the demand for a wage increase and advised the bus workers to concentrate on grappling with the whole problem of duties and spreadovers.[9] He made it clear that Union policy was the prerogative of the T&GWU's Executive Council, not the London Bus Section.

The left wing militant approach of the London Bus Section, which continued at least until the second world war, had originated with the London & Provincial Union in 1913, long before the foundation of the Communist Party of Great Britain in 1920. Quite why the London bus workers and their leaders adopted such left wing positions in the first place is difficult to discover. This left wing political radicalisation and influence was less pronounced among their colleagues on the trams and railways. But it is clear that the combination of a militant approach and a Company in a strong trading position, which was willing to negotiate with the Union and unwilling to jeopardise profits by holding out in strikes, led to better than average rates of pay and conditions, ensuring that the Union continued to have strong support among the staff. And the London Bus Section did not trust Bevin.[10] Many bus militants did join the Communist Party (CPGB). George Sanders, for instance, came to play a leading part in the British bureau of the Red International of Labour Unions.[11]

Negotiations dragged on. Bevin pointed out (correctly addressing the issue of speed up and increase in the size of buses): "The development of petrol propulsion has grown with such rapidity that every vehicle which comes on the road is an intensification of the one already there. It is the same front and back". The introduction of diesel engines from 1930 would further intensify this trend. On 15th August 1924 Pick, then a director of the LGOC, agreed that wages would not be reduced below their present level. Finally, in January 1925 it was agreed that not less than 75% of duties would have a maximum spreadover of 9 hours and a further 15% of duties could have a maximum spreadover of 10 hours. But the Company refused to make Union membership a condition of employment. Bevin refused a London Bus Section request in 1927 for a strike on the issue, but a notice was posted in all LGOC garages saying: "Whilst there is no obligation on the part of any employee to belong to a Trade Union, the Company find it mutually convenient to have some organisation to represent the staff collectively on their behalf. The Company therefore recognises the Transport Workers Federation (!) for drivers and conductors and inside staff other than craftsmen". And in 1929 the Operating Manager issued a statement which confirmed the Company's undertaking to call into the office any employee leaving the T&GWU and to recommend re-joining, in addition to the old undertaking to point out to new employees the advantages of membership.[12] Despite the improvements achieved there was a rash of local disputes in early 1925 over schedules, in particular at Seven Kings and Hendon garages. The London Bus Conference in 1925 rejected the agreement, and after amendments the membership again rejected the January agreement by 7,401 votes to 6,968. The Union campaigned for acceptance among its members and finally signed the Agreement in March 1926.[13]

Sir Albert Stanley (later to become Lord Ashfield) with umbrella and top hat in the 1920s

On the Underground it is worth noting that technological advance in the form of replacement of steam engines with electric propulsion on the Metropolitan and District resulted in less pay for drivers on the grounds that less skill was required to drive an electric train than a steam one. And there is no record of any increase in pay following replacement of manual gates with air worked doors on tube trains.

Following the 'Black Friday' betrayal of the miners on 15th April 1921 with the failure of the Triple Alliance to support them, the three railway Unions in May 1921 'reluctantly' agreed the suspension of the guaranteed week achieved in 1919. Further cuts followed, including redundancies and short time working; in the main clerical workers were given a minimum of three days' work per week.[14]

The NUR General Secretary J.H. Thomas MP had been waxing lyrical about the Railways Act of 1921. He declared on 12th August 1921 that the Act was "As near perfection as the brain of man can make a Bill in its passage through Parliament". Perfection it was certainly not, but it did safeguard the rights of railway workers made redundant as a result of the grouping of the railways into four regional conglomerates (the Underground, including the Metropolitan, was not included in this). Such persons were to be paid compensation for loss of wages and also for loss of prospective super-annuation.[15] The National Wages Board in its award of 3rd June 1920 had stated: "In practice security of employment for the ordinary railway employee extends beyond the guaranteed week and, provided he is able to perform his work, he is practically immune from the vicissitudes of short time and unemployment.[16] As the crisis hit, the Railway Companies cut staffing, hours and rates of pay. The NUR Special General Meeting on 17th March 1922 agreed to reduction of railway wages by between 16/- and 20/- a week in order to safeguard jobs by allowing the Companies to reduce fares. They decided not to refer the issue to the new Wages Boards and accepted revised conditions of service.[17] This is a graphic illustration of the differences between negotiating with a successful and profitable bus company and anti-union railway companies, with a Union that saw London Underground railways and their staff as inferior and strictly subsidiary to the big four national railway companies (this attitude lived on into my time in the NUR in the 1970's).

In 1923, following reference to the National Wages Board, further cuts were agreed by the NUR and RCA but the ASLE&F called a strike from 19th January 1924. The effects of the strike were uneven as in most cases NUR drivers did not support it, although in some cases they did. The strike did not affect the Underground and it ended on 29th January with minor concessions to locomotive staff.[18] An article in the Railway Review pointed out that the Railway Companies had increased their divi-dends in 1922, and the NUR in December 1924 launched a new all-grades programme for improvements in pay and conditions. But in the light of the general depression and the growth of road competition, the claim was met with a flat 'No' at Xmas 1925. The Executive Committee of the NUR had a joint meeting with the Executive Council of the T&GWU on 1st March 1923 and had tried to build a degree of unity, as employers in the road transport industry were demanding reductions in lorry drivers' wages and conditions[19]. But nothing was done in the case of the London Bus Section, who as we have seen were more successful than most in defending and advancing their position. However, the pledge of support from the NUR in the successful 1924 tram strike gives a taste of what might have been achieved if the attempts at co-operation had been followed through and developed.

The General Strike

The very brevity of the post war boom and its rapid turn round into depression in 1921 set off a period of great social and industrial unrest which culminated in the general strike of 1926. Called by the TUC on 3rd May 1926, its immediate cause was another attempt by the mine owners to impose further wage cuts on the miners, but its impact was felt right across the country, and not least on London's transport system. Lord Ashfield wrote in a notice: "The regrettable dispute which has arisen with regard to the terms and conditions of employment in the coal mines cannot justify the stoppage of those services which are essential to the public welfare. While it is recognised that the support which has been shown by all classes of workers to the miners is admirable, it should not be forgotten that there is a wider and greater loyalty which should be shown to the nation at large. In this crisis each man must decide for himself but we hope that we can rely upon the staff remaining at work. There is no difference between the Companies and their staff, but both have a duty to the public which they should discharge. The Companies are bound to discharge to the best of their ability and resources their duty in providing public passenger services. Those members of the staff who do likewise are assured of their positions". It all sounded so reasonable until you read the threat in the last sentence. And as we shall see, it was no idle threat. A general strike does, of course, put into question the legitimacy of the state power, a point not lost on NUR General Secretary J.H.Thomas during the 1919 strike.

Extract from General Strike daily strike bulletin dated Thursday morning 6th May

FELLOW TRAMWAY WORKERS

Reports show that the strike is rapidly extending and is now taking a further step forward. Up till now STOPPING WORK for the bosses has been the most important thing. Now we are faced with a second task, that is ORGANISING WORK FOR THE TUC.

A START was made last night, when the Herald offices produced the TUC official bulletin, THE BRITISH WORKER, which sold by the thousand late last night and early this morning. Early last night the Government sent a force of police who batoned the crowds out of the way and occupied the Herald offices, stopping the production and distribution of the paper.

LATER the paper was released, thus showing clearly that the Government is divided among itself, one section having the wind up and the other, with Wix thinking he is going to be Mussolini, wanting to fight to the death.

THE BRITISH WORKER is a fine eight page production which completely beats the Government plus O.M.S. plus scab Labour BRITISH GAZETTE.

SO WE HAVE NOW TO STOP THE SCAB SERVICES AND ORGANISE OUR OWN. LET EVERY MAN LEND A HAND AND OBEY THE INSTRUCTION OF THE TUC AND THE STRIKE COMMITTEES.

The London Tramwaymen Communist Group

Author's Note O.M.S. (Organisation for the Maintenance of Supplies) was a right wing group established in 1925 to provide volunteers in the event of a General Strike and was taken over by the Government during the 1926 General Strike.

The Underground group stated that 9,610 'volunteers' were enrolled, 78% of them described as 'persons normally employed but available for service during the strike' (the politest description of a scab that I have ever heard), 19% students or persons of independent means, and 3% unemployed. 39,000 men of the Combine were on strike. By 14th May 116 trains of the 315 scheduled were running on the Underground and Metropolitan, along with 638 LGOC buses, 318 Tillings and 349 Independent buses. The municipal trams ran less than 100 of their 2,269 cars. Barker & Robbins say that on the railways despite 'incidents' due to over enthusiasm and under training of 'volunteers', a 'reasonable' service was operated at a flat fare of 3d. On the Metropolitan 80% of staff struck but they ran trains every 15 minutes to Harrow and every 20 minutes on the Metropolitan side only of the Circle; these figures increased as the strike went on. At Fulwell depot only 6 trams went out, with 5 others returning to Chiswick depot reported damaged by egg and brick throwing, which gives an idea of the passions aroused. Buses, they say, had 'difficulty' getting in and out of garages and a large number were parked in Regents Park.[20]

The RCA, in what its General Secretary A.G. Walkden described as its "first real baptism in a general withdrawal of labour" (being generally opposed to strikes) declared the response of its membership to be "most encouraging". 3,000 new members were recruited in the first days of the strike. But by 12th May when the strike ended only 55% of the RCA members were still on strike.[21] Malcolm Wallace in his history of the RCA/TSSA writes that when the strike was called 95% of London Underground staff responded. By the end of the strike on 12th May only 37% of trains were operative.[22]

Bagwell quotes a comment in the 'Westminster Worker' (a strike bulletin) commenting on the slowness and infrequency of the District Line during the strike: "We understand that luncheon cars are to be put on trains running between Westminster and Blackfriars".[23]

Stan Collins records 'incidents' at Clapham depot on May 7th and at New Cross on May 13th and 14th, when 'volunteers' attempted to bring cars out. 'Riots' were recorded in the Walworth Road and around a convoy of trams briefly operating between Hampstead and Kings Cross. Power for these trams came from the LCC's Greenwich generating station, which was manned by 37 Naval Ratings. The LCC assisted the 'volunteers' and beds were made up for them on the floor of the Chief office but Stan Collins notes that the LCC was "embarrassed ... and at best made merely a tactical gesture". When the strike finished the Metropolitan District Council of the Tram National Joint Industry Council met to arrange the return to work. London managers attempted to impose new conditions on re-engaged staff but this was squashed by the T&GWU. One of the East London municipal managers (I wonder which one) attempted to use the occasion to withdraw two unprofitable services with a number of redundancies, but a T&GWU delegate reported that the other London managers "plied him with alcohol" until he changed his mind.[24]

On the buses Ken Fuller notes that 3,300 buses were moved into Regents Park for 'volunteer' crews, mainly students. It was estimated that 1 in 4 of the normal quota of buses was running by 12 May. Farman in 'The General Strike', London 1972, is quoted as saying that although there were 300 buses operated by 'volunteers' on the Tuesday of the strike, this was down to 40 by the Friday.[25] Clearly the situation was fluid and both 'pirate' (independent) and 'volunteer' buses were liable to attack. Jack

Dash in J. Skelly's book 'The General Strike 1926', London 1976, recalls an incident at the Elephant & Castle: "All eyes were turned in one direction. Coming in from the direction of Westminster were car loads of Special Reserves, all steel helmeted and truncheons at the ready, the trucks protected by a kind of wire cage over the top to protect them from missiles aimed by the strikers. They were followed by mounted police, escorting a General omnibus with passengers, driven by a University student. Stones began to rain down from the tops of the adjacent tenement buildings ... The mounted Reserves and Police were unseated from their horses. Running fights took place with the foot police. The bus was halted, the passengers were dragged out and a great crowd of men overturned the vehicle, which caught fire and began to blaze away. There were casualties everywhere. Eventually reinforcements arrived and the Police, Special Constables and Army Reserve men regained control".

The Government, having failed to get the trams running due to their greater vulnerability to strikers, concentrated on trying to get buses moving. But apparently Lord Ashfield was reluctant to expose his buses to damage from strikers and 'volunteer' crews and only released older models. By 5th May 47 General buses were put out of action and the Government would not try to run buses into the 'wilds of the working class regions' (Skelly). Bill Jones, later to be Chairman of the Central Bus Committee and a member of the T&GWU Executive Council, was in his 20's and recalled: "Blacklegs rode with Police escorts, including the man who later became

'Volunteer' B Type bus in the General Strike. Note barbed wire on bus

Operating Manager, the bastard. He was an undergraduate. The blacklegs were in the main students. Of course we turned the bastards over when we could – turfed 'em off when the Police weren't around. I lived at that time just off Kingsland Road, and we used to turn 'em over like nobody's business down there. Because they didn't all have Policemen riding with them – there wasn't enough Police for that. And if they didn't have a Policeman, that was their lot. One of the lads would get in the bus and drive it anywhere – any side turning out of the way – so it would sometimes take 'em an hour to find the bus". (Skelly)

The strike lasted for nine days. The TUC had no desire to challenge the Capitalist system and called the strike off despite the miners violently opposing the terms of the settlement. The LCC at first refused full reinstatement for their regular tramway staff and on 13th and 14th May had tried to run trams from New Cross with 'volunteer' staff. Backing up Stan Collins account, Skelly notes on page 274, : "Once again, huge crowds assembled outside the yard. Police battled with pickets to clear a way, but the tram was halted after a journey of just 20 yards. The Police ordered the work to stop to prevent riots. The LCC Tramways Department settled with its employees on Friday 14th May.

Some Tillings bus workers returned to work to find themselves working along-side blacklegs. They were swiftly called out by colleagues who marched on Catford garage, staying out until terms for a return to work were agreed. The LGOC settled on 14th May on terms which guaranteed no victimisation.[26]

After the strike "Railway managers were determined to exact their revenge and refused to take all the former strikers back. Railway workers were enraged at the reception they received and thousands spontaneously continued the strike".[27] "The three Railway Unions and the T&GWU formed a national strike committee to resolve the new situation ... The settlement, finalised on 14th May 1926, can be ranked amongst the most infamous in the history of industrial relations".[28] "By 22nd May 1926 6,321 members of the RCA (nationally) were still waiting to be reinstated ... In April 1929 the RCA took action in Parliament against Bills proposed by the Underground Electric Railways Co. Ltd. which resulted in Lord Ashfield giving an undertaking to restore one clerk to his former position".[29]

Although the General Strike did not directly impact on the wages and conditions of London's transport workers, the militant response to it and the widespread failure of management's appeals to the loyalty of staff show that there was much discontent, especially among busworkers, who organised to resist the conciliatory approach of their General Secretary Ernest Bevin. In 1928, against the advice of their committee, the membership voted in a ballot for the termination of the 1926 agreement and for a claim for higher wages, more holidays, an increase in meal reliefs to 30 minutes and abolition of spreadovers. Bevin urged caution, warning that the Company might use termination of the agreement to worsen conditions. Figures were produced which showed that for an average duty of 8.5 hours, paying drivers 92/6 and conductors 84/- a week, the actual hours worked were: Mon–Fri 6 hours 39 minutes, Sat 6 hours 45 minutes, Sun 6 hours 31 minutes. The Company pleaded poverty, claiming that revenue had declined by £100,000 in Jan/Feb 1929 compared with 1928 and petrol costs had increased by £375,000 per year. Frank Pick agreed to increase the minimum meal relief to 30 minutes and to employ 100 extra crews to facilitate this. Two extra days holiday had to be taken in winter, making a total of 10 days a year.

An increase in penalty payments for very early and very late duties was offered, but no increase in basic rates. These proposals were agreed in a ballot on 10th May and a new agreement was signed on 31stMay 1928.[30] At a time when most workers were being subjected to wage cuts and prices were falling, the standstill in London bus workers' wages represented an increase both in absolute and relative terms. They felt that this was justified by the increase in size and speed of buses mentioned previously. The larger and faster new buses cost no more to operate than the old ones and brought much increased revenue into the LGOC. Details were kept out of the public realm, but the LGOC's profits continued to subsidise 'unsatisfactory' results on the Underground railways and the Company tramways. Fuller notes that LGOC profits in 1929 were £671,000, allowing an 8% dividend to be paid to shareholders, while in 1930 profits increased to £740,000. They could have afforded a pay increase and this was the root of disaffection with Bevin's leadership of the T&GWU. The possible effect of this on their fellow workers on the Underground and trams seems not to have entered their consciousness. London bus workers still saw themselves as 'aristocrats', and very left wing aristocrats at that.

Bevin's main concern was protection of conditions at a time of economic difficulty, especially the hard-won guaranteed week which the railway Unions, with their conciliation boards, had so signally failed to defend. He participated in the Mond-Turner talks of 1928 with a group of 20 leading industrialists headed by Sir Alfred Mond of ICI, as part of the TUC's scheme to discuss ways in which the two sides of industry could co-operate. The report of these talks argued that rationalisation and 'rustification' should be welcomed and encouraged, and that a National Industrial Council should be established under which a system of compulsory arbitration should operate. In return the employers would take a 'sympathetic view' of Trade Union recognition. According to Emmanuel Shinwell the Labour MP: "The Trade Union keeps the men in order, the employer in return agrees to employ Union men only".[31] This of course was anathema to the London Bus Section with its strong Socialist and Communist influences, great self confidence and a highly profitable but not unsympathetic employer.

CHAPTER TEN

THE FORMATION OF THE LONDON PASSENGER TRANSPORT BOARD

Testing the 'deadman's handle' at Northfields Depot, Piccadilly Line, 1937

Co-ordination of all London's passenger transport by one body was obviously a desirable objective, for which all the Unions had campaigned for many years, but it meant different things to different people. And from the very start the main line railway companies made it clear that their suburban railway operations would not be included. The Southern had an extensive programme of electrification but the other companies were much slower off the mark and some sections of their lines were only to be electrified by incorporation into the Underground.

The 1924 London Traffic Act had already introduced regulation of buses and the routes they ran on but the highly profitable nature of the business meant that there was still considerable competition for the LGOC from independent operators, which were often called 'pirates'. The LGOC was of course keen to eliminate this competition and no less than 56 independent bus companies were absorbed into London Transport in 1933.[1] The LGOC was a part of the Combine, as the Underground Electric Railway Company was known to its staff. The Combine owned all the underground lines except the Metropolitan and two large and one small tramway companies, the LUT, MET and South Metropolitan.

But this still left the municipal tramways (chief among them the LCC) outside their control. In 1920 the LCC had 149 miles of tramway, and in 1921 took over the operation of the Leyton system. Some short extensions brought the total to 167 miles by 1932. Through services were developed by operating agreements with East Ham, West Ham, Walthamstow and Croydon municipalities along with the two large Combine owned companies. Barking council had closed their solitary route to Beckton gasworks in 1929, leaving the municipal operators of Ilford, Bexley (who had taken over Dartford's trams) and Erith as separate entities. The decrepit fleet of open top cars operated by the SouthMet company showed the worst of tram operation. By comparison, the LCC invested heavily in modernising its fleet – some 850 trams received the 'Pullman' treatment in the late 1920's, and new faster cars were introduced in 1930. The LUT and MET Companies brought in 100 fast comfortable 'Feltham' cars in 1931, but the amount of investment necessary to bring the whole of the tramways up to a modern standard was not likely to make as good a return for private capital as diesel buses. The drive to incorporate the mostly loss-making municipal tramways (only Ilford and Walthamstow were shown to be profitable), with their cheap workman's fares, into a Combine controlled LPTB thus has to be regarded as a privatisation, not the nationalisation which the Unions had campaigned for.

The LCC had recognised that the future operation of an effective tram system in London would require the construction of expensive subways under the central part of London, where surface operation continued to be denied them. On this subject, see Ed Humphreys' articles in Tramfare (journal of the Tramway and Light Railway Society), Nos 272, 273 and 274 for a full examination of the proposals. The one subway which had been built, under Kingsway, was rebuilt in 1930 to accommodate double deck cars but the expense deterred any further developments in this direction. In any case, the tide had begun to turn against trams. Herbert Morrison, the former Labour leader of the LCC, and Minister of Transport in the 1929 Labour Government, often cited as the architect of the LPTB, came out against trams. The 1931 Royal Commission on Transport recommended their gradual removal. Thus, the Combine was very firmly in the driving seat of the new organisation and municipal influence was practically excluded.[2]

In fact, the demand for a joint municipal authority was explicitly rejected by Morrison himself. If the alternative had been full outright nationalisation this fault might have been attenuated, but the Act provided for London Transport stocks to be issued in return for the shares in the constituent private companies. The local authorities concerned were paid sums equivalent to their outstanding loan obligations or issued with an agreed amount of London Transport stocks. The stocks would pay a rate of interest of not more than 6%. There were three types of stock. Holders of 'C' stocks, for instance, received 3.5% in 1933/4, 4% for the next two years, 4.5% in 1936/7, 4% in 1937/8, and 1.5% in 1938/9.[3] In its first year the LPTB made a profit of £4,778,782 (Fuller P135). The terms were sufficiently generous to secure the assent of 95% of the private interests involved in terms of capital owned. An independent and self-supporting Board was established on the lines of the Central Electricity Board of 1926 and the BBC of 1927. It has been claimed that London Transport was nationalised at this time, but the private ownership through the issue of stocks shows that it was a far cry from the nationalisation which the Unions and Labour-run municipalities had demanded. A study of the facts shows Morrison in a different light to the socialist hero he is sometimes portrayed as. The Daily Telegraph aptly described it as "Nationalisation in Disguise".[4] The bus workers rank and file movement described it as "State Capitalism". (Clegg P 35) Nationalisation proper was not to come until the 1948 creation of the British Transport Commission.

The Unions demanded statutory representation of the workforce on the Board, again opposed by Morrison at the 1932 TUC and Labour Party conferences.[5] Morrison was able to convince John Bromley, Alexander Walkden and Charlie Cramp, General Secretaries of the three railway unions ASLE&F, RCA and NUR, to drop the claim for representation on the LPTB on the basis that the introduction of Trade Unionists would enable capitalist interests to demand similar rights. This was monstrous, considering that 'capitalist interests' would own the Board through their stocks, and Board members such as Lord Ashfield had widespread financial interests and directorships. Perhaps Morrison wanted to obscure the fact that the LPTB continued to be privately owned. It was accountable to no-one. Even the stockholders had no annual meeting, their only right being to call in the receiver in the unlikely event of bankruptcy. Nationalisation would at least have brought in accountability to a Government Minister, as it did in 1948, but in 1933 this 'interference', as they described it, was rejected. Morrison told the T&GWU that worker directors were 'bad socialism'. They were not persuaded but their resolution at the TUC was remitted (referred to the Executive).[6] The issue dragged on until 1944, when the TUC, as part of the planning for the post war nationalisations, quietly dropped the demand for worker representation on the Boards of Nationalised industries (see Clegg P 34).

Interestingly, when the Bill to establish the LPTB came before the House of Commons on 14th February 1933 the Labour opposition abstained. Lord Hailsham, the Lord Chancellor, is quoted by Barker & Robbins as saying: "This measure is one which is Conservative in its structure".[7]

John Cliff, the Assistant General Secretary of the T&GWU, was appointed to the Board, and given special responsibility for staff matters, but not before he had been obliged to resign his Union position.[8] Bill Jones (of the T&GWU) recalled that Cliff was very much his own man and never saw eye-to-eye with Bevin, who urged him to take the post on the Board because he wanted to get rid of him (see Fuller P 134).

The new Board decided not to unify road and rail operations but to leave them as separate entities subject to a single overall policy at top level, and once again the Unions did not make any moves to unify their activities across the road-rail divide, thus losing another opportunity for co-operation. Historic ties to different negotiating systems were broken in the case of the trams, who withdrew from the National Joint Industrial Council for the tram industry, but despite being in the same Union as the bus staff, formed a separate negotiating structure, the Tram and Trolleybus Council. This united the former Company and Municipal operations, and inherited the commitment to cheap workmen's fares and the possibility of staff changing routes during the day which was strenuously opposed by the Central Bus Section. Stan Collins says (P 73) that while the buses had a 'single road schedule', on the trams some duties were called a 'married road' where the second half of a duty could be on a different route. Staff could also be sent to a different depot to cover vacancies. He says that the LCC "was a fair employer at the top, but the Inspectors were bastards, they were harsh, and you worked under constant fear of losing your job" (P 77). "They used to book you for the least little thing in the old tram days. If you were booked for running early you had to go and see the Guv'nor – he'd want to know why....If you were a minute late back off your relief you'd get booked" (P 79). The LCC staff contracts had no set retirement age and ex-LCC staff retained the right to work to whatever age they chose; some continued to a ripe old age; I recall a shunter at Ealing Common Depot where I worked who had started his career as a tram driver on the LCC who was 85 when he retired.

The Central Bus Section continued much as it had before under the LGOC.

Feltham and Standard E1 type trams in Telford Ave Depot, Streatham, 1938

The other area of change was in the country area. The LGOC had expanded into the rural areas around London as suburban developments had spread, and had established the Green Line coach network in 1932, taking advantage of the new arterial roads which the Government was building. But the LPTB Act greatly expanded this area of operations and the LPTB took over routes from a number of non-London companies, namely Aldershot & District, Chatham & District, Eastern National, East Kent, Hants & Dorset, Maidstone & District, Southdown, and Thames Valley. The staff of these disparate parts were welded together into the Country Services Committee. Wage rates were generally levelled up, but remained considerably less than in the Central (red bus) area. One person operation of buses in both country and central areas was inherited from some of the constituent companies, but was restricted to single deckers with less than 20 seats. A flat rate bonus of 5/- per week was paid to the drivers of one man buses. The LPTB Annual Report of 30th June 1935 notes on P58 that Leyland Cub buses seating 20 passengers had been introduced in February 1935 "controlled by a Driver-Conductor". The first woman bus driver did not start until 1974, so until shortly before this the term 'One Man Operation' (OMO) was in common usage.

Conferences of the three road service sections met every other month. Each section had a Committee elected by ballot every two years, thus the T&GWU was able to

The bus training school at Chiswick, 1935

extend its enviable democratic structure from the Central buses to the rest of the road services. Frank Pick laid down that each section had to be self-supporting ie no cross subsidisation (Clegg P 73).

On the Railways the Unions insisted on retaining the Staff Councils Scheme. The Metropolitan line was simply tacked on to the scheme inherited from the Combine. NUR Political General Secretary J.H.Thomas MP claimed that he had threatened to resign from the Labour Government if Herbert Morrison, then Minister of Transport, did not set up a Staff Councils Scheme similar to that on the main line railways. As Bagwell drily remarks, the Craft unions and the T&GWU "had no great enthusiasm" for this.[9] On the fall of the Labour Government Thomas joined the 'National' coalition Government on 14th August 1931. The National Executive of the NUR on 31st August instructed him to abide by the decision of the Parliamentary Labour Party to become the official opposition. He did not do so and resigned as General Secretary the same day, preferring to support former Labour leader Ramsay MacDonald and become Secretary for the dominions in what was effectively a Tory Government.[10]

The three railway Unions felt more attached to their members on the main line railways than to their colleagues on the buses, and when dealing with their members on the Underground tended to follow the policies and decisions of the main line railways.

The canteen at Chiswick bus Works, 1000 seats, 1922

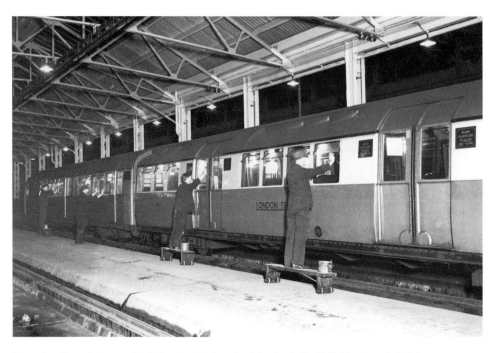

Cleaning the windows of a 'Standard' tube stock train at Northfields Depot, 1937

The nine Sectional Councils established on 13th February 1934 for railway operating staff dealt with day to day matters. For full details of staff represented and a flavour of how the scheme functioned see the Machinery of Negotiation 'Blue Book', as it was called, appended. A Negotiating Committee dealt with rates of pay and conditions of service, including hours of work. An independent Wages Board at the top acted as an arbitration panel. It was clearly specified in the agreement: "No withdrawal of labour or lockout or interference with efficient operation shall take place until the cause of dispute has been dealt with under these proposals and unless a settlement has not been reached within 28 days after the result of the deliberations of the Wages Board has been published". This agreement ensured that no significant industrial action took place on the railways for many years. Despite the often glacial pace of negotiations some advances were achieved. The contrast with the situation on the buses could not have been greater.

As many of the Sectional Councils were the province of a single Union the election process, although it seemed quite democratic to the activists in the Unions, was quite opaque to most of the members. Sectional Council No 1, Clerical and Technical staff, was wholly run by the RCA. Sectional Council No 2, Booking Office staff, was mostly RCA with partial NUR representation, as was No 6, Operating Supervisors, so there were sometimes elections. Sectional Council No 3 was hotly disputed between the NUR and ASLE&F with fiercely fought elections. Sectional Councils No 4 Station Staff, 5 Engineering Supervisors, 7 Signal Engineering, 8 Permanent Way, and 9 Mechanical Engineering Wages Grades, were wholly organised by the NUR.

It is noteworthy that Sectional Council No 1 – Clerical and Technical staff – covered, among others, 'common' posts ie those at Head Office (55 Broadway) and elsewhere which covered bus staff as well as railway staff. The RCA was generally very reluctant to engage in industrial action and did not attempt to utilise this commonality to breach the 'road – rail divide'. To reflect the RCA's increased coverage of clerical, technical and supervisory staff on the buses and other non-railway areas the RCA became the Transport Salaried Staffs Association in 1951.[11] Clegg notes (P 42) that the T&GWU had a clerical section but the RCA aimed to cover Head Office staff in the Underground group. The T&GWU recognised the RCA's right to organise Country Service depot Inspectors and clerks, but elsewhere competition existed.

Apart from the Staff Councils scheme, there was a veritable plethora of negotiating structures for workshop staff and other departments. Barker & Robbins observe that the LPTB, under its Act of Parliament, was obliged to set up negotiating schemes with the various Unions, but it is clear that the wily Lord Ashfield and the stickler for detail Frank Pick were not going to go out of their way to help the Unions by pulling the various negotiating machineries together.

As we have seen, the Craft Unions did not wish to participate in the Staff Councils scheme. In 1932 no fewer than 13 Craft Unions* came together to form the London Transport Joint Trades Committee, which covered the whole of the LPTB with separate sub-committees for railway, bus and tram sections. The structure displayed a high degree of unity, marred only by the separate organisation of the more numerous semiskilled and unskilled grades on the railways in the NUR, with their own series of Departmental Committees. There was thus a whole series of negotiating committees in the various workshops. Chiswick Bus works had a Works Council recognised by management. (Clegg P 22) Other departments had separate Negotiating Structures, including Power Generation and Distribution, Canteens, Commercial Advertising, and all the Supervisory, Control and Managerial grades also had separate structures.

The LPTB was aware of the importance of staff facilities in maintaining good staff relations. The first Annual Report on 30th June 1934 noted that staff canteens were provided for recreation as well as refreshment and, I would add, to keep the staff out of the pub. The 1935 Annual Report says on Page 28 that there had been "Three labour stoppages without any notice from the staff" and "not supported by the Trade Union concerned". "Practically the whole of the Board's staff are now covered by Negotiating Machinery acting through the Trade Union representation or their elected staff councils or committees". "The Board's relations with the Trade Unions, Staff Associations and other bodies representing the staff continue to be satisfactory". The 1936 Report says that Negotiating Machinery had been established for Engineering Supervisory staff and Traffic Supervisory staff (Country buses and coaches), and Garage Wardens (Central Buses). These areas were mostly represented by the RCA whose influence was spreading from being a purely rail Union to the

---

* The Amalgamated Engineering Union, Electrical Trades Union, National Union of Vehicle Builders, Transport & General Workers Union, National Union of General and Municipal Workers, Boilermakers and Iron & Steel Shipbuilders Society, Associated Blacksmiths Forge and Smithy Workers Society, National Union of Sheet Metal Workers and Braziers, National Society of Metal Mechanics, Amalgamated Society of Woodworkers, Amalgamated Union of Foundry Workers, Amalgamated Society of Wood-Cutting Machinists, National Union of Enginemen, Firemen, Mechanics and Electrical Workers – Clegg P 53.

buses. The 1936 Report also records five minor labour stoppages without notice and not supported by the Trade Union concerned ie unofficial. (P 23) It notes an increase of staff of 1,466 over the previous year due to the granting of extra holidays, additional service requirements and additional work in the engineering departments.

The bus workers' Rank & File movement took a principled position in favour of unity but was unable to achieve much in practice, even among the road services staff. The hierarchies of the many different Unions had their own interests and power structures, so they were not going to pursue the goal of unity.

The Rank and File newspaper 'Busman's Punch' said (12th August 1932): "Every opportunity should be taken to keep all sections of London Passenger transport – buses, trams, railways and coaches – in close touch with each other, so that the employers' old policy of 'Divide and Conquer' can be defeated." In its March 1933 issue the 'Busman's Punch' said: "The issues of the seven hour day, no spreadovers and the definite limitation of speed (with compensation for speed) – these are the practical issues". The Rank & File movement called a TOT Conference (Trams, Omnibuses, Trains) in July 1934 which attracted delegates from 31 bus and tram branches and 5 rail branches, demanding among other things busmen's rates for tram workers. The achievement of this demand ought to have been facilitated by the LPTB's decision in 1934 to replace trams with trolleybuses. The Central Bus Committee attempted to persuade the T&GWU's National Trams Council to recognise trolleybuses as buses not trams so they could press for bus rates of pay. Selective interference with the conversion programme would have given some industrial muscle to persuade management. But the T&GWU's Trams Council refused to agree (we are not privy to the reasons for this perverse decision but we may presume that they were 'protecting their own turf'). Certainly this has to be classed as a disastrous own goal on the part of the T&GWU. Fulwell Depot, where the first trolleybuses in London had been running since 1931, refused to be represented by the Trams Council. Their Rank & File delegate, Mr Burr, pointed out: "Our conditions are different, our uniforms are different, and we do one and a half days more work a week than they do. The conductor takes approximately an average of £10 more a week than he did on a tramcar. The intensification has increased from 10-15% more compared with the trams".

The Communist Party had built considerable influence within the busworkers' Rank & File committee, initially through its industrial front organisation the 'Minority Movement'. In 1932 they changed policy and abandoned the Minority Movement as they considered it "appeared as a body outside the Trade Unions, dictating to the Trade Unions as to what they ought to do". It was replaced with rank and file movements "growing up from within the Unions". The 'Busman's Punch' in May 1933 said: "The statement is made that the movement is dominated by communists and its policy is that of the Communist Party. This is definitely untrue". (Clegg P 108)

So even the unofficial Rank & File committee seems to have had great difficulty in building any unity between tram, trolleybus and (diesel) bus workers, let alone with the railway staff. Incidentally, diesel buses were not referred to as such at this time, possibly so as not to draw attention to the German nationality of Herr Diesel; they were called 'heavy oil' or 'compression ignition' engines.

In 1935 a Western Divisional Trolleybus Vigilance Committee was established, prompted by their distrust of General Secretary Bevin, who refused to meet the Trams council to discuss the Central Bus Committee's demand for central bus rates to be paid to trolleybus staff. According to a report to the 16th September 1935 conference of the Rank and File Movement: "Bevin is coming back with an offer of a hybrid grade. We must resist this." It was reported that trolleybus workers had set up their own group because only 5 out of 35 branches were affiliated to the Rank &

Interior of former NS type bus used as a mobile canteen, 1937

File Movement and some of the other branches were scared of the term 'Rank & File Movement'. Then in September 1935 a 'Justice for tram and trolleybus' committee was set up. It seems that progressive tram and trolleybus workers suspected (rightly) that the support of busworkers for the 'levelling up' principle might prove 'less sincere' as time went by. At a joint conference in October 1935 Rank and File leader Bert Papworth called for a single Rank & File Movement using the conversion to trolleybuses, which was now in full swing, to raise their wages to the bus rate. But there were issues with conditions. Tram workers took their meal reliefs on the car and were said not to be willing to adopt the busworkers' practice of meal reliefs in the canteen, though later they were happy enough to adopt this practice. The tram conductors were paid the same as drivers and bus drivers were sceptical about abolishing the differential they had. The key demand for bus workers was for the seven hour day, to gain some compensation for the speeded up schedules they were being subjected to. The Union seems not to have addressed the impact on staff of a considerable speed up for tram staff converting to the much faster trolleybuses.

Eventually at the end of November 1935 Bevin met the Trams Council. The Rank & File Movement demanded an all-in bus and tram agreement and an increase of 7/6 a week for the tram staff. The negotiations resulted in an increase of 4/- a week being agreed. The Rank & File Conference in December was informed that "no member of the London Trams Council ... the Joint Divisional Committee ... or the Negotiating Committee was aware of this settlement or that it had been signed by the Executive Council of the T&GWU prior to the Tuesday of the week it was posted in all depots by the Board". An unofficial strike was proposed but did not happen. Negotiations were reopened but the demand for 7/6 was not met.

'Diddler' trolleybus at Fulwell Depot with crew in summer uniform, 1934

The divisions in the Union position, the machinations of Bevin and the resultant failure to achieve 'all in' agreements on rates of pay and conditions between trolleybus and (diesel) bus staff were to have serious consequences for the staff. Any thoughts of unity with rail staff were overshadowed by this failure. The November 1935 increase brought the top rate for tram and trolleybus drivers and conductors up to 78/- a week (£243.17 in 2014 terms), compared to 88/6 for a bus driver and 83/6 (£260.31 in 2014 money) for a bus conductor. Tram and trolleybus rates went up further to 80/- in 1936 and finally in December 1939 tram and trolleybus crews achieved parity with central bus conductors, but not drivers, although their conditions of work remained more onerous.[12]

The new LPTB had a vast disparity of wages and conditions to deal with across all the various undertakings it had absorbed. The policy generally was to deal with the most unfair examples by levelling up the lowest paid. The wages at the worst paying municipal tramways were immediately brought up to the LCC level. In 1933 the LCC, West Ham and the three Company tramways paid 73/- a week (£221.89 in 2014 money), while the others paid 71/- or less, down to Erith at a mere 65/-. Stan Collins notes that in 1935 the LPTB accepted the principle of bringing tram and trolleybus crews' wages up to the level of a central bus conductor (not driver), and this was achieved by 1939.[13] Where necessary the wages of country bus crews were brought in line with the LGOC country rates. A partial attempt to improve the lowly position of country bus conductors was made in 1936.

The following chart, compiled from Clegg PP 71 and 77, shows the comparison between bus and rail rates, and how the differentials changed.

	1933	1936	1939
Central bus driver	86/6	88/6	94/-
Central bus conductor	79/6	83/6	88/-
Tram/trolleybus driver/conductor	73/-	80/-	88/-
Country bus driver	72/6	72/6	76/6
Country bus conductor	60/-	64/-	68/-
Coach driver	80/-	80/-	84/-
Railway motorman	93/-	93/-	97/- (1940)
Railway guard	68/-	68/-	72/-
Railway porter	46/-	46/-	56/-

A bonus of 5/- per week was paid to drivers of one man operated buses with less than 20 seats which did not increase until the one man operation of larger buses came about in 1953.

In 1934 the LPTB found itself with a total of 75,468 staff paid, on average, 77/6 a week. By 1939 this had risen to 86,456 at 82/10 a week on average (£242.91 in 2014 money).[14]

The misgivings of the Trolleybus Committee in 1935 were certainly justified. Despite the principled position of the Rank and File Movement's leaders, many bus staff and their representatives were concerned to maintain their 'aristocratic' status, which they feared might be threatened by fighting for parity for tram and trolleybus staff. How wrong they were was to be seen in 1937.

CHAPTER ELEVEN

THE RANK AND FILE MOVEMENT AND THE CORONATION STRIKE

Striking bus crew march on the May Day demonstration, 1937

By the mid 1930s the industrial depression had begun to ease. Particularly in the Midlands and South of England new industries were being built up. Car, lorry and bus manufacturing expanded greatly, along with component and accessory production such as electrics (CAV at Acton for instance) and tyres (Firestone on the Great West Road in Brentford, Dunlop in Birmingham). Domestic appliances such as washing machines and vacuum cleaners began to be manufactured on a large scale. Industrial food production spread rapidly (Heinz tinned foods, Smiths crisps etc.) Many of the new factories were situated along the new arterial roads that the Government had been building partly as a way of alleviating unemployment. In the main the people who worked in these factories used public transport to get to and from work so the demand for bus and coach travel increased greatly. In some cases trams also benefited from the increase in passenger numbers eg the LUT's Boston Road route 55 which went from a lightly used link with one man operated single deck cars to a busy route with double deckers serving the new factories on the Great West Road.

The gradual increase in wages and granting of paid holidays allowed many workers to go away in the summer for a week or at least a day trip. This increased demand for leisure travel, which would often be by coach. As we have seen, the introduction of the diesel engine and other technical improvements allowed larger and faster buses and coaches to be operated.

In January 1932, still in the depths of the depression, the LGOC had proposed a wage cut of 1/- a week. Pete Glatter in his article in International Socialism No 74 (January 1975) estimated that at this time the Communist Party had no more than a dozen bus staff as members, but they were able to pass a resolution at Enfield garage branch of the T&GWU against the cuts, and issue a call for a mass meeting. So strong was the feeling that the LGOC withdrew from their position and issued modified proposals. On 31st July 1932 the LGOC proposed to dismiss 800 men, but numerous mass meetings threatening strike action forced the Company to postpone the dismissals. Continuing the long tradition of rank & file unofficial organisation on the buses Bert Papworth, secretary of Putney Chelverton Road garage branch of the T&GWU, called a conference of garage delegates for 12th August. Papworth worked with the Communists but did not join the party until later.[1] About half the garages were represented at the conference and a Rank & File Committee was set up to run a campaign against the pay cuts. Demonstrations were organised in central London and the Central Bus Committee held a ballot in which the cuts were rejected by 16,500 votes to 4,000 despite an official Union recommendation to accept. The Rank & File conference called for a strike from 23rd September 1932, the day the cuts were to come into force.

Against this background T&GWU General Secretary Bevin was able to persuade the LGOC to agree to withdraw the pay cuts, cancel the proposed redundancies, reduce maximum time on duty from nine hours to eight, and to increase payments for Sunday duties. But crucially, Bevin agreed to the principle of speed up which was the main issue in the LGOC's rationalisation programme. Average scheduled speed on central buses increase from 9.67 mph in 1927 to 10.24 mph in 1933/4 and 10.42 mph in 1936.[2] Thus this 1932 settlement was known forever after as the 'Speed Agreement'. Dissatisfaction continued to increase among the workforce as the Company tried to implement the speed - up and the economy gradually began to improve. A reduction of overtime following the Agreement reduced take home wages.[3] The Union claimed that the Speed Agreement had allowed the Company and then the LPTB to improve takings while reducing wages.

The Rank & File Committee went from strength to strength. Garage Committees sent delegates to the central Rank & File Committee paralleling the official T&GWU organisation. Communist Party influence grew as the Party abandoned its crazy 'Third Period' ultraleftism, along with the Minority Movement. The Rank & File Committee became strong enough to take over the 'Busman's Punch' magazine, which had been founded by Communist Party members at Holloway garage, and extend its influence across the LGOC. A Communist Party member won a seat on the T&GWU's Central Bus Committee.[4]

The Rank & File Committee, in its first pamphlet, calculated that as a result of the speed-up the Company was saving seven minutes per hour, or 56 minutes per day. Including 'build up' time they said this gave an extra 90 minutes per day saving the LGOC £911,000 per year. The Committee claimed that the new schedules were based on an average speed of 14.3 mph, requiring a speed of 30 mph between stops. They claimed that by taking 10 minutes off each journey route 110 had been reduced from 24 duties to 16. However, Ernest Bevin is quoted in Ken Fuller's book as saying to the LGOC that: "he did not object to a change being made in the running times, he would advise the staff that they must accept it, but this must be accompanied by concessions in time and/or in money".[5]

In January 1933 new schedules were introduced at Forest Gate garage. All 500 workers there struck and a mass picket of 300 men was put on the gate. Next day these 300 marched the short distance to Upton Park garage where 1,000 joined the strike. The Rank & File Committee called mass meetings at Barking, Seven Kings, Romford and Dalston garages, which all joined the strike. By 31st January 1933, thirteen thousand men at 26 garages (over half the fleet) were on strike despite repeated orders from Union officials to return to work. Lord Ashfield posted a notice at every garage stating: "In this strike we stand in the same position as the Union leaders".[6] On 23rd January a deputation organised by the Rank & File Committee met officials at Transport House, T&GWU Head Office, where Assistant General Secretary John Cliff gave an assurance that the grievances at Forest Gate would receive immediate attention. However, he also pointed out that: "Members who accept any of the offices of a branch ... Central Bus Committee or Representative to Delegate Conference are not entitled and would not be allowed to serve on unofficial committees ... determining the trade policy of this Union".[7] Despite this warning the Rank & File movement won 10 of the 13 elected London Bus delegates to the T&GWU Conference, and when the Rank & File members of the Central Bus Committee were asked by the Union's Finance & General Purposes Committee to dissociate themselves from the Rank & File movement their refusal to do so was left unchallenged.[8]

Members at Forest Gate are quoted by George Renshaw, the Communist Party London Industrial Organiser in a pamphlet entitled "The London busman's victorious strike", as saying: "it would have been worth a three months strike to win such schedules". But despite a number of other disputes over schedules the LPTB's introduction of speeded up schedules was generally successfully achieved. According to a chart in Fuller's book miles per crew increased from 60.2 in 1930 to 62.8 in 1936, while wages per car mile fell from 2.9d to 2.8d for drivers and 2.7d to 2.67d for conductors over the same period.[9]

George Renshaw claimed that before the establishment of the Rank & File movement the Communist Party had 12 supporters over the whole fleet and influence in only one garage (Enfield), but by October 1932 it had about 40 members in the London Bus Section.[10] Pete Glatter quotes Renshaw as claiming that they had recruited 60 members in the early days of the Rank & File movement but that the majority of them had soon left the Party. In 1934 another abrupt policy change (the Popular Front) had led the Party to downplay industrial work.[11]

The Rank & File movement, however, continued to grow and campaigned for a 7 hour day, pointing out that the cost (£1 million) could have been covered by reducing the interest paid on the LPTB's stocks to 3%. But one far-sighted delegate pointed out that the 7 hour day could not be achieved without the support of the trains and trams staff. And the Rank & File movement had been unable to build a base among those staff. Another delegate noted that the large number of rest days being worked made the 7 hour demand unrealistic.[12] The wage cuts made in 1921 had been fully restored by 1934, and an interesting list of disputes between 1933 and 1937 recorded by the LPTB shows that nearly all of them concerned changes to schedules.[13] Clegg notes that "a fleet stand down was called in 1935 when a conductor at Norwood refused to join the Union, but this was averted when he was finally persuaded to join".[14] Eleven garages struck for 2 days over disciplinary action against two members at Nunhead garage.[15]

The Movement also made attempts to organise among the Country Services section and the 'Busman's Punch' carried articles covering the Country area. Green Line services were expanding rapidly. As workers' wages rose a little and hours were reduced weekend trips to the countryside around London became a popular pastime. This meant that for many Green line services Saturdays and Sundays became the busiest days of the week. Laurie Akehurst has studied the timetables in detail. Route P ran from Farnham Common to London once an hour on Mondays to Fridays while route O ran three times an hour from Windsor giving a combined service of four times an hour from Slough. A timetable change on 3rd July 1935 introduced a double run to the popular tourist spot of Burnham Beeches giving two coaches an hour on Saturday afternoons and Sundays. Route O was stepped up to four coaches an hour giving a combined service of six an hour (one every ten minutes) from Slough to London. This was the straw to break the camel's back as it meant there would be few if any Saturday or Sunday rest days at Slough Bath Road garage. On 26th July 1935 Slough and Windsor Green Line coach garages struck over insufficient rest days and speed. The LPTB refused to negotiate until the staff returned to work. The next day two more Green Line garages came out in sympathy and by 28th July 24 of the 33 Country area garages totalling nearly 3,000 men were on strike.[16] Bevin denounced the strike as the work of the Communist Party and the (now defunct) Minority Movement. Rank & File leaders Bert Papworth and Frank Snelling met T&GWU full time officials, and as members of the Central Bus Committee were sent to Slough Country Area garage, where they advised a return to work so that talks could take place.[17]

It is easy to see how the dispute spread so rapidly as more than one garage would be involved in operating such long routes. Laurie Akehurst notes that the position was eased from 2nd August 1936 when route Y3 was introduced on Sundays running from Brentwood to Windsor via Trafalgar Square. This was worked by Romford London Road garage, which had very high Monday to Friday commuter traffic so that the rotas could be balanced. As well as showing the weakness of the Union leadership in the Country area this episode also indicates what can happen when Rank & File leaders are placed in a position to negotiate on an official basis and make compromises. Papworth and Snelling were obliged to resign from the Rank & File Committee, but were reinstated on the grounds that they had "acted in good faith".[18]

Unrest on the buses was not confined to London. On 14th April 1937 bus staff at Maidstone & District struck for better conditions at Tunbridge Wells and other depots, joined by crews in Sussex, Essex, Luton Corporation, Bedford, Cambridge, Norwich, Oxford, Northampton, and on 3rd May East Yorkshire. On 1st May London bus workers were on strike "to a man" and joined a massive May Day march. But the T&GWU refused to make these strikes official and Bevin got them back to work by 5th May on the promise of no victimisation and a resumption of negotiations.[19] The Rank & File movement had proved unable to sustain prolonged unofficial action and concentrated on trying to commit the official structures of the T&GWU to support industrial action. Meanwhile, the negotiations for the 7 hour day dragged on. The T&GWU Executive reduced the official demand to 7.5 hours in 1937 and this was accepted by the bus delegates. But no agreement was reached and thus the scene was set for the 'Coronation' bus strike.

The mood of the Central bus staff had not been improved by the laudable moves by the new LPTB to close differentials, increasing the pay of the Tram and Trolleybus section and the Country bus conductors in particular. These staff were also represented by the T&GWU which obviously had an interest in seeing their wages increased. This would bring them closer to Central bus rates if not actually achieving parity. The failure of the Rank & File movement to come to terms with this issue was to prove fatal. Fuller writes that "The differential between bus workers and tram workers was the most immediate identifiable token of the formers' aristocratic status ... Some wanted a differential between themselves and their colleagues on the trams. For the bus workers to stand still while the tram workers caught up with them would have meant that their status vis a vis other sections of the working class would have been lowered."[20] The demand for the 7 hour day had been central to the Rank & File movement's entire reason for existence since 1931, so it could not be abandoned. Fuller also notes that Bevin was patiently waiting for a suitable opportunity to crush the Rank & File movement which enjoyed such great support from the Central bus staff and whose militancy caused Bevin and Union officialdom so much trouble.[21]

The 'Coronation' strike.
King George VI was to be crowned on 12th May 1937. The May issue of 'Busman's Punch' accused the LPTB of "Deliberately engineering a deadlock, creating a strike position, at the period of the Coronation, in an attempt to alienate public opinion from the busmen". This prescient intervention went unheeded. The strike started on 1st May, Cup Final day. Another own goal. Football fans had little difficulty in reaching Wembley as the underground, trams and trolleybuses were working normally. Fuller notes that the strike was unable to have any significant effect on the movement of travellers into and around the capital.[22] The LPTB Annual report for 30th June 1937 shows a direct loss of 86 million passengers due to the strike, compared to a total of 278 million who had been carried the previous year.

The Government appointed a Court of Inquiry whose first hearing was on 3rd May.

It found that the medical claims that speed up caused increased stress were inconclusive, but agreed to further investigation of the issue. However, on the main claim, now for a 7.5 hour day, there was no compromise. The terms offered were placed before the membership on 9th May. The response was extraordinary. At Putney Chelverton Road 377 members out of a possible 441 attended the meeting and voted 374 to 3 to continue the strike. At Leyton 900 of a possible 947 attended and voted 898 to 2 to continue the strike. Only three garages – Old Kent Road, Palmers Green and Harrow Weald – voted to resume work. The overall vote to continue the strike was 15,684 of a total staff of 25,050. These figures were collated by the LPTB from local 'intelligence reports' ie spies. On 13th and 14th May a second round of branch voting recorded a total of 15,596 to 1,927 for continuation of the strike, with only Tottenham joining the three who supported a return to work.[23]

Bevin and the Executive of the T&GWU had signed an agreement for an increase of 4/- a week for Tram and Trolleybus workers in November 1935 (the claim had been for 7/6) without reference to the London Trams Council, the Joint Divisional Committee or the Negotiating Committee. Crucially, the principle of bringing tram wages up to bus conductors' rate was also enshrined in this agreement. Early in 1936 14 Tram branches had lobbied the Trams Council to press for the full claim, but the threatened unofficial strike did not happen and the agreement stood.[24] Now, on 5th May the Tramway & Trolleybus delegate conference had requested that they be joined to the busworkers claim, only to be told that the November 1935 agreement could only be terminated with six months' notice and that this notice could not be given until mid 1938. Bevin said: " the breaking of the agreement would create an impossible situation and make matters worse for the busmen in dispute, and in the light of the agreement existing it was in fact impossible to join the tram and trolleybus workers with the claim".[25]

Then, following a visit by Bert Papworth and Frank Snelling, a meeting of the London Trams Council on 18th May referred the bus workers' request for solidarity action to a full conference of the Tram and Trolleybus section. Having had the possibility of being officially joined to the busworkers' claim ruled out, the conference voted 34-9 against an unofficial sympathy strike. Bevin's view was that the dispute could not be won even if the trams had decided to lend their support. He urged the Central Bus Committee and the London Bus Conference to consider ending the dispute on the basis of the Court of Inquiry's interim report and undertakings by the LPTB to look into the question of hours of duty and the working day. From the perspective of history this looks like a sensible proposition, but at the time conference expressed its 'indignation' at the Executive's reaffirming the decision not to extend the dispute to the Trams section. Finally, in an act of desperation, the conference called upon the tram and trolleybus branches to picket their depots to ensure that no extra journeys were run or overloading allowed. Finally, they called upon the NUR and ASLE&F for support. Why they had not done this at the outset can only be ascribed to arrogance. The Underground operating staff had already achieved an 8 hour day with half an hour paid meal break which made it equivalent to a 7.5 hour day, but as we shall see later they had many other grievances.

Bevin met the LPTB on 26th May. Lord Ashfield held to the view that they had already made a firm offer on 8th May. Having withdrawn 'plenary' powers from the London Bus Conference the T&GWU Executive instructed the members to return to work on 28th May following a Rank & File conference which was left with no alternative now that the plenary powers had been withdrawn.[26]

Thus was the strike lost and the London busworkers Rank & File movement destroyed.

Ashfield, Pick and Bevin

Interesting insight into the way LPTB Chairman Lord Ashfield, Vice Chairman and Chief Executive Officer Frank Pick and T&GWU General Secretary Ernest Bevin acted and interacted is given in Christian Barman's biography of Frank Pick.

Sir Alan Bullock's "Life and times of Ernest Bevin" describes the London bus workers' Rank & File movement as "One of the most militant groups in the Trade Union movement of this country". Herbert Morrison is quoted as recalling how Lord Ashfield, if he had decided for peace, "would be prepared to pay any price to avoid trouble ... .But there were other occasions when he would judge a strike to be desirable and then would order his managers to stand firm; if necessary he might even arrange for a strike to be deliberately provoked. Here clearly was one of those occasions ... Perhaps the moment had come when it would be possible to secure that the power of the Committee should be broken. Only one person was capable of doing the breaking, Ernest Bevin, the architect of the T&GWU and still its General Secretary ... Bevin in this present game was an opponent indeed. He had spoken long and passionately in support of the busmen's claim. Ashfield, however, was one of the few intimates who were aware that beneath that great show of loyalty there lay a sense of cold disapproval – more than once in the past ten or twelve years the Central Area Committee had been warned by Bevin that it must moderate its rapacity. If London Transport continued to stand firm, was it not possible that Bevin might decide that his Union, like London Transport, had had enough? And that is precisely what did happen. In the fourth week of the strike the Union's General Executive was persuaded to withdraw the powers that had put this predatory committee in its position of strength, and the committee, thus shorn of its special status, was unable to prevent the Union from ordering the strikers back to work." (A biography of Frank Pick by Christian Barman, David & Charles 1979, PP 158/9.)

Apart from illustrating the distaste and contempt in which senior management held that section of their workforce, this account shows how closely the interests of Pick and Bevin were allied. The Central Bus Committee and the Rank & File movement clearly overreached themselves, hamstrung by the 7 hour day demand and their consequent inability to get the tram and trolleybus staff onside, and comprehensively outmanoeuvred by Bevin. They had failed to absorb the lessons of the exemplary organisation of the successful 1924 tram strike which bus workers supported and for which verbal support from the Railway Unions was obtained. Lord Ashfield had conveniently taken sick leave in the period when the negotiations broke down. He had read his opponents well and proved a highly skilled operator and judge of character.

Pete Glatter in his article lays the blame for the defeat squarely on the shoulders of Ernest Bevin saying that he "stabbed them in the back". It is not my intention to debate the ethics of Bevin's actions, but it is clear that there is more to it than this. Bevin did what he did in the context of the Rank & File movement's failure to build support among the tram, trolleybus and Underground staff, without which the dispute could not have been won, and in turn this places in question the demands on which the dispute was based. The Central bus workers' view of themselves as 'aristocrats' provided a shaky foundation on which to build. It seems the lessons of the 1935 Green Line strike were also not taken on board, when the Rank & File leaders had been obliged to negotiate a compromise. Leaders, be they official or unofficial, have to lead and sometimes this means taking difficult decisions that the Rank & File may not support at the time, although later they may see the sense in them. Pete Glatter's view that the problem lay with the Rank & File movement organising the strike through official structures of the T&GWU rather than relying on the independent unofficial movement thus misses the point, though the fact that Bevin was clearly a clever, devious operator was a factor. Lord Ashfield's deft manoeuvring and understanding of the dynamics of the situation was clearly also a major factor. Glatter also points out that the Communist Party's Popular Front policy led it to cease active support for Rank & File Trade Union movements. Given the Communist Party's abrupt changes of policy at Moscow's behest this loss of political guidance is a factor whose significance should not be overestimated.[27]

Trade Union officials, even ones as autocratic as Bevin, have their role to play when negotiations lead to compromises having to be made, as they have to be. A Rank & File movement runs the risk of becoming a prisoner of the high expectations created by an inflexible demand around which the movement is built. This is what explains the massive popular votes to continue the strike when Union officials, and some of the Rank & File leaders, could see that a compromise would be necessary if the strike was not to be lost and the unofficial movement destroyed. The same dynamics were in operation in the 1989 unofficial strikes on the Underground. First those strikes were made official by the Unions, then a compromise was agreed and the strikes called off. But despite the compromise being a very favourable one, the writer, as an NUR Executive member at the time, was denounced as a traitor for not having achieved the full claim. The 1949 unofficial strike which did unite tram trolleybus and bus workers is examined in a later chapter.

Pick and Bevin negotiated a fresh agreement on rates of pay in June 1937 which also granted longer holidays and a reduction in maximum time on duty from 8.5 to 8 hours. By agreement, differentials between central bus staff and tram, trolleybus and country area staff were gradually reduced as can be seen in the chart at the end of Chapter 10. The medical effects of speed-up which had been such an evocative issue before the strike proved inconclusive when further investigated.[28]

The T&GWU expelled Bert Papworth, Frank Snelling and Bill Jones, and debarred three others from office until 1942 and one other until 1940. The 'Busman's Punch' reappeared in September 1937 but this was to be its final issue. The Central Bus Committee was re-elected at a series of district meetings rather than through the branches. Papworth and Jones, both now members of the Communist Party, applied for re-admission to the T&GWU rather than join the breakaway National Passenger Workers Union which was supported by the anti-Communist Frank Snelling, a member of the Socialist Party of Great Britain. In 1942 Papworth and Jones were re-elected to the Central Bus Committee and the General Executive of the T&GWU, and later to the TUC General Council. Fuller notes that the LPTB continued to collect "intelligence" regarding the activities of the Rank & File movement until it was sure it was dead.[29]

Tram driver Stan Collins says that "busmen's conditions – the point of the strike – were undoubtedly better than those of the tramwaymen, and there was a feeling that the increasing and profitable use of trolleybuses by London Transport (operated at tram wages and conditions) posed something of a threat to established busmen and their services. The notional solidarity of transport workers in London Transport was rather tenuous at this time".[30]

Meanwhile, on the Underground

In stark contrast to the frenetic activity and militant demands of the bus workers Rank & File movement through the T&GWU and its Central Bus Committee, the cumbersome conciliation machinery on the railway side of the LPTB was not immune to the pressures on living standards and demands for wage increases that the gradual recovery was bringing. Bagwell notes "Owing to the speedier and uninterrupted improvement in the passenger traffic receipts of the LPTB, it proved possible to restore the wage cuts in the London area at an earlier date than was the case with the main line companies. The first improvement was introduced at the same time as the agreement was reached with the main line companies in August 1934. The second deduction of 2.5% on those earning over 40/- a week was restored in two stages, at the beginning of October 1934 and at the beginning of January 1935. Full restoration of the remaining deductions from earnings resulted from discussions between the Unions and representatives of the LPTB held on December 18 1934, when Mr Pick, for the employers, proposed that from the beginning of April 1935 the first 2.5% reduction should be reduced to 1.25% and that from the first pay week in July the remaining 1.25% should be restored, thus completing the return to the position as it was before July 20 1932 when the deductions were first imposed in London. At a further meeting on 8th Jan 1935 Mr Pick agreed to advance to the beginning of June 1935 the date for full restoration of the cuts. For the LPTB staff the cuts had come a year later and were fully restored two years earlier than was the case with the men employed by the main line companies."[31]

A special conference of LPTB conciliation grade staff on 25 and 26 August 1936 demanded a minimum wage of £3 (60/-) a week (£185.94 in 2014 money), a 6 hour day, a 36 hour week, time and a half for duty between 10pm and 5am, time and a half for overtime, double time for Sundays, a general wage increase of 3/- a week, improved mileage rates for drivers and more pay for signalmen. Was the busmen's Rank & File movement aware of this militant programme? Did they not see how it could dovetail with their own demands? The abstract appeals to Unity and Solidarity beloved of Communists and other left wingers do not cut much ice with most workers unless they can be shown to have a practical value in advancing their own interests. The material, practical basis for a campaign uniting the bus, tram/trolleybus and Underground workers clearly existed and could have been highly effective, as 1924 had shown. But it would have taken a brave Rank & File leader to tell the bus workers to abandon their pretensions to aristocratic status, which they were bound to lose sooner or later, and throw in their lot with fellow workers on trams trolleybuses and trains.

Bagwell notes that the LPTB received the demands of the special conference on April 26 1937 but "there was a delay owing to the dispute with the London busmen and the negotiating committee did not meet until June 25 1937". Far from co-ordinating their efforts, the rail Unions saw the Coronation bus dispute as merely 'causing a delay in negotiations'! Claims were also submitted jointly by the NUR and RCA on behalf of the clerical grades. Mr Pick said the cost would be £2.5 million and it was impossible to concede the claim. He also said the proposals were "in excess of those submitted by the same Unions to other transport undertakings with which the Board was in close partnership". They would have to await the result of the claim on the main line railways. The three railway Unions agreed to delay the claim. The NUR delegate conference for LPTB staff declared they were "in favour of the Executive Committee continuing negotiations to obtain the utmost improvement in the wages of the lower paid grades" (no aristocracy here).

Eventually an agreement was signed on Feb 28 1938. All 'conciliation' employees earning less than 46/- a week (£142.65 in 2014 money) were to receive an increase of 4/- a week from the beginning of 1938 and a further 2/- a week from Jan 1st 1939.There was to be a scaling upwards of many other rates of pay. The NUR also endeavoured to obtain 12 days holiday for all conciliation staff but only achieved an extra 3 days on top of the existing one week. They were again held back by the main line companies' refusal to grant 12 days holiday. Looking at these figures, it is small wonder they were reluctant to support bus staff's attempt to further improve their already far superior wages and conditions. On the main line railways the claim continued to be pursued as the companies' receipts continued to rise. By August 1939 talk of strike action was in the air, which may well have involved LPTB rail staff. The ASLE&F called a strike for August 26 1939 and only called it off following lengthy talks with the Minister of Labour. NUR delegates were in militant mood at a conference on August 22nd, but as Hitler's armies invaded Poland the second world war began with the claim still unresolved.[32]

Finally, on October 18th 1939 an award was made. It was agreed in advance that Railway Staff Tribunal (main line companies) wartime awards would be binding on both sides. The claim for a 50/- a week minimum wage for all rail staff was granted for London only and applied to LPTB rail conciliation staff, shopmen, power generation staff, and other ancillary services. Increases were also awarded to salaried and supervisory staff. Further increases were granted throughout the war, but in all grades the war wage paid to women was below that paid to men.[33]

CHAPTER TWELVE

THE SECOND WORLD WAR

Air raid precautions at Chiswick bus Works, 1939

Stan Collins notes that things were better organised in 1939 than they had been in the first world war, when many London County Council tramway staff (among others) had volunteered for 'Kitchener's Army', as Stan calls it, or from 1916 had been conscripted. Conscription began again in 1939 and there had already been prepared a schedule of reserved occupations which exempted certain ages and grades of transport workers (among other essential services) from conscription.[1] Nevertheless, 22,580 staff left for full-time service in the armed forces and civil defence. By the end of the war the LPTB had recruited 16,500 women to replace them. There were 11,250 women bus, tram and trolleybus conductors out of a total of 18,800, 950 of 1,150 porters on the railways, 400 booking clerks, and 3,000 in engineering departments. Wallace tells us that equal pay had been granted for "some women within the railway conciliation grades as early (!) as 1940". The RCA General Secretary, presenting the case for equal pay for clerical grades to the Railway Staff National Tribunal on 16/17th February 1942 said: "Where women clerks are performing duties similar in character and value to male clerks, they should be paid in accordance with the male clerical staff agreement". The claim was turned down. The proportion of women members of the RCA nationally had fallen as low as 5.5% between the wars, but by 1944 it was 25.3%.[2]

Passenger numbers varied dramatically. By the end of 1940 LPTB total car miles had fallen by 17% and passenger numbers by 23% due to evacuation of children and air attacks. But in 1942/3 greater mobilisation for war work, holidays at home, cessation of private motoring and the arrival of large numbers of US forces led passenger journeys to rise to 6% above the pre-war level, but car mileage on buses and trains fell further to 22% below the pre-war figure. By 1945 passenger mileage was 13% above the pre-war figure but car mileage was 19% below. In the country area, by 1945 passenger miles were up by no less than 90% but bus mileage was only 32% above the pre-war level. This situation produced massive overcrowding, with associated stress for passengers and staff alike.[3]

Stan Collins recounts some stories of the courage and resilience shown by staff during the blitz. One night the bombing had blocked the tracks on the way back from Victoria. Stan took his Feltham tram on a lengthy diversion to get back to the depot at Telford Avenue Streatham, including traversing roads which the long Feltham tram was not officially allowed to run along. He eventually got home at 6.30 the next morning, and taking up duty again at 4pm the same day was told he would not be paid any overtime for his efforts the previous night. Only after the T&GWU Secretary at Telford Avenue intervened was payment secured.[4] The only industrial dispute during the war that Stan can recall was a one day token strike over brakes not working properly. The brake blocks and shoes had worn so thin that even with the magnetic track brake drivers had lost half their braking power. The depot had no replacement brake blocks or shoes due to a shortage of 'steel' (in my experience brake blocks are made of iron but Stan uses the term 'steel'). Pamphlets were printed advising the public what the strike was about (an issue of safety) and after the one day strike steel (iron) was delivered to Charlton Central Repair Depot and plenty of new brake blocks and shoes were produced.[5]

On the road services, there do not appear to have been separate pay rates for women. A chart of rates of pay for road service staff from 1891 to 1966 produced by the London Transport Board (undated) carries a note stating: "Women 90% of male rate upon starting, reaching maximum rate after two years (this clause deleted by agreement 3rd Jan 1951)". The total war wage for salaried and supervisory staff was £66/6/- pa , but only 21/6 a week for women staff.

Basic rates for railway conciliation staff rose by 56% during the war compared to 44% for all industries, but actual earnings rose only by 65% compared to a national average of 79%, although railway workshop staff kept pace with the industrial average. (Bagwell PP 587, 589)

Rail staff wages rose by 21/6 a week between 1940 and 1944 for motormen and guards, £56 pa. for a Booking Clerk 5, and 26/- a week for a porter, the lowest paid grade.[6]

But Clegg shows that LPTB staff fell behind the average during the war. He gives the following index of actual earnings (NB this is not the same as basic rates of pay):

	All workers	Males	All LPTB staff	Central bus drivers
1938	100	100	100	100
1944	182	180	134	131
1948	220	200	164	149

This fascinating table also shows how central bus drivers fell behind compared to both other LPTB staff and other workers. It also indicates that women's wages advanced slightly faster than men's.[7]

Another interesting comparison in Clegg's book shows the relative increases in pay rates for road service staff over the period from 1933 to 1948:

Central bus driver	49%
Central bus conductor	57%
Tram/ trolleybus driver/conductor	71%
Coach driver	53%
Country bus driver	63%
Country bus conductor	88%

Earnings, of course, could be considerably higher with weekend enhancements and spreadover payments.

The TUC had declared an industrial truce for the duration of the war and in July 1940 strikes were banned and compulsory arbitration introduced. Despite the defeat of the 1937 strike and the demise of the rank and file movement, on the buses, trams and trolleybuses schedule alterations led to various local disputes e.g. Hanwell depot on strike for three days in late November 1939, Edmonton out for two days in May 1940, Victoria garage in December 1940. Grays and Northfleet country area garages also saw disputes. War conditions intensified the workload of staff and necessitated transfers from garage to garage to maintain services. As long as the USSR was in alliance with Hitler's Germany the militants tried to stir up industrial action, but as soon as the Nazis attacked the Soviet Union in June 1941 the USSR became our ally and the Communist Party line changed again. Now all impediments to war production were to be removed. With the threat of invasion there was not much stomach for industrial action though the Kent miners and Teesside shipbuilders struck in 1943, some ending up in prison for their trouble. The Communists were allowed back on the Central Bus Committee from January 1942. Joint Production Committees were formed to eliminate inefficiency and boost war production. Bill Jones recalled that

Women bus conductors passed out on 4th November 1940

Air raid damage at Bexleyheath trolleybus depot 29th June 1944

they were "a real waste of time. Very little came out of them. They couldn't interfere with wages and conditions. They were a way of letting off steam and kidding yourself that you were really doing something on the question of productivity. They were a joke." But he also notes that "you gave away conditions to increase wages eg increase the number of standing passengers to get a 4/- wage increase."[8]

In October 1941 a Production Conference was organised by the Communist Party influenced Rank & File paper "The Transporter", which was designed to appeal to all LPTB workers but whose influence in practice was confined to the Central buses. With 89 delegates from 33 garages and depots the conference "drew the unanimous conclusion that the LPTB alone cannot be relied upon to give the kind of service that is needed. Speaker after speaker emphasised how essential it is that the workers in the industry who know its problems and possibilities from the practical point of view, must have a share in management".[9] Garage consultative committees were, however, not established until 1946. The militants started to take a negative attitude to strikes, to further the 'interests of the war'. By March 1942 a temporary amendment was agreed whereby 20% of all duties could be regarded as outside the main agreement, with a maximum spreadover of 13 hours. Maximum time on duty would be 8 hours with all spreadover time over 8.5 hours to be paid. Fuller notes drily that "These proposals were not greeted with universal acclaim". As the war dragged on resistance to wartime conditions grew. There was a half day strike at Sutton garage over new schedules. Some critics accused the Communist Party of having participated in a sellout of the British working class after June 1941, but support for the Soviet Union, encouraged by both Government and Unions, remained strong.

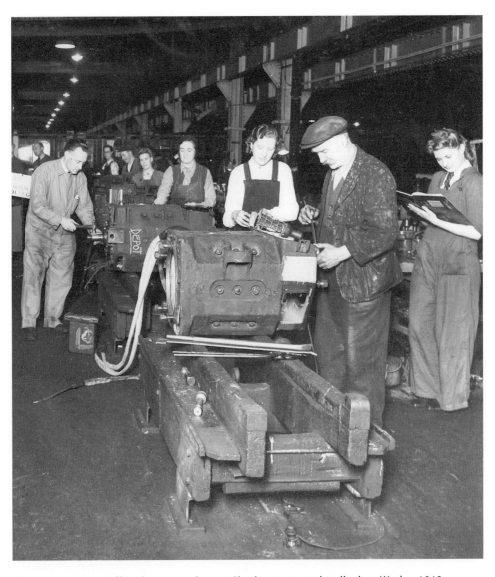

Men and women staff in the motor shop at Charlton tram and trolleybus Works, 1943

Figures in Fuller's book[10] (price data derived from 'British Economy Key Statistics') tell their own story.

	Retail prices	Central bus driver average earnings	Average male earnings
1938-41	+27%	+10%	+44%
1941-45	+16%	+21%	+22%
1938-45 overall	+48%	+34%	+76%

Transport workers in general, and central bus drivers in particular, were worse off in real terms by the end of the war, both in absolute and relative terms.

CHAPTER THIRTEEN

AFTERMATH AND NATIONALISATION

Conductor on country area STL type bus, 1950

The second world war left the country exhausted and effectively bankrupt and London Transport and its staff had suffered badly. Equipment, vehicles and staff were worn out, but staff had high hopes for a new future free of the pre-war privations suffered by so many.

In 1944 the TUC programme for post war reconstruction called for nationalisation of key industries, price controls, and a National Industrial Council with Trade Union representation, though not Trade Union representation on the boards of nationalised industries. Fuller notes that many workers were persuaded that the construction of a socialist society would be on the agenda.[1] In Germany post war reconstruction of industry, largely under British tutelage and with the involvement of the British TUC in rebuilding the German Unions, led to a system of worker representation on the Boards of all large industries, not just nationalised ones. This successful scheme is known as co-determination and is still in place today. Yet the TUC and the Labour government were unable to place their trust in British workers to enable them to participate in any similar scheme here. That failure was to have immense repercussions in constant industrial unrest in the years that followed, not least on London Transport.

Under Government control during the war the LPTB had not been earning enough to pay any interest on its stocks, and two of the four railway companies (the London & North Eastern and London Midland & Scottish) were essentially bankrupt. Nationalisation had become inevitable quite independently of any ideological considerations of the Labour government. Stockholders were to be compensated by the issue of Government bonds on the basis of recent stock exchange quotations.[2] The compensation payments to the former private owners became the first charge on the new nationalised industries amounting to £3.8 million p.a. for the LPTB, which the T&GWU's Bill Jones felt crippled their ability to pay improved wages and conditions.[3] Bagwell notes (P604) that "The takeover of the railways was an unduly expensive one". He says Labour MP Richard Crossman quoted no less an authority than Winston Churchill as saying that 'we nationalised at the wrong time; if we had waited two years at least two of the railway companies would have been in the hands of the receivers and we would have got them cheaper'.

The Attlee Government's failure to accept the concept of public transport as a public service and its decision to include in the 1947 Act the condition that the British Transport Commission was to pay its way as a commercial concern did not seem to be a problem at first. The profitable British Road Services (BRS) would cross subsidise the railways. But interest on BTC stocks, which were compensation to the shareholders of the pre-nationalisation companies, had to be paid. In 1953 the Conservative Government sold more than half the BRS fleet to private road haulage companies at knockdown prices, destroying the profitability of BRS. They would have sold the whole fleet if a public outcry had not stopped them. The level of wages and conditions of those employed in public transport was dependent on the profitability of the BTC, and by 1954 its overall finances were in the red to the tune of £11.9 million. (Bagwell Vol 2 PP159-160)

However, in 1946 the Labour government repealed the 1927 Trade Disputes Act. This had shackled the Unions with financial responsibility for losses incurred by strikes and had made the closed shop (compulsory Trade Union membership) illegal. For months there had been a series of local disputes at bus garages where T&GWU

members had refused to work with non-members, many of whom were in the break-away NPWU. On 26.08.46. the LPTB agreed to make T&GWU membership a condition of employment on the road services "in order to avoid industrial conflict and restore discipline in the garages". The Economist magazine found the Board's attitude "as prudent as it was unheroic". The breakaway NPWU fought on for a while, but the majority of their members joined the T&GWU.[4]

As we saw in Chapter 12, status, conditions and pay of busworkers had declined during the war, especially when compared to workers in other industries. Militancy had been curbed during the war and there was pressure from the post war Labour government to continue the constraints on industrial action. People felt that they were not getting a just reward for their wartime sacrifices; the country was 'in hock' to the Americans, who lent us $3.75 billion on strict conditions, including free convertibility of the pound and removal of restrictions on foreign trade.[5] The LPTB took 'full advantage' of this situation to refuse even 'quite modest' demands and disillusionment with the Labour Government began to grow as it became apparent that the construction of a socialist society was not going to happen.[6]

Learning the lessons of the previous divisions the three T&GWU sections – Central Buses, Trams & Trolleybuses and Country Services – elaborated a programme for a new common agreement which called for a 40 hour week without loss of pay, levelling up of tram & trolleybus and country services wages to the level of central buses, time and a half for Saturday afternoon, Sunday and Good Friday working, three weeks holiday, and increased stand time, an "objective to be reached in stages".[7]

In March 1946 the NUR asked for a meeting with the T&GWU to discuss the nationalisation of transport. New T&GWU General Secretary Arthur Deakin, a dour individual who had replaced the ebullient if controversial Ernest Bevin, declined.[8] Another opportunity for the Unions to agree a mutually beneficial approach was lost. Basic rates for railway staff had risen by 56% during the war compared to 44% for all industries but actual earnings for conciliation grades had only risen by 65% compared to a 70% national average, although workshop staff managed to keep pace with the industrial average.

The NUR had submitted a National Programme for improved wages and conditions of service along with the two other railway unions RCA and ASLE&F. An agreement operative from 30th July 1945 revised basic wages from 77/- to 84/- a week in rural areas, 78/- to 85/- in industrial areas and 80/- to 87/- (£168.14 in 2014 money) in London including the underground. Sunday duty rate was increased from time and a half to time and three-quarters, hours for night duty payment extended to 10pm – 6am, and paid holidays up from 6 to 12 days per year. Salaried grades gained an increase of £12 - £15 pa and increase in holidays from 12 days to 15 days. Railway workshop staff finally achieved a guaranteed day and week and an advantageous simplification of grades. The NUR EC on 20th November 1946 threatened strike action and after interviews with the Ministers of Transport and Labour gained consolidation of war wages into basic rates as well as other gains.

The Guillebaud Court of Inquiry was set up to consider claims for a pay increase and a reduction of the working week from 48 to 40 hours on the railways. It finally reported on 4th July 1947. As the wartime National Arbitration Order No 1305 of 1940 was still in force, making Railway Staff National Tribunal decisions 'final and binding', the NUR EC and General Secretary John Benstead were not prepared to refer the claim to the Tribunal which they suspected would not respond favourably. That is why the Minister of Labour set up the Guillebaud Inquiry, at which Mr Benstead showed that since the lifting of the Essential Works Order in 1946 railway staff were free to move to other industries, where wages were 68% above those of August 1939 while the wages of railwaymen had only risen 54% in the same period. He showed that 13,486 members of permanent staff had left the railways for other jobs in only six months (Bagwell P 608). The Inquiry recommended an increase of 7/6 a week on the basic rate from 30 June 1947 and reduction in hours to 44 for wages grades and 42 for clerks, which applied to the LPTB as well as the main line companies. Under the astute Benstead the NUR had proved quick off the mark to achieve these improvements. The association with the main line companies with their important freight traffic on this occasion provided valuable leverage with the Government. In effect the improvements were paid for by the treasury. The NUR also showed that it was possible to bypass the Conciliation machinery given the will to do so.

Permanent Way gang at work 1951

John Benstead had been elected General Secretary of the NUR in 1943 on the retirement of his predecessor. Clearly highly intelligent and a skilful negotiator his success in the early post war period was noteworthy, and for the first time it is possible to detect a faint note of envy from bus staff, who had been accustomed to seeing themselves as the leading force on London Transport. Their own Union had rejected approaches from the NUR for a joint campaign and as we shall see was to tear itself apart in an anti-communist witch hunt. The NUR had gained a "catalogue of concessions" from the railway companies and the LPTB in the last months of their existence when they were still enjoying the Government guarantee of net revenue of £43 million pa. Any deficit the railway companies might incur, including any as a result of wage increases, was made good by the Treasury. From 1940-45 the Companies had earned a substantial surplus over the £43 million guaranteed revenue but in 1946 and 1947 earnings fell far short and in 1947 the Treasury paid out almost £60 million to the railway companies. (Bagwell P 608)

Woman porter flags off train at Chancery Lane station in 1940. Uniform has not yet been issued.

There were high hopes in the 1948 nationalisation of transport, including London Transport. But as Bagwell notes on P 608: "From the time that the British Transport Commission (BTC) took the railway companies over (1st January 1948) the Union encountered much heavier weather in its wage negotiations". The NUR still took the view that "workers participation in management is an indispensable requisite to ensure the success of a publicly owned transport industry" (Bagwell P 623) and even now it is difficult to take issue with this view. But this phrase, of course, means different things to different people and the Labour government was certainly not contemplating any form of workers control or participation. The TUC had stated in 1945 that members of nationalised industry boards were to be appointed "at the discretion of the Minister solely on the grounds of competence and ability ..." (Bagwell P 624). John Benstead became the only Trade Unionist appointed to the BTC, which had five members. He was obliged to step down as NUR General Secretary at the end of 1947 as the NUR AGM carried by 72 votes to 2 a resolution demanding "50% workers representation at all levels" (Bagwell P 625). His successor, the left wing Jim Figgins, found it necessary to deny that he was a member of the Communist Party. He continued to press for workers control of the railway industry, albeit without success. John Benstead served on the BTC from 1947 to 1961. He was knighted in 1953 and became deputy chairman. He rapidly became involved in management and was perceived as having 'joined the other side'.

Despite the good 1947 settlement railway wages continued to lag behind those in other industries. The Government decreed that 'there should be no further general increase in the level of personal incomes' unless it could be clearly shown that productivity had increased or that an industry was undermanned. The NUR again showed its concern for lower paid staff by submitting a claim in July 1948 for a flat rate increase for all staff. This was resubmitted in April 1949 as a 10/- a week increase for all staff. This time the Railway Executive insisted on the claim going through the internecine Conciliation machinery which was still subject to the wartime National Arbitration Order No 1305. This also brought the other railway Unions into play. The RCA, ASLE&F and CSEU (Confederation of Shipbuilding and Engineering Unions) in the workshops all saw the flat rate claim as reducing their differentials and declined to support it. The NUR had neglected to seek their support when it lodged the claim; it knew what the response would be. The claim was rejected by the Railway Board of Conciliation in September 1949 and given the total lack of support from the other unions the NUR had to accept this. But the cost of living had risen by 11% in the little over two years since the 1947 award and the 10/- claimed would barely have offset that rise (Bagwell P 611).

The NUR immediately submitted a further claim for 'an improvement in wages for low paid employees' the aim being to achieve a £5 per week minimum but a proposal for industrial action to back up the claim was voted down on the grounds that "such a policy would considerably undermine whatever little chance they had of economic recovery and political independence ... and injure the chances of the Labour Party in winning the next General Election" (Bagwell P 612). But this time the support of the RCA was gained although the ASLE&F would not agree to a joint meeting. An increase of 3/6 on the basic rate was achieved on 15th August 1950 which also applied to the LTE. The length of time taken to reach agreement on even so modest an increase is extraordinary.

Bagwell notes that the Railway Executive recognised that they would have to increase wages if the 'dangerous' drift of labour away from the railways was to be arrested. The Labour government policy of wage restraint, in the context of the 1949 devaluation of the pound, was endorsed by the TUC General Council, who (amazingly) advocated "rigorous restraints on all increases of wages, salaries and dividends". Thus the Labour government sought and lost support. The NUR opposed the TUC position and submitted a further claim for a 10% increase this time in concert with the RCA and ASLE&F. Bagwell notes that the endorsement of the TUC position by other unions made the climate of opinion for this claim more hostile (P 613). An offer on 7th November 1950 to raise basic rates in conciliation grades in London to 100/6 a week was conditional on productivity economies, which was unacceptable to the union. Eventually yet another Committee of Inquiry was set up following a deputation to the Minister of Labour. NUR General secretary Jim Figgins told the Court of Inquiry that since 1947 not only had railwaymen's rates of pay fallen behind those in comparable outside industry but their average earnings at 135/9 a week (£209.34 in 2014 money) compared most unfavourably with the 145/9 a week (£224.77 in 2014 money) average of all other industries. In consequence there was a very rapid turnover of labour (by January 1951 an average of 20% per year). The wage increases on offer amounted to about 5%, only half what the NUR considered the minimum necessary, and the offer was rejected.

A new Minister of Labour, Aneurin Bevan, appointed a new Chairman of the Railway Executive. Mr (later to become Sir) John Elliot would become chairman of London Transport in 1953. General Secretary Figgins described him as "a very adaptable fellow" (Bagwell P 615), and eventually an increase of 7.5% was agreed, still well short of the Unions' claim and not enough to compensate for the price increases, while the Unions had to recognise the 'imperative need' for increasing efficiency and productivity. The resentment felt by railway workers was not surprising. The Times newspaper, no less, stated on 17th February 1951: "If railway charges are kept artificially low at the expense of employees it would appear that the railway workers are, in effect, subsidising other industries" (Bagwell P 616). By the end of the Labour government in October 1951 the early goodwill and idealism had dissolved. In December 1950 the NUR EC called for the removal from his post of Minister of Transport Alfred Barnes.

Unlike the situation at the end of the first world war the NUR did not object to the continued employment of women staff, though they do not appear to have worked as guards in the second war as they did in the first war. Bagwell notes (P 618) that by September 1950 many more 'coloured men' were being employed, especially on London Transport. The NUR EC stated (unanimously) "that we have no objection to the employment of coloured men in the railway industry", who had been "satisfactorily employed on the railways over a long period". But there was considerable racism at the workplace level. English railwaymen working in the goods department at Kings Cross objected that coloured men, as they described them, were being taken on above the starting grades and that if they became senior to white men "they would not stand for it". The NUR EC reaffirmed its policy of opposition to the colour bar and unanimously agreed to co-operate with the Railway Executive in the 'removal of obstacles to the employment of coloured persons' (not just men this time). This policy would also, of course, apply to London Transport.

In October 1952 the railway Unions submitted a further claim for a 10% increase in wages. NUR General Secretary Jim Figgins told the Railway Staff National Tribunal that the cost of living had risen by 35% from June 1947 to May 1952; railway wages had only risen by 16.1% over this period while wages and salaries in outside industries had gone up by 29% (Bagwell P 645). The Tribunal awarded a flat rate increase of 7/- a week for adult salaried and conciliation males, 5/6 for adult females, 4/- for junior males and 3/- for junior females. It solved nothing and yet another claim was submitted for a 15% increase. The failure to deal comprehensively with the continued falling behind of the wages of all transport workers is shocking and caused untold problems for the industry. The NUR threatened a strike on British Railways and eventually a 6% increase was awarded, which would set the precedent for London Transport. This was still inadequate and after yet another strike threat finally in January 1955 further increases were granted which came close to the claim for 15% above the level of December 1953. Increases of 7% in January 1956, 3% in November 1956 and 5% in March 1957 were achieved without recourse to industrial action.

The British Transport Commission (BTC) was created with the aim of co-ordinating all transport, road, rail and canal, in the most efficient way so that each mode would fulfil the role it was best suited to. But so great was the damage to Britain's main line railways during the war, with delayed or missed maintenance and little new rolling stock, and so great was their importance to the economy, that all efforts were concentrated on re-equipping the main line railways. Initially, London Transport's rail workers, as we have seen, gained some advances in pay and conditions largely as a result of being associated through their unions with the main line railways. But Barker & Robbins note that London Transport's financial needs for investment were treated as an added extra above what the BTC could provide. Constraints were placed on wages and salaries on London Transport which, in the opinion of Barker & Robbins, LT would have wished to improve. This was done in order to avoid 'repercussions' which would have been 'unwelcome elsewhere' ie political pressure to hold down wages.[9] Successive governments of both political persuasions insisted on nationalised industries complying with their views on limiting pay rises. Staff shortage rapidly became a major issue for LT management. Barker & Robbins note that from 1950 there was difficulty in recruiting and retaining suitable staff for operating buses, limiting the services that could be provided at a period of high demand. The shortage of labour was particularly acute in West and Northwest London caused by what Barker & Robbins call 'unbalanced industrialisation', especially near the North Circular and Great West Roads and around Heathrow Airport. Lack of provision of suitable housing for manual workers and the removal of large numbers of such workers from inner London to new estates and new towns were also cited. Immigration from Commonwealth countries alleviated but did not solve the problem.[10]

The number of women staff had reached 25% of the total by 1944. After the war there was no policy of dismissal of women in favour of men returning from the forces as there had been after the first world war but initially no further women were recruited and the figure had dropped to 9% by 1947.[11] By way of comparison, the figure was 22% in 2004.[12] In 1951 the wartime policy of engaging women conductors (at equal pay) was resumed. Long term the solution was to be the general adoption of one person operation but with LT's complicated system of graduated fares and the existing fare collection technology this was not practical for busy routes in the 1950s. Management calculated that too much revenue would be lost by adopting flat fares as was commonplace in the USA, and the concept of a zonal structure much used in many continental cities was not to be considered for many years. It will be recalled that one man operation of buses had been restricted to vehicles with 20 or less seats. The arrival of GS type buses in the country area in 1953 increased the seating to 26, and one man operation of full size single deckers (40 seat RF's) began in 1954.[13] Further flexibility in the country area was given by crews being allowed to change routes during their shift. But in the central area the need for higher capacity vehicles, whether double or single deck, led to the last five 20 seaters on routes 238 and 252 being replaced by crew operated T type single deck buses on 19th July 1949.

So the staffing problems continued. Clegg gives a useful breakdown of staff numbers on 31.12.47.

Central bus operating	27,800
Central bus inside (maintenance)	5,200
Tram & trolleybus operating	13,400
Tram & trolleybus inside	2,900
Country bus & coach operating	5,800
Country bus & coach inside	1,000
Road workshops	7,300
Road services total	63,400
Railway operating	8,100
Railway workshops	4,200
Railway other	5,000
Railways total	17,300
Power generating and distribution	2,400
Canteens etc	5,000
Supervisory, control, clerical, technical and executive	8,800
Total	97,000

The LPTB annual report of 31.12.47. notes that the Board accepted "without reservation" the principle of collective bargaining (PP 198/9). The same report claims that common conditions of service had been established for bus tram & trolleybus and country bus & coach staff (P36), though clearly some anomalies remained. Stan Collins says that the tram & trolleybus and bus administrations were formally merged in 1950, marking the LGOC takeover of LCC ways of doing things on the trams, which were about to be replaced by buses.[14]

The medical organisation, established in 1934, was to be expanded to provide a comprehensive industrial health service covering the whole of the staff (known to generations of staff as the Company Doctor). The canteen service was also greatly expanded with expenses borne by the Board as a welfare charge to keep the cost of meals low. Improved standards of lavatory and washing accommodation were provided and sports grounds developed. The 1947 Report also notes pay settlements for road and rail Workshops, Generating & Distribution, Works & Buildings, Police, Head Office Clerical & Technical (including work formerly carried out by men in the two lowest grades to be carried out in future by women), Supervisory & Control, and various other grades. It notes a "spirit of mutual trust and understanding" but regrets unofficial disputes that occurred on 6th July and 12th November (PP38/9). And that was the heart of it.

The bus staff had not had the benefit of the link with the main line railways and the astute leadership of the NUR's John Benstead to secure a reasonable increase in the immediate post war period. Fuller quotes Larry Smith, a bus driver at Victoria garage who became London District Secretary and eventually National Passenger Secretary of the T&GWU, as saying: "We weren't too enamoured of the BTC because they (London busmen) saw themselves being soaked up by a larger organisation … As time went on they saw it as very much a drag anchor on their own possible progress with London Transport". London busmen still thought they could make better progress without seeking unity with other transport workers. In June 1947 agreement on a 44 hour week was reached with the LPTB, but a flexibility clause allowed the employer to schedule up to 46 hours weekly, although the average time on duty across the fleet could not exceed 41 hours 15 minutes. The claim for enhanced payment for Saturday afternoons (when many men would expect to be free to attend a football match) was refused, and payment for Sundays remained at time and a quarter. On Sunday 6th July 1947 18,849 central bus drivers and conductors and 3,724 tram & trolleybus crews took unofficial strike action in support of the demand for time and a half for Sundays, and in November 2,600 crews struck over new schedules.

Bus washing at Victoria Garage, 1950

In February 1948 the Labour government introduced wage restraint so, to some extent, the focus shifted to hours and conditions. In 1948 the demand for time and a half for Sundays and Good Fridays was conceded, along with one additional day's holiday with pay for each Bank Holiday worked. But the settlement fell well short of the demand for an increase to £6/16/- for drivers and conductors on both buses and trams & trolleybuses (a united demand at last). Tram & trolleybus crews and central conductors received £6/5/- while central bus drivers advanced to £6/9/-.(£220.05 in 2014 money).[15]

In October 1948 the claim for time and a half for Saturday afternoons was resubmitted, but again, as Larry Smith observes: disenchantment "was as much against the current full time leadership of the passenger group in the Union and of course the General Secretary, who tended to lean towards a pay policy with the Government, and indeed accepted the (Chancellor) Stafford Cripps pay freeze. They blamed the Passenger Group leadership for the slippage which occurred in the wage rates for London busmen at that time". The Area No1 (London) Passenger Group Committee of the T&GWU disowned the General Executive Committee's endorsement of the Government's wages standstill. Meetings were held with Lord Latham, chairman of the LTE and John Cliff, former T&GWU Assistant General Secretary and now vice-chairman of the LTE but the claim was again rejected. The committee recommended to go to arbitration but the London Bus Conference of delegates had already recommended that strike action be taken on Saturday 1st January 1949. Garage meetings were held at midnight on 31st December and most decided to go ahead with the strike. LT's spies recorded that 13,531 drivers and 13,602 conductors took part in the action. Lord Latham had notices posted in all garages which threatened with dismissal all staff "who did not keep good faith and honourable observance of the agreements", a reference to the 1940 wartime arbitration agreements. Pressure was also brought to bear by T&GWU General Secretary Arthur Deakin, who told the London Bus Conference: "I will not move one finger to seek a discussion with the LTE so long as you have taken your decision, which is flat contradiction to the policy of the Union". Conference agreed to lift the strike and the matter went to arbitration. The Tribunal agreed to the application and enhanced payment for work completed after 1pm on Saturdays was introduced on 5th March 1949. We may speculate whether this would have been achieved if the strike had not happened.[16] As before on the buses, frustration after the long hard war years and the restrictions imposed by the Labour Government found expression in rank & file organisation resisted by the hierarchy of their Union. But things were to get worse.

Fuller notes that Trade Union leaders were continually exhorted by the Government and press to consider the effects of Trade Union activity on the community, and an anti-communist witch-hunt as the cold war began was the political counterpart of the Government's wages standstill. But the T&GWU was the only major Union to actually implement a ban on Communists. The 1949 conference decided: "No member of the Communist Party or Fascist parties shall be eligible to hold any office within the Union, either as a lay member or as a permanent full time officer". The ban was not rescinded until 1969. The ban had serious consequences for the London bus section. Fuller quotes Max Egelnick, Communist Party North West London Area secretary, saying that in his area the Communist Party was very much involved in Hendon, Cricklewood, Middle Row (North Kensington), Willesden and Edgware garages. The

Party's decision to wind up industrial branches seems not to have been implemented. Dalston and Merton among others also had large Communist Party branches. The reaction of the T&GWU membership was mixed, but they did realise that in many cases they were losing popular and effective leaders. Nine full-time officials were sacked for refusing to sign the declaration that they were not Communists. Much time and effort was expended fighting the ban, but to no avail. The leadership of the London bus staff was severely weakened.[17] One upshot of the ban was the founding in 1949 of the unofficial journal 'The Platform'. Some of those behind it were Communists, but not all. One of the leading lights was George Renshaw, formerly of Red International of Labour Unions fame (or infamy, depending on your point of view), who was no longer a member of the Communist Party. The Party had started to lose members at an increasing rate. But despite the popularity of 'The Platform' no mass rank & file organisation was built around it.

From a peak of 4,631 million in 1949 total passenger numbers on LT began gradually to fall as more Londoners started using motor cycles and cars, which in turn led to road services being slowed up by traffic congestion. But staff shortages meant that even reduced schedules could not be maintained. Fares were increased, leading to further reductions in passenger numbers. The LTE's approach is justifiably described by Fuller as "unimaginative".[18] An application in June 1950 for sick pay was described by vice chairman John Cliff as "a financial burden which LTE are unable to shoulder" and he was "unable to accede" to the demand. Instead of improving wages and conditions to compensate for increasingly unpopular shift and weekend work LT advocated increased overtime, a relaxation of the staff loan and transfer agreement, and recruitment of women conductors, all of which were resisted by militants in the Union. They still regarded recruitment of women staff as a means for LT to avoid payment of a more attractive wage rate. LT said they would go ahead with the recruitment of women despite Union opposition, and a joint conference of all three road transport sections in September 1950 reluctantly agreed. Similar fears were expressed about recruitment of staff from the Caribbean but there was no active opposition.[19]

Rates of pay for London bus drivers continued to fall relative to average pay rates for manual workers as shown below[20]

	Manual average	London bus driver	
1950	100	100	44 hour week
1951	109.2	106.25	
1952	118.8	111.4	
1955	143.4	131.25	
1956	155.5	142.9	42 hour week
1958	167.5	149.26	
1960	190.1	162.58	

Ever since the main line railway companies had started acquiring bus companies and road freight companies in the 1920's the RCA had been growing in those areas. On the LPTB the RCA gradually obtained negotiating rights for clerical, supervisory and control grades in road services and by the end of the war it was becoming more difficult for an organisation called the Railway Clerks Association to recruit in those areas. Thus in 1950 it changed its name to the Transport Salaried Staffs Association (TSSA)[21]

CHAPTER FOURTEEN

THE CHAMBERS REPORT AND TWO STRIKES

Bus inspector using roadside phone 1956

So much industrial unrest made it clear to all that the way London Transport was structured and run following nationalisation in 1948 was not working well. Ken Fuller's description of LT's management as "unimaginative" can be seen as something of an understatement. There was no Lord Ashfield, no Frank Pick, to give the kind of visionary inspired leadership that was needed. In the 1950' and 60's the Unions, each resolutely ploughing its own separate furrow, did not show any sign of original thinking to exploit their strong position at a time of zero unemployment and serious staff shortage. With the benefit of hindsight it is easy to see the potential for productivity deals to improve the position of staff, but these were not to come into vogue until the 1970's.

So the Government did what it usually does – it appointed a commission of inquiry. The Chambers Committee, chaired by S.P. Chambers, vice chairman of ICI (Imperial Chemical Industries, a large and successful industrial company), was appointed in April 1953. The Committee was charged with reducing costs "with a view to ascertaining what practical measures can be taken ... to secure greater efficiency or economy". Such a formulation was not exactly designed to appeal to the Unions and the T&GWU duly refused to co-operate. (The Committee only looked at bus operations). The 1955 Annual Report singles out the main conclusion as being that LT was "conducted efficiently and with due regard to economy...London has one of one of the best passenger transport systems in the world...they regard an increase in fares as the lesser evil". (P13) This complacency was not supported by the figures on P13 of the same Report, which noted a 10% loss of passenger traffic in the year (mostly on central buses and trolleybuses). Fares had risen by 113% compared with the pre-war figure while prices generally were up by 150%, making fares in real terms considerably cheaper than they had been before the war. The problem was that the cost of private motoring was falling in the post war period. After paying financial and administration charges to the BTC LT found itself with a net shortfall of £0.5 million in the year of 1954.

In its report in February 1955 the Chambers Committee rejected LT's proposals for wholesale introduction of one man operation. They felt it would be impractical in central London, leading to serious delays and a reduction in service efficiency. Without major changes in fare collection methods and technology this was certainly the case. They proposed that only some routes in the country area should be converted to OMO. A flat fare system was examined and found 'inappropriate' as London was so big that it was felt too much revenue would be lost. The Greater London Chambers of Commerce suggested to the Committee a 'Wheel Plan' which would divide routes into a central area and suburban radial services with passengers having the inconvenience and expense of changing buses at the interface. It was not adopted, although the idea of central area distributor routes serving mainline termini with high capacity one man operated single deck buses was eventually successfully put into practice, albeit years later. The Committee also concluded: "Unless, in fixing remuneration, LT take into account the remuneration of staff at all levels in comparable employment in industry, it will be impossible to attract and retain the right men and women ... If the present policy, which in our judgement produces a false economy, is maintained, there will be a chronic inability to get staff of the right quality and a fall, both qualitatively and quantitatively in the standard of service given by LT, which in turn will encourage the use of other forms of transport with its attendant consequences for LT in the shape of diminished revenue, increased traffic congestion and difficulty of operation." [1] Instead of acting on these prescient words, spelt out for them in black and white, LT management tried to press ahead with a programme of OMO. The T&GWU leadership recommended acceptance of a scheme with a proposal for a bonus payment, but this was rejected by the membership.

In 1959 the Central Bus Committee indicated that they would accept an OMO scheme subject to each individual route being considered on its merits, no standing passengers, a maximum seating capacity of 39, and allocation of staff on a rota basis to prevent a separate grade being established. LT offered an allowance of 15% but refused to agree to the 'no standing' condition.[2] It looked as if agreement was not far away, but the opportunity was let slip and the proposal was dropped.

In 1954 LT decided to replace the fleet of high capacity six wheel 70 seat trolley-buses with diesel buses seating only 56 or 64 passengers. As they still required a crew of two this clearly would increase operating costs and reduce operating efficiency in the interests of reducing the high capital and infrastructure costs of the trolleybuses. Between 1950 and 1952 LT had replaced the remaining trams, which typically had 84 seats and room for many standing, with 56 seat buses. At a time of severe labour shortage simple economics would indicate that investment in the capital costs of replacement and improvement of the trams and trolleybuses in the interests of reducing operating costs may have been beneficial, rather than more labour intensive buses. Certainly, the closure of the tram subway under Kingsway was nothing short of folly. The new Routemaster bus, designed in 1954, had an open rear platform so could not be adapted for OMO. It seems that LT management not only failed to implement the recommendations of the Chambers Committee but they also failed to think through the implications of their plans for OMO.

Interviewing job applicants in Barbados 1956

The 1954 Annual Report tells us that the total number of staff at the end of the year was 90,448, a decrease of 4,157 over the year. Turnover was 18.2% compared to 12.7% in 1953. Reconstruction of the Administrative and Supervisory Superannuation (pension) Fund brought retirement benefits into line with those of the former main line railway companies. A male wages grades pension fund had started on 1st October 1954 – all new employees were expected to join it and 40% of existing staff had joined. Half the cost was to be met by members' contributions and half by the employer. Twelve months' notice of termination of the railway salaried and conciliation Machinery of Negotiation was given by management for reasons that are not clear. The 1957 Report states that unspecified improvements to the Machinery had been agreed and that a formal negotiating and consultation machinery for Control grades had been introduced. Four new canteens had been opened, making a total of 186, but it was noted that trade continued to decline as food supplies eased and rationing ended. There were 10 sports grounds.

Despite the opening of four staff hostels in 1954, and the direct recruitment of staff in Ireland in 1955 and Barbados from 1956, the staffing position on the buses continued to deteriorate throughout the 1950s and 60s. There were fears among some staff that immigrants from the Caribbean would be less Trade Union oriented than native staff but Fuller quotes a woman conductor saying (P207): "They stuck by the Union in the big strike (1958), although no-one expected them to. It was OK after that." In 1963 there was a campaign to recruit staff from Malta. The T&GWU London Bus Section opposed this, laying themselves open to accusations of racism, which they denied. The T&GWU Executive refused to support the position of the London Bus Section.

A chart in Fuller's book tells the story of staff shortage more eloquently than mere words:

Drivers	Establishment	Shortage	%	Recruitment	Wastage
1954	19,874	1,074	5.5	1,768	3,127
1955	18,829	1,538	8.2	1,393	2,776
1956	18,463	1,396	7.6	1,724	1,169
1957	18,329	1,113	6.1	1,396	1,861
1958	17,594	1,405	8.0	912	2,274
1959	16,074	1,203	7.5	1,021	2,106
1960	16,063	2,153	13.4	1,470	2,186
1961	15,888	1,955	12.3	2,021	1,525
1962	15,719	1,639	10.4	2,149	2,218
1963	15,604	1,849	11.8	2,001	2,717

Figures for conductors were similar.[3]

In 1956 an 84 hour 11 day fortnight was introduced – a great advance for busworkers along with, at last, a sick pay scheme, although this was the work of the much maligned BTC, covering not only LT but British Railways, docks, waterways, hotels, catering and British Road Services.

But dissatisfaction on the wages issue continued to simmer in the bus section and by 1954 had reached boiling point. Dalston garage proposed a ban on overtime and this spread throughout the fleet. When some members at Willesden garage broke the ban the garage went on strike for three days. A circular issued by 13 T&GWU

branch representatives and one branch secretary stated: "It is our desire to place this movement, which is now practically fleet wide, on an organised basis. We realise that this cannot be done through the present machinery of the T&GWU so we intend to call a meeting of all representatives of garages and depots … " (an attempt to rebuild a rank & file leadership). LT introduced emergency schedules, resulting in an 8 day unofficial strike involving 16,550 crews (half the fleet), but it seems nothing was achieved. In February 1955 there was a three day stoppage at Bexley, Highgate and Ilford trolleybus depots and Loughton bus garage over schedules and in May a one day stoppage by 29 garages over revised Sunday schedules.[4] No disputes are recorded in the next two years. There was a 5% pay rise in 1957 compared to the 3% Government 'norm' achieved by the railwaymen but resentment was again building up among the bus staff.

In 1955 T&GWU General Secretary Deakin had died, and was replaced in May 1956 by the left wing Frank Cousins. Cousins was against wage restraint, arguing: "We (the T&GWU) are not prepared that our members stand still whilst the Government continually hand out largesse to those who are more favourably placed".[5] In October 1957 Chancellor Thorneycroft announced that public spending would be cut and

The canteen at Hounslow bus garage, 1957

wage rises subject to a 3% ceiling. The pay claim for London bus staff was almost 12% and was rejected by LT. Following talks an inquiry was agreed to, but a week later Minister of Labour Iain McLeod announced that this had been overruled by the Cabinet. Fuller says that LT Chairman Sir John Elliot later admitted that without Government interference LT would have negotiated. I wonder ... Anyway, the bus conference delegates voted 83-48 for a strike, not a ringing endorsement and short of the two thirds majority necessary for action, so they decided to go to arbitration. On 13th March 1958 the Industrial Court awarded 8/6 for central bus crews but nothing for 'inside'(engineering) staff and nothing for Country Services staff. And they said the costs of the award would have to be found internally, which in practice meant by service cuts. Cousins requested that the amount awarded be spread out evenly over all LT busworkers, giving them each 6/6 but this was refused by Elliot. The bus conference set 10/6 as its final claim and voted 128-4 for strike action. The T&GWU Finance & General Purposes Committee granted the London Bus Section plenary powers to conduct the strike and LT was given notice that it would start on 5th May.[6] Elliot must have realised that his refusal of further talks to spread the award more evenly would lead to a strike. Was there a parallel with 1937? Did LT management pick a fight they thought they could win? We can only speculate, but they were unable to stand up to a restrictive Government pay policy. Were they also unwilling to do so?

Trolleybus crew, 1957

Sir John Elliot in his autobiography gives some tantalising clues. He says on P 95 that as the Union had asked for arbitration, he had accepted the outcome of the arbitration, and that is why he would not negotiate further. He also says that he knew there were voices on the Union's Executive urging Cousins to accept the arbitration award. Elliot also says he sent out a personal letter to every London busman setting out "the facts of the case"; it looks as if this had a negative impact. In the sixth week of the strike Elliot says Cousins asked him to reopen negotiations so he would have "something to go back to his people with" if he were to call the strike off. Elliot says he replied that if Cousins called the strike off on the basis of the arbitration figure he would be free to come back with a new application covering the grades which had been left out. This would cause Elliot no problem as the BTC had just agreed an increase for main line railwaymen which would also apply to Underground staff. Elliot also says that the Cabinet had agreed that the LTE could offer a settlement but they said if any increase that was given was out of line with Government policy on wages they would have to disown Elliot and BTC Chairman Sir Brian Robertson. Elliot decided to "pay no attention to it" (P97). A fascinating and rare glimpse into the way Government and management co-operate and collude. Elliot then notes that the strike was called off and staff returned to work on the basis of the arbitration award. Technically and formally this is true, but Fuller says that on 4th June 1958 Elliot offered to come to terms on the basis of a mutually agreed figure for Green Line staff and an immediate review of the excluded grades. Quoting a Press Association statement of 4th June, Fuller says Elliot added that this statement was made on his own initiative and that he had had no contact with any minister.[7] A very murky episode. In his book Elliot also says he came in for some flak from Tory backbenchers for not using the opportunity to discredit Cousins, but "the deed was done". (P98) Sidney Greene, General Secretary of the NUR, advised Elliot that the NUR members would only stop work if LT tried to run extra trains.[8] The attitude of the Underground staff and their Unions was a critical factor given management's assessment that on its own a bus strike could not cripple London.[9]

During the strike the number of passengers brought in to central London by Underground and British Rail suburban services rose from 72% to 85%, and 3% of this increase was retained by them after the strike. Personal transport (bicycle, motorbike, car) rose from 7% to 9% by the end of the strike.[10] Barker & Robbins note that although they caused great inconvenience, neither a strike by BR footplate staff in May-June 1955, nor the 1958 bus strike, nor a one day Underground strike in 1962 (I think they mean 1960), or a three day stoppage in 1964, had brought London to a standstill. There was always an alternative mode. This may be taken as management's official line. On P 357 Barker & Robbins state: "The foregoing contains a mere sketch of LT's corporate and official outlook on some of the policy issues of the 1950's and 1960's". The Times reported "London takes bus strike in its stride".[11] Not until 1989 did the Unions manage to achieve simultaneous industrial action on all three modes.

Although Cousins recognised that the situation was 'bleak' there was great enthusiasm for the strike among the rank and file. LT's reports indicated that no more than a handful of members showed up for work on any one day. Cousins could see little chance of the busworkers achieving victory on their own, but the TUC, fearing that it might develop into a "headlong confrontation between the TUC and the (Tory)

Government", declined to help. Members of the TUC General Council had been communicating regularly with Prime Minister Harold MacMillan. When the TUC leaders met him formally he suggested they accept the 8/6 offer with the inclusion of Green line coach staff in this deal and negotiations over those not included. Sound familiar? So much for Sir John Elliot's 'no contact with any minister'. Troops' leave was cancelled in case the T&GWU-organised oil tanker drivers should take solidarity action. Talks produced no concrete offer for Country Services staff but the TUC were not prepared to spread the action to other areas and intimated that Cousins should retreat. A week later the bus conference voted to return to work, although many still wanted to stick it out. The agreement signed on 19th June 1958 by Elliot and Cousins stated: "In so far as the Country Services staff are concerned, it is not the intention that any decision arising from the review shall leave the wages of such staff in an unfavourable position with other staff inside the LTE road services or comparable grades elsewhere".

After the return to work these words were belied by the award of 7/6 to Green Line coach drivers but only 5/- to other Country Services staff, compared to the central busworkers' 8/6.

Fuller notes that it was a defeat of major proportions. An all-out seven week strike achieved virtually nothing. Fuller tellingly says: "No matter how it may affront lingering aristocratic sensibilities, the London bus section needs allies in any major confrontation".[12] There must have been people still around who had memories of 1937. 20 years reflection on that defeat might have better informed their actions in 1958.

At the same time yet another crisis had developed on British Railways. Although recognising in April 1958 that railway wages were 'low in comparison with those cited in nationalised industries, public services and certain private undertakings', BR management were not prepared to offer any advance in pay.[13] BTC financial deficits as a result of the BR modernisation plan were cited as the reason. After yet another strike threat (25th May 1958) 3% was offered and an inquiry established to 'make a comprehensive examination of the wages structure'. The Inquiry dragged on and patience was becoming exhausted. Finally, the NUR called for its members to withdraw their labour from 12.01 am on Monday 15th February 1960. Their frustration after such incredibly long delays must have been palpable. The London District Council of the NUR called for a 24 hour stoppage on 1st February, and on that day NUR members obeyed the unofficial call and most London Underground staff stayed away from work. Only 85 of the scheduled 493 trains ran. The stoppage had a devastating effect on London and served as a warning of what might happen if the call for an all-out official strike were to be activated. The TUC, as ever fearing a major industrial confrontation, got involved and agreement on the detailed application of the Guillebaud Report finally resulted in an 18% increase for most grades which, briefly, brought railway wages nearly, but not quite, up to par with comparable jobs in outside industry. It had been 21 months since their last pay rise, which itself had been way behind the 'going rate' in outside industry.[14] Nevertheless, the lessons were clear.

CHAPTER FIFTEEN

ANOTHER INQUIRY – PHELPS BROWN AND OMO

Replacing trolleybus supply cabling, Grays Inn Road, 1954

The 1958 strike was indeed a defeat of major proportions for the T&GWU, but the victory, if it can be so termed, for London Transport was a hollow one. The Annual Report of 31st December 1958. concludes:

i. People shifted to other forms of transport during the strike
ii. Personal transport was unable completely to take the place of buses
iii. The railways are indispensable to the daily life of London

For LT management to leave it at that smacks of complacency. The underlying problems of staff shortage and comparatively low wages had not been addressed. Management stubbornly failed to see the connection between the two. Management and Union had a common interest in dealing with the staff shortage but were unable to work together to deal with it. The London Bus Section of the T&GWU became much more cautious in its approach to major industrial action. Fuller notes that "the Section's future could not be determined by industrial strength alone but it would depend on a combination of industrial muscle and the political advances of the labour movement as a whole".[1]

This period of reflection led the T&GWU in 1960 to call for another committee of inquiry into LT buses. A public campaign was organised which gained the support of 52 garage branches. Every London MP and borough council was circulated and a petition was launched. There was a lobby of Parliament and T&GWU General Secretary Frank Cousins supported the campaign. There was a shortage of 5,200 staff on the buses and LT offered an increase of 18/- on basic rates. The Government, however, refused an inquiry and LT continued to cut services to try to match them to the staff available. The LT Annual Report of 31st December 1959 notes that staff numbers continued to fall. It records 3,484 vacancies, almost entirely on the road services.

The 1960 Annual Report notes a staff shortage of 7.4% in the wages grades, mostly on road services. Before the October wage settlement the shortage of drivers and conductors had reached 15%. It also records a serious shortage of railway booking clerks and recruitment in Ireland and Barbados on a larger scale than 1959. A bonus scheme for bus crews was recommended by the T&GWU's Negotiating Committee but rejected by a Delegate Conference of garage representatives. In March 1960 a settlement gave a10/- a week increase to drivers and conductors and after rejection of the bonus scheme rates of pay were further increased by 18/- a week. There were also improvements in conditions of service. The Report says:" The primary objective of this second settlement was to remedy the serious deterioration in London's bus services brought about by the acute shortage of drivers and conductors" (P 56).

At this time the pay and conditions of the Electrical Generation and Distribution Department were brought in line with the excellent rates paid in the Electrical Supply Industry (ESI). I was told by staff representatives that this followed a strike though this is not recorded in the Reports. Certainly, pay negotiations in this department which I was involved in consisted of 'How much did ESI get? OK, that's what you're getting.'

The 1961 Annual Report notes that Booking Office vacancies had been reduced to 49. Direct recruitment of guards and station foremen began in August 1961 – up to then everyone had had to start as a railman and work their way up. A new scheme for Railway Operating Apprentices (boys of 15 or 16) was introduced. The working week was reduced to 42 hours for railway workshop, garage maintenance and canteen staff from October, and a two hour reduction in the working week for railway salaried, conciliation and booking office staff started from 1st January 1962. In December 1961 the last stage of the scheme for equal pay for equal work for women administrative, technical and clerical staff, agreed back in 1954, was finally implemented. The Report also notes that each year about 700 staff are recommended for alternative employment on medical grounds, either temporarily or permanently.

There was the threat of a strike in 1961 but the service cuts continued. The T&GWU's campaign also continued, demanding a single authority for London with responsibility for public transport. A Government policy of moving industry out of London supposedly to ease traffic congestion reduced passenger demand still further and is politely described by Fuller as 'misguided'. A ban on overtime and rest day working in protest against service cuts was started by Southall garage in September 1963. This was deliberately chosen to put pressure on the Government in the run up to Christmas. It rapidly spread to other garages and put real pressure on the West End shops as bus services were severely affected. The Annual Report of 31st December 1962 notes that there had been a failure to agree a productivity allowance for the larger 64 seat Routemaster buses (compared with the 56-seat buses they were now replacing), OMO in the outer suburban area, experimental standee buses and faster schedules following the Ministry of Transport raising the maximum speed of Public Service Vehicles from 30mph to 40mph. The Report also says that bus mileage lost due to staff shortage had reached 1.5% by the year end. Reductions in schedules led to the shortage of drivers being reduced from 8% to 7% and of conductors from 7% to 4%. Improved working methods and an incentive scheme allowed reductions in the staff establishment and numbers of staff employed in the engineering departments. In June the Country Area had introduced a 5 year operating apprenticeship scheme which included three years as a conductor, boys entering service at 16 years of age. A two year scheme for booking office apprentices was introduced in September 1962 (I was offered one but turned it down!). Pay increases of 3% from April 1962 for all rail staff were granted. Following an increase of 6% for BR staff in November 1962 a similar increase came in for LT railway conciliation and workshop staff. Two one day strikes on the Underground are recorded in the 1962 Annual Report, one of them official also supported by the Craft Unions, over the BTC policy of closing BR branch lines.

The 1963 Annual Report records that the shortage of bus drivers rose to 12% causing 3% of Central bus scheduled mileage not to be operated, rising to 7% at the end of October and no less than 15% as the ban on overtime and rest day working began to bite. The Report also states that there were 165 canteens employing 1,500 staff at a cost of £690,000. The number of staff employed had been reduced by 60 as a result of an incentive bonus scheme and installation of automatic vending equipment. The impression given by these Reports is of a management constantly trying to play catch-up without any overall strategy.

In November 1963 the Government finally agreed to establish a Committee under Professor Henry Phelps-Brown of the London School of Economics to review the pay and conditions of LT bus drivers and conductors. The overtime ban was not lifted until an interim report was published with great promptitude on 16th December with the recommendation that LT should negotiate wage increases. The final report, published in February 1964, recognised what everyone already knew, that LT's

Effra Road, Brixton,
ticket works, 1957

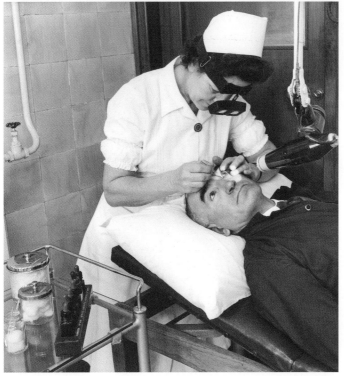

The industrial health
centre at Chiswick Bus
Works, 1963

inability to recruit and retain staff was "evidence of the relative inadequacy of pay". It even quoted the 1955 Chambers Committee's statement that "unless LT … take into account remuneration of staff … it will be impossible to attract and retain the right men and women". The 1964 Annual Report says Phelps-Brown concluded "that it would be more reasonable to compare the earnings of LT busmen with skilled and semi-skilled workers rather than those of wage earners as a whole and that on this basis the earnings of the LT busmen did not occupy a high position in the scale of actual pay despite their relatively high basic rates". The Committee drew attention to the inconvenience of shift and weekend working and "expressed the view that the increased disadvantages … of busmen's employment needed to be offset by higher pay". They also noted "the persistent difficulties experienced by the Board in finding enough staff to fill its establishment we regard as evidence of the relative inadequacy of pay". The Report stated that average earnings generally had risen 3.8 times between 1938 and 1963 while bus drivers' earnings had risen only 2.6 times and Underground staff 3.1 times. Phelps-Brown recommended the phased introduction of the 40 hour week and a total increase of 31/- a week for drivers and 26/- a week for conductors on the basic from July 1964.[2] Average rostered earnings for a 42 hour week were increased overall by 38/- per week. An average 40 hour week would give bus crews an additional rest day every 4 weeks. Scheduled earnings would increase by 17% and the whole package was equivalent to 23%.

Following the pay rises staff shortage on the buses fell from a high of 15% to 10% by December 1964 (still not good). For the first time the Underground saw a serious staff shortage amounting to 6% by the end of 1964. Phelps-Brown stated that "the labour force required in the London bus service is at least as great as the present establishment" but LT continued to cut rosters and the staff shortage continued. The 1965 Annual Report notes that staff recruitment was still a major problem. "Morale of staff running road services was adversely affected by the difficult operating conditions", it says. The catering service also suffered from a worsening staff position despite considerable amounts of rest day working. The 1966 Annual Report notes that recruitment of staff from Barbados had been greatly reduced due to the operation of the Commonwealth Immigration Act of 1962. Phelps-Brown also repeated the Chambers Committee's recommendation for standee flat fare buses with automatic fare collection equipment, extension of OMO in suburban areas and conversion of some country area routes to OMO with double deckers. To enable these changes to take place agreement was reached for larger front entrance buses. Experimental Daimler Fleetlines and Leyland Atlanteans were acquired to enable trials to take place but they were crew operated on busy central area services.

A great deal of overtime was still being worked and overtime bans were called at various garages in 1964 over service cuts and schedule disputes. On 6/7/8th January 1965 at least 70 garages were affected by an overtime ban. The implementation of the 40 hour week was postponed until October 1965 in return for an extra 21/3 per week from 17th March. In this agreement the Union agreed to the compulsory working of one rest day per month and the right of LT to take "any action" against any garage imposing an overtime ban. A strike call for Boxing Day was withdrawn although six garages (Chalk Farm, Hackney, Putney, Palmers Green, Peckham and Turnham Green) went ahead with unofficial strikes. Eventually LT agreed that all Boxing Day duties would have a maximum length of five hours. The 5 day 40 hour week had still

A conductor collects fares on an RT type bus

not been implemented and the T&GWU called an official overtime ban at 67 Central area garages that lasted for five weeks. In February 1965 Catford, Camberwell and Stockwell struck against attempts to break the ban and Southall and Hanwell struck against service cuts; Hounslow also struck in this period. The 5 day 40 hour week was finally introduced in 1967.[3]

The 1965 Annual Report notes that pay negotiations took place against the background of the Government's Prices and Incomes policy and the 'standstill' meant that no settlement had been reached on the buses. The agreed 3.5% increase on the railways was not paid until March 1967 despite LT agreeing to bring it forward to September 1966. The 40 hour week had been agreed in principle for conciliation staff but not yet introduced. Similar situations existed for workshop and garage maintenance staff.

In April 1966 one-man single-deck flat fare 'Red Arrow' buses were introduced on new short central area routes, with great success except for problems with the fare collection machines. Initially Ministry of Transport regulations did not permit OMO on double deck buses but LT eventually persuaded the Ministry to relax the regulations and the first one man double deckers appeared in Croydon in 1969.[4] Under the Bus Reshaping Plan of September 1966 there were to be flat fare networks of short routes in various suburban centres feeding Underground stations and trunk routes. The trunk routes would continue to be operated by Routemasters with conductors but some routes would be shortened in an attempt to improve reliability of services.

There was considerable public resistance to the new standee single deckers which had 25 seats and room for 48 standing. This led to some friction with drivers. The new flat fare routes were successful although greatly slowed down when the troublesome fare collection turnstiles (passimeters) had to be replaced by driver collection of fares, even though no change was given. The failure to find a workable mechanical system of fare collection until the Oyster card system many years later meant that any productivity gains from abolition of the conductor would be marginal. As previously noted, OMO on small buses on lightly trafficked routes had existed since before the foundation of the LPTB in 1933 and an allowance of 5/- had been won before the war for OMO drivers. So the T&GWU were unable to mount opposition to OMO as such, though they supported various public campaigns against it. But what was now proposed was clearly on a completely different scale.

Following Phelps-Brown an allowance of 15% plus a productivity allowance of 1d per seat per day was agreed. Many T&GWU activists were against OMO in principle (the redoubtable Bill Jones in particular) so there seems not to have been a Union campaign at this time to increase the OMO allowance for fear of legitimising the introduction of OMO.[5] It was still seen as a limited introduction, maybe on Sundays only, but the door was ajar and in the negotiations which followed it was to be kicked wide open. In March 1967 a Joint Working Party was set up – these devices always presuppose agreement on the main point at issue and focus on the details of implementation. The devil, as always, was in the detail, and the big question was how the supposed savings from OMO should be divided up. The T&GWU thought that crew drivers and conductors should also gain some benefit from OMO. LT proposed that the benefits should be split three ways – one third each to the employer, staff and public. As LT was nationalised, the T&GWU argued that the employer and the public were one and the same and so the split should be 50:50 with staff.

The Government then intervened with its Prices and Incomes report No 50, which recommended the 10/- payment to all bus staff already agreed by LT plus a premium for OMO drivers of 20% for single deckers and 22.5% for double deckers (similar amounts had been agreed by the T&GWU for Manchester and Liverpool). But they said the double share of the receipts bonus and the 1d per seat capacity allowance should be discontinued. The T&GWU found themselves negotiating with the Government, that most immovable of employers even though it was a Labour Government. Eventually, following a strike threat by both central and country areas, the Chairman of LT agreed to meet T&GWU Assistant General Secretary Jack Jones and the Union's National Passenger Secretary and a formula was agreed. Single deck OMO drivers would receive an allowance of £4/10/- a week rising to £4/14/- in 1970. All drivers and conductors would get 10/- a week, to be consolidated in January 1969, plus a further 10/- for other productivity items. When double deck OMO operations started drivers would receive between £5/7/- and £5/12/- (26% above the crew drivers' rate) according to the type of bus they drove. Later these allowances were consolidated to give OMO drivers a separate basic rate. The receipts bonus and capacity allowance were to be shared among the staff. The Union were not happy with this 1968 agreement but could see no way of achieving anything better given the Government's hard line on productivity. No jobs were threatened as the staff shortage was so severe. The principle of OMO on central area routes was thus firmly established. Although the cost to management may have been close to their formula of one third of the savings for the staff, OMO drivers did not receive anything like this amount because the Union had insisted on part of the savings going to other staff, particularly crew drivers and conductors.

Bus mechanic works on rear engine DMS type bus, 1978

The following year the T&GWU claimed £1 on the basic rate plus 12/- for London weighting. With the staff shortage still numbering 5,000 an overtime ban was very effective and following strikes at seven East London garages 17/- on the basic was achieved plus a further 3/- from October subject to agreement on a new type of OMO bus.[6]

However, despite the increasing use of OMO buses and consequent pay rises the staff shortage persisted then got worse, reaching 19% overall in 1969 and over 30% in some garages in West and North West London. OMO buses were considerably slower than crew operated ones, especially on routes with graduated fares. This factor required more, not less, drivers to carry the same number of passengers. Many conductors were unwilling or unable to change over to driving. The staff shortage was most acute for drivers partly because of the worsening traffic conditions in London. Ken Fuller notes considerable revenue losses following conversion of some outer London routes to OMO in 1966[7]:

Route	201	31% loss
	206	27% loss
	216	26% loss
	250	25% loss
	237	36% loss
	251	39% loss

It was also becoming more difficult to recruit and retain engineering staff in the garages. With the purchase of new 'off the peg' buses whose reliability was nowhere near as good as the LT designed traditional buses the shortage of 'inside' staff was becoming a critical factor. The experimental front entrance rear engine Routemaster (the FRM) unfortunately remained unique. Increasing traffic congestion also became a major issue delaying buses. When this was temporarily eased during the fuel rationing occasioned by the Suez crisis in 1957 LT said that the faster running would have allowed it to save 200 buses. The introduction of the Piccadilly/Pall Mall one way traffic system in 1961 resulted in 10% ridership losses in the area but LT did not call for bus lanes until 1964 and the first ones did not appear in London until 1968.

The BTC had become almost entirely concerned with the problems of British Railways and LT had been left largely to its own devices. The lack of strategic leadership had become palpable and it was becoming obvious that if a satisfactory service was to be provided for London subsidies from the public purse would be needed. So the Transport Act of 1962 reconstituted the London Transport Executive as the London Transport Board, reporting directly to central Government. The Annual Report of 31st December 1963 notes that the new Board was subject to Ministerial control. It would have no stocks or loan obligations, past debts being cleared, but it would have a duty to "secure that revenue is not less than sufficient to meet all charges ... "

A change of Government in 1964 might have provided an opportunity for some strategic thinking but the Labour Government in 1966 introduced a prices and incomes freeze, which among other things prevented the LTB from increasing fares. The commitment under the Guillebaud settlement on the railways to keep rail staff wages on a par with wages outside was also abandoned at this time. An application for a pay increase by the railway unions was referred to the Government's Prices and Incomes Board, which stated that improvements in pay and conditions were dependent on "a direct contribution to increasing productivity". On the basis of the increase of railway traffic and the reduction of manpower from 1963 to 1964 the NUR calculated that productivity had increased by 13%, more than enough to justify the 10% pay increase that would have been due under the Guillebaud formula. Over the three years from 1962 to 1965 productivity had increased by at least 26%. But the Prices and Incomes Board came to the conclusion that with the exception of clerical staff the pay of railway staff "did not require adjustment".[8]

Negotiations at 10 Downing St ensued on 11th and 12th February 1966 (the famous 'beer and sandwiches' episode). Following passionate appeals from Prime Minister Harold Wilson and Transport Minister Barbara Castle, in the early hours of the morning the NUR Executive Committee was persuaded, by the narrowest of margins (13-11), to call off a threatened strike and accept a most unsatisfactory settlement. Harold Wilson promised that he would himself chair meetings to discuss improving productivity and wages and, having 'cleared the decks' of any industrial strife, the 1966 election was called. The Pay and Efficiency talks, as they were called, took up the next two and a half years. But having prevented LT from increasing fares and now being responsible for the finances of the new LT Board the Government was obliged to subsidise LT if further service cuts were to be avoided. The Transport Finances Act of 1966 allowed grants of up to £16 million up to the end of 1968.

Neasden No.1 branch of the National Union of Railwaymen, c1940s

The number of passengers and mileage travelled declined both on buses and Underground, but the effect on the buses was much more severe, falling by 42.5% from 1960 to 1979 compared with a 15.2% fall on the Underground.[9] The bus side of LT's operations plunged into the red while the Underground, for a while, still earned a surplus.[10] The proportion of staff on the buses fell from 47% in 1969 to 42% in 1979, while rail staff rose from 18% to 20% and workshops (road and rail) rose from 32% to 35%.[11]

In the 1967 Annual report there is reference to the need for a rapid extension of OMO. We also learn that a new LT Pension Fund for male and female wages grade staff had started on 1st January and a five day week for catering staff had been implemented in October.

The Annual Report of 31st December 1968 records significant progress with improved labour productivity, in particular the general introduction of OMO. The fall in passenger numbers had been all but halted, but a downward trend on Green Line coaches was noted, where all single deck routes had been converted to OMO. Automatic ticket issuing and collection was to be installed on the new Victoria Line. The 1963 report notes that the first automatic entrance barrier with a device to read tickets was to be experimentally introduced at Stamford Brook station on 5th January 1964. In the 1964 report we learn that automatic entrance barriers of different types had been installed at Stamford Brook, Chiswick Park and Ravenscourt Park stations, in association with the Advance Data Systems Corporation of Los Angeles. The 1965 Report noted the first automatic exit barrier had been trialled at Acton Town while automatic entrance and exit barriers were installed at Turnham Green. The Productivity scheme on the Underground had resulted in pay increases of between 3% and 15% in return for increased versatility, efficiency and productivity, especially acceptance of the principle of OMO on conventional (non-automatic) trains on the Hammersmith & City and Circle lines. Some railway staff had a work to rule and overtime ban from 24th June to 6th July and there had been a one week stoppage in the Lifts and Escalators Department in the autumn.

Back in 1955 an acute shortage of station staff had led LT management to try, without success, to get local staff representatives to accept regular rest day working. The full-time officials of the NUR, however, agreed a scheme whereby staff would be assumed to be willing to work their rest days unless they notified 'manpower officers' to the contrary. The NUR EC endorsed this action as a similar scheme operated on British Railways. But at the NUR AGM (conference) an appeal against this policy for the Underground was carried unanimously. The traincrew had, and still have, a long standing policy of refusing to work rest days which has stood rail staff in good stead over the years when arguing for a decent basic rate.[12] Fuller notes that in 1966, two years after Phelps-Brown had brought substantial increases for bus drivers, a weekly increase of £4 would have been necessary to re-establish parity with an Underground train driver, let alone the pre-eminence they used to enjoy.[13]

Both the Chambers and Phelps Brown reports were about the problems on the buses, but Chambers in 1955 had noted that LT should look at "improved public transport both above and below ground". Since the Underground extensions to outer suburbs, largely undertaken under state control due to the failure of the private railway companies with the notable exception of the Southern, to electrify their suburban services, little attention had been paid to the Underground. In 1964 LT railway staff received 3.75% (5% for supervisors from 23rd December), interim payments of 10/- to 15/- a week and 9% in December following similar increases on BR. LT Wages Board Decision No 3 of 1955 laid down that LT must have 'regard to rates for similar duties on BR'. Railway workshop staff achieved the 40 hour week from 17th March 1965 plus 1 additional day's leave. The 1964 Annual Report notes that some unofficial strikes occurred over reductions in services.

The 1965 Annual Report notes that the Race Relations Act had come into force in November and a voluntary machinery had been set up to deal with complaints of discrimination. Eleven references were made, they say, and no evidence of any discrimination was found. In the light of what we know about the racism and discrimination that did exist at that time and subsequently it is very clear that this machinery was totally ineffective and LT was somewhat complacent if not complicit on the issue.

As far back as 1954 the LTE had sought enabling powers for a new Underground 'Route C' from Victoria to Walthamstow. The Annual Report for 1954 states: This "cannot be expected to earn the interest on the capital invested in it...It will relieve overcrowding on the most heavily used sections of the Underground and (bring) considerable relief to road services over a wide area". This is a fascinating and unfortunately rare example of joined up thinking and recognition that profitability is not the only justification for extensions. The 1955 Report notes that powers had been granted to build what was now known as the Victoria Line, but not until 1962 was Government authority, with the necessary financial commitment, finally given. Its significance from the point of view of labour relations was that it was designed from the start to be operated automatically, without a driver or a guard. The very first experimental automatic operation of trains in passenger service started on 8th April 1964 between Stamford Brook and Ravenscourt Park Eastbound on the District Line.

The rail Unions were able to persuade LT that a member of staff needed to be on the front of the train to deal with any emergencies or breakdowns that might occur, and to allay the fears of a sceptical public. Nevertheless, the Victoria Line would have the first trains without a crew of two. The 1964 Annual Report records the decision to adopt Automatic Train Operation (ATO) on the new Victoria Line, stating on PP 4-5: "Since 5th April 1964 4-car trains with automatic driving equipment have been running on the Hainault-Woodford section of the Central Line with one train operator who controls the train doors and presses buttons to activate the automatic control mechanism." Effective communication between the Operator and Control room staff was essential, at this time by carrier wave through the running rails. The minutes of the NUR EC for 21st February 1964 note re. Automatic driving of trains: "to accept the offer of the LTB for a rate of pay for men operating these trains of 372/- per week (£340.03 in 2014 money), 65/- above the maximum basic for train drivers." This was the equivalent of a Supervisor Class 1, but without supervisory status or conditions. On 4th May they voted to "accept the arrangements". The 1965 Annual Report of the LTB notes on P 15 that ATO "will reduce by half the number of train crew required".

In March 1964 the railway Unions applied for a 40 hour week, though this was not agreed until 1967. The NUR EC minutes record that on 7th December 1964 the abolition of extended turns agreed to as long ago as 3rd September 1947 had finally been agreed, but abolition of split turns (known to bus staff as spreadovers) was not agreed – the NUR gave three months' notice of action on this.

Staff check signal relays at Earl's Court Interlocking Machine Room, 1966

However, as the construction of the Victoria Line progressed, both Unions (NUR and ASLE&F) applied on 29th November 1967 for a further increase in the ATO rate of pay. Application was also made on 9th May for three weeks annual leave. It was noted that the reduction in qualifying period for the extra three days granted in the last year from 10 years to 12 months had necessitated extra staff. The claim was left in abeyance awaiting the outcome of a similar claim on BR. On 8th October 1968 a revised pay structure for ATO was agreed. This gave the ATO operator 463/- per week (£367.08 in 2014 money) and extended the ATO allowance of 30/- per week to all related staff such as Carriage Examiners, who needed additional training to qualify to deal with the ATO equipment on the trains. The conventional (crew) driver/ motorman rate increased from between 304/- and 357/- to 385/- per week, a carriage cleaner 232/- to 266/- (with consolidation of many benefits), Automatic Equipment Technician (signals) from 433/- to 463/- and Station Foreman 'A' from 317/- to 326/-. These figures give an interesting picture of the various differentials, and show that the OMO rate was just over 20% above the crew drivers' rate. But the agreement also included a commitment to discuss "an understanding on the operating and technical requirements for OMO on the Hammersmith & City and Circle lines."

Also contained in the 1968 agreement was a commitment to modify the 1947 agreement to increase (not abolish) split turns from 4% to 8% on a Line basis. And still further, to "make savings by introduction in the period 1968-1970 of automatic fare collection equipment on the Victoria Line and at stations from Acton Town to Hammersmith inclusive". Further staff saving measures and efficiencies included reduction of the rolling stock seven daily examination gang (where I started my railway career) to two Leading Car Examiners and two Car Examiners for three trains of 7 or 8 cars or 4 trains of 6 cars. There was also a revised structure and rate of pay for booking office staff.

The demonstration railway at White City Railway Training Centre, 1971

On 5th January 1971 a Wages Board Decision accepted that: "all conciliation staff in the operating department shall be allowed 30 minutes meal time included in their 8 hour working day, such meal time to be taken as and when circumstances permit". It will be recalled that there had been a bitter strike over this very issue just after the first world war. The paid meal break was abolished unilaterally by management in 1992 under the 'Company Plan'.

Meanwhile, the claim for an increased differential for OMO which had been lodged back in 1967 was still wending its tortuous way through the labyrinthine negotiating machinery. Finally in January 1971 Wages Board Decision No 7 awarded an increase of 9/- backdated to 1st May 1970. This brought the ATO rate up to 21.7% of a guard's wage above the crew drivers' rate, although of course there had never been guards on the Victoria Line. The NUR EC minutes record that the claim at LT's Railway Negotiating Committee (RNC) on 20th January on pay, annual leave and hours of duty was still awaiting settlement of the BR claim, while part 2 of the Pay and Efficiency scheme was continuing, with a 'scientific' study into staff motivation. A review of station staff establishments and other productivity measures was in progress. Finally the minutes record that the RNC had agreed holiday pay to be paid at the rate of time plus one eighth, and the following increased pay rates, now decimalised:

Railman (bonuses consolidated)	£16.10 - £18.10
Station Foreman 'B'	£19.25 - 21.65
Automatic Train Operator	£28.05 - 32.05
Train Driver	£23.05 - 26.60
Carriage Examiner	£18.65 - 20.95

The top ATO rate is equivalent to £432.42 in 2014 money.

LT management clearly saw this settlement as a green light to start the process of removing guards from other lines, especially given the staff shortages which were becoming more and more serious on the Underground. Discussions on 'labour economies' on the Hammersmith & City and Circle Lines had begun on 9th October 1968. New rolling stock ('C' Stock) which would be suitable for OMO was about to be ordered, and Bagwell confirms (Vol 2 P 290) that the Unions had already agreed to the principle of OMO on these lines. Implementation, though, would have to wait until the new rolling stock was available and agreement was reached on a rate of pay for OMO on conventional (non-automatic) trains. In May 1971 LT sought agreement but the economic climate had now changed and unemployment, for the first time since the war, was becoming a major problem. The view of the membership of the NUR and its London Transport District Council began to move against OMO. Finally, on 11th November 1977, after protracted negotiations, the NUR EC passed a resolution stating that: "this Union no longer wishes to pursue OMO". Against the wishes of the Unions the LTB unilaterally referred the question of the rate of pay to the Wages Board, indicating that they "cannot accept this as they feel that the establishment of a rate of pay should be taken to conclusion". The LTB also stated that "agreement to OMO on the H&C&C was reached in 1968 and this agreement is widely known". The NUR EC resolved that "we reiterate our previous decision that we no longer wish to pursue OMO...and inform LTE that if they go unilaterally to the Wages Board they will find themselves in dispute with this Union...and to advise other Unions of our decision" (NUR EC minutes 11th November 1977). But no action was taken on either side. Eventually, in the summer of 1979 the NUR EC recognised that previous commitments left it no alternative but to re-enter negotiations. By 13th September 1979 it had agreed that OMO could be implemented as soon as possible on the H&C and Circle lines and extended to the District and Metropolitan lines "in due course", ie all the sub-surface lines, "subject to that form of operation proving to be satisfactory". A review before any further extension of OMO would take place six months after the start of the H&C&C scheme. Train Operators would receive the same rate of pay as ATOs (then £89.42 per week). Further, they agreed the principle of the extension of OMO to the deep tube lines subject to any restraints imposed by the Railway Inspectorate. There were voices in both Unions that believed that the Railway Inspectorate would never allow OMO on the deep tubes, but the necessary technical requirements (especially train radio) were put in place.

In return, a flat rate sum equivalent to 7.5% of the basic rate was given to all staff in the Traffic division of the Railway Operating Department, ie all those who may have been considered to be in a line of promotion to the new grade of Train Operator. This overall payment was probably the critical factor in the NUR EC's acceptance of the scheme in the face of furious opposition from some workplace activists and the District Council. A minority on the NUR EC opposed OMO on principle but were heavily outvoted as the EC recognised "our responsibility to negotiate" on OMO.[14] One Person Operation on the H&C and Circle eventually started in 1984. The first woman train driver had started work in 1978, and the first woman bus driver in 1974, leading to the change in terminology. However, the issue of OPO and the rate of pay was to arise again as implementation of what was by now called One Person Operation (OPO) proceeded in the 1980s.

Comparisons between rates of pay for OMO on buses and trains are extremely difficult to make accurately due to the difference between basic rates and actual earnings, but these early 1970s figures suggest that the bus driver was not as far behind the train driver as is sometimes suggested.

Train Driver (crew)	up to £26.60	Bus driver crew: £29
ATO/OMO Train Operator	up to £32.05	Bus driver OMO single deck £33 (14% diff)
Differential	20.5%	Bus driver OMO double deck £36.50 (26% differential)
Source: NUR EC minutes May 1971		Source: LT records 1972

On 12th March 1979 LT Railways decided to establish a new separate cleaning organisation to improve the standard of cleaning on stations and other property. The grade of railman, with its low rate of pay, was abolished.

CHAPTER SIXTEEN

THE ENGINEERS STRIKE OF 1969

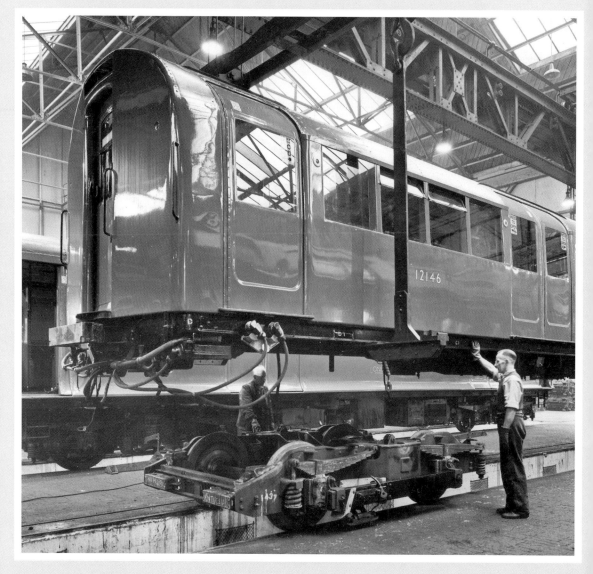

A 1950s view of an overhauled 1938 stock car being lifted back on to its bogies in Acton Works.

As related in earlier chapters, the pattern of labour representation and negotiation in the railway workshops developed separately from the operating side of the railways, due largely to the opposition of the Amalgamated Engineering Union to the conciliation scheme and their insistence on a shop steward system to represent their members. Thus, the engineers, electricians, bodymakers and other skilled trades were represented by their own separate craft Unions co-ordinated by an Allied Crafts Committee. Unskilled and semi-skilled grades were organised by the NUR, and just to make things more complicated some skilled grades such as brake fitters not covered by any of the craft Unions were also organised by the NUR. The T&GWU did not organise on the railways until it absorbed the National Union of Vehicle Builders, who represented the bodymakers, in 1972, when the T&GWU became part of the Craft Alliance. The craft Unions protected the status and the passing on of skills to their members by insisting on proper apprenticeships, and there was no possibility of unskilled or semi-skilled staff progressing to skilled status (and pay). But there were always exceptions to the rule and some members of the craft Unions had acquired their skills without an indentured apprenticeship, for instance through the Army. As long as they had an AEU card they were considered eligible for skilled jobs, access to which was jealously controlled by the AEU and other craft Unions. To complicate matters even further, in workplaces where it held sole negotiating rights the AEU had taken semi-skilled and unskilled workers into its membership. A complex and unstable system of grading had been allowed to develop in LT's workshops.

Not surprisingly the NUR had lodged a claim for their semi-skilled members to be allowed promotion into the skilled grades hitherto reserved for the craft Unions. The TUC Bridlington Agreement of 1939 prevented the Unions actively poaching each other's members so an uneasy status quo prevailed. (Since the 1993 Trade Union Reform and Employment Rights Act gave workers the right to join the Union of their choice it has become difficult for the TUC to enforce the provisions of the Bridlington Agreement). The NUR argued that if their members were being refused access to skilled grades because they had not served an apprenticeship (ie were 'unindentured') logically the management should not allow unindentured members of the AEF (Amalgamated Engineering and Foundry workers as the AEU had become) to be recruited into skilled jobs. The NUR argued that semi-skilled workers, after a number of years' experience, were as capable of performing certain skilled jobs as non-indentured craftsmen employed from outside LT, and should have the opportunity to apply for promotion to such posts.

In an attempt to solve this predicament LT management decided to require all non-indentured craftsmen recruited from outside LT to undertake a 'trade test' before offering them employment. LT claimed that this did not conflict with any agreement with the AEF, but the AEF felt that this "intruded on their rights" as LT phrased it in their 1969 Annual Report.

An AEF fitter at Acton Works had been promoted to a position as an apprentice instructor. LT said that the applicant from outside for the resultant vacancy, an AEF member, did not have sufficient engineering experience, so they would not take him on. In turn, the fitter whose place was to have been taken by the applicant could not take up his promotion. So in the view of the AEF technically it was not an inter-Union dispute, although LT saw it as such. The AEF claimed the right to say who could be taken on in the skilled grades, so for them the strike was over LT not honouring an agreement on promotion and recruitment. The AEF claimed it was "the wanton and deliberate breaking of an agreement by the LTB who by this unprincipled act refused to employ an unindentured craftsman" (Strike Chairman Don Cook in AEF Pamphlet 'LT (Railway Workshops) Dispute Sept 24 – December 20 1969'). Following a "series of skirmishes with LT management over the previous 18 months" according to Don Cook, or "a year of endeavours to reconcile the views of the two Unions" according to the LT Annual Report, a mass meeting of AEF members at Acton Works at 10am on September 24th 1969 unanimously agreed to take strike action.

The other craft Unions and the NUR had no problem and continued to work. Showing great loyalty to their Union, AEF members in the Depot workshops and other departments joined the strike along with unskilled and semi-skilled AEF members. Regular day-to-day maintenance of rolling stock was carried out by NUR-organised conciliation staff and along with non-AEF workshop staff they ensured that there was not a great effect on the train service. Acton Works mainly carried out five yearly overhauls of trains so it would have taken a very long time for any serious effect on services to be felt. But overhaul of equipment was also carried out at Acton Works, and LT management recognised problems due to non-availability of 1938 stock on the Northern and Bakerloo lines due to problems with aging hydrovane compressors which were not being repaired at Acton Works. There was also some effect on Lifts and Escalators but the overall impact was limited.

The organisation of the strike was exemplary. It was recognised by the AEF nationally. Strike money was paid and a District levy was organised. LT referred the dispute to the Department of Employment and Productivity and several meetings took place. The support of TUC General Secretary Vic Feather was enlisted. A mass meeting on December 15th decided on a 'formula' which was eventually agreed at the DEP. The AEF claimed that this was the "AEF formula without exception", which for them represented "complete victory on a principle which is vital to the interests not only of our members on LT but to our Union as a whole". The dispute ended on December 22nd. The AEF had certainly secured its position in the workshops for a few more years, but had won no friends in the other railway Unions.

The lessons activists in the railway Unions drew were very different from those of the AEF, namely that to achieve anything worthwhile collective support across the Unions would be necessary. To stop the railway from running would require action from traincrew, signalling staff and/or other staff in critical positions. To claim, as the AEF Pamphlet does, that withdrawal of all skilled mechanical craftsmen left the railways "without mechanical maintenance of any sort" (P4) is to exaggerate severely the significance and impact of the dispute. However, the LT Annual Report does note that the effects of the strike were not "overtaken" until the spring of 1970.

But for the NUR that was not the end of it. The EC minutes of 8th October 1969 note that the AEF represented 250 of the 1,400 staff at Acton Works and that a Line of Promotion to craftsman for semi-skilled staff existed in the Civil Engineering and Signal Engineering departments. NUR members at Acton Works were advised to only carry out work appropriate to their grade during the strike. The minutes of 27th November 1969 express 'serious concern' at the decision of the LTB to reduce the wages of their members at Acton Works to 75% of normal from 7th December and sought an 'urgent meeting' with management. On 18th December they note the re-establishment of previous practice and seek immediate talks on this and the NUR's claim for semi-skilled staff to be considered for craftsman vacancies "in the absence of indentured applicants". "If the matter is not settled in a manner acceptable to the majority of the workers in the Chief Mechanical Engineers Department, the matter...must be referred to arbitration" they say.

An incredibly long drawn out series of interchanges then takes place, indicating the stark contrast between the results obtained by the AEF's strike and the non-results obtained by the NUR's patient requests for talks.

To their request on 18th December 1969 for "immediate talks" the LTE Chief Industrial Relations officer finally replied on 17th August 1970 that "it had not been possible" for a meeting with the AEF to be arranged. The NUR EC decides that "we see no useful purpose in pursuing this with the LTE or the AEF as it is apparent that the AEF are only interested in delaying tactics...We therefore insist that this matter be referred to the Department of Economic Affairs and the TUC seeking their assistance for this case to be put before a Committee of Inquiry or similar". On 23rd October the NUR decides to take up the Secretary of State for Employment and Productivity's suggestion to refer the matter to the Commission on Industrial Relations. In March 1971 they note that the AEF and NUVB (National Union of Vehicle Builders) oppose the reference to the Commission and the TUC defers a

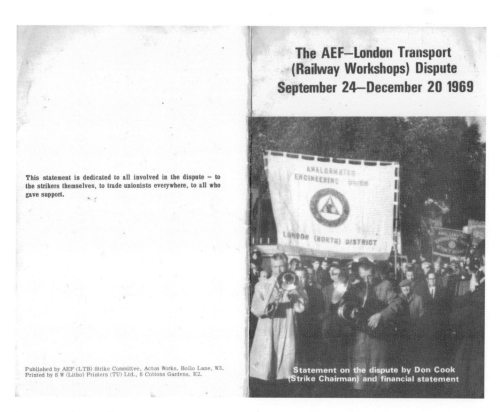

Report on the Amalgamated Engineering and Foundry Workers Union dispute at Acton Works, published June 1970

'C' stock car on accommodation trucks at Acton Works

decision on the issue in the light of the Industrial Relations Bill possibly becoming law. The NUR reply to the TUC that "we are still desirous of resolving this question as it is still a source of friction between the TU's concerned". In August 1971 the TUC decides to recommend Unions not to co-operate with the Commission on Industrial Relations and the issue is referred back to the TUC. In December 1971 they arrange an informal meeting of the Unions concerned. It takes until December 1972 for the TUC General Secretary to advise that the other Unions thought "no useful purpose was likely to be achieved by such a meeting and therefore he had not pressed the matter". The NUR decides to seek a meeting with the other TU's with a TUC Council member in the chair.

Another lengthy delay ensues before the TUC General Secretary advises in August 1973 that the newly renamed AUEW were not prepared to take part in an informal meeting. The NUR decides to pursue it through the TUC. In August 1974 the NUR note that the AUEW are still unwilling to meet and the TUC is unable to do anything. The LTE agree to discuss the matter separately and an "immediate" meeting is sought, which finally takes place on 3rd February 1975. LT agree to reconsider the claim.

Nothing is then minuted until December 1978 when the AUEW are willing to meet the LTE to discuss the matter but LTE are "mindful of the sensitivity of the matter and that the present procedure for recruitment of mechanical fitters and turners… is covered by a 1958 agreement with the AEF". That much was known in 1969. Further meetings are to take place. In August 1979 the NUR EC note with concern the continuing delay and the commitment made by both LTE and AUEW in 1970 to enter into 'meaningful discussions'.

The saga continues. In August 1981 the NUR "seek an urgent meeting with LTE to break down this long outstanding barrier which debars semi-skilled staff from taking promotion to mechanical craftsman". A minute of 25th November 1982 notes that the AUEW consider it "inappropriate to involve themselves in discussion concerning the line of promotion". On 5th May they note that the NUR had accepted proposals from the LTE in February 1982 but still awaited a response from the AUEW, who saw no possibility of progress.

On 29th November 1984 we learn that management have stated that it is not a matter for the Joint Negotiating Committee but for the individual TU's involved. The NUR insist on a meeting with LRT, saying that "a matter of principle…cannot be blocked by another organisation". On 19th July 1985 the NUR are still pressing for a meeting with LRT, but receive the news that in future train overhaul is to be carried out in the various depots. Acton Works will be closed and replaced with a new Equipment Overhaul Shop. Finally, in December 1985, 16 years after the end of the strike, the NUR EC minutes note that: "the long standing aim of this Union to achieve promotion to craftsman of suitable semi-skilled staff is catered for under items 3.1 and 3.3 of the LUL document".

Victories, if so it can be termed, do not come any more pyrrhic than this. What seemed like a long strike in 1969 was a great deal more effective than the strung out process which the NUR followed.

This chapter could not have been written without the help of Billy Taylor, who was the Appeals Organiser for the Strike Committee and later became a full time official of the Engineering Union.

CHAPTER SEVENTEEN

THE GLC TAKES OVER

Hannah Dadds, the first woman train driver, boards an 'R' stock train at Ealing Common Depot, 1978

Two new Transport Acts in 1968 and 1969 re-organised public transport in Britain again, and the Transport (London) Act of 1969 provided for the Greater London Council (GLC) to take over responsibility for London Transport from 1st January 1970. The London Transport Board once again became the London Transport Executive. When we recall that demands for the LPTB, when it was established in 1933, to be controlled or even influenced by the GLC's predecessor the LCC were considered dangerously radical, it is slightly ironic that no such objections were raised in 1969. It would be interesting to speculate how different an organisation might have been built had the LCC rather than the LGOC been put in charge in 1933 but I must resist that temptation. Importantly, the Transport Act also established the right and duty of local authorities (including the GLC) to pay subsidies to public transport operators. However, in 1968, when agreement for the transfer of London Transport was reached between the Ministry of Transport and the GLC, the Conservative-led GLC made it a condition that fares should be increased to bring LT back into financial viability. The 1970 Annual Report notes (P4) that the new LTE had "an overriding duty to conduct its affairs on a commercial basis, including making proper provision for the depreciation or renewal of assets". The accumulated capital debt of £269.8 million was, however, written off on 31st December 1969.

The GLC was given the duty of laying down 'principles' of transport operation and of giving 'general direction' to the new Executive. The Country Bus Services, which mainly operated outside the GLC boundaries, and the Green Line coaches, were transferred to London Country Bus Services, a new subsidiary company under the nationalised National Bus Company.[1] 5,463 staff were involved.

On the eve of its transfer London Transport was adrift with no leadership strategy. The impression was very much given of a Government desperate to offload a loss making organisation. Voices were raised against a local transport provider, albeit in the capital city, being subsidised by the national taxpayer. There were declining service levels, worsening regularity of buses, still increasing staff shortage and a bus reshaping plan that was clearly not working. Increasing traffic congestion and insensitive traffic schemes took buses away from traffic objectives. LT was in crisis.

Political control of the GLC swung from Labour to Conservative and back again, causing LT Chairman Ralph Bennett to complain in the 1979 Annual Report that "it had proved difficult to establish long-term policies and objectives for the future of public transport in London because of changes in political control and priorities".[2] But the changes reflected real issues affecting public transport. In particular, under the prevailing Government policy of encouraging road building which had held sway since the war no matter which party was in power, a motorway box had been proposed for inner London which gave rise to massive public protests. The elevated motorway through Notting Hill (now part of the M40) was to be the first part of the motorway box, which was part of the Conservatives' programme. But following the mass 'Homes Before Roads' campaign Labour adopted a policy of support for public transport and opposition to more road building and gained a majority in the 1973 GLC elections. This was the first time that the policy of 'solving' traffic congestion by building more roads was challenged and heralded a major change in transport policy. The GLC had rapidly to set up a team of officers to administer, evaluate and monitor subsidy payments to LT. It also set up a new unit to design and implement bus priority schemes. At last, some degree of strategic planning was evident.

The 1970 Annual Report somewhat over-optimistically states: "By the end of this decade every LT bus will be operated by one man and the total bus operating staff reduced by 10,000...enabling fares to be at a lower level...Higher pay should help attract and retain staff and so overcome staff shortage...It would be unrealistic, however, not to recognise that OMO will have its disadvantages as well as its advantages. The most serious problem is obviously that of getting passengers, who have to pay their fare on entry, on the bus without undue delay. Part of the solution to this must lie in equipping the buses with the simplest and most reliable type of ticket issuing machine...All new vehicles delivered in 1970 were designed for split entrance...those passengers with the correct fare obtain their tickets from the automatic machine and pass through a turnstile while the others obtain their ticket from the driver" (P12) The faith of the LT management in OMO to solve all their problems was short sighted to say the least, but in the absence of any clear overall direction they were clearly struggling and they were right to identify the effectiveness of fare collection machines as critical. The Report also states (P13): "Staff who have transferred to OMO have, almost without exception, welcomed the change. Obviously the pay is better but...drivers have preferred the direct contact with the travelling public which is involved in ticket issue to the isolation of the drivers cab on a two-man bus". If this was ever true is doubtful, but certainly with the increase in staff assaults often occasioned, but not excused by, poor services, staff morale rapidly became a problem and a major factor in the inability to retain staff which OMO had been supposed to solve.

An OPO bus driver issues a ticket, 1974

Just prior to the GLC takeover the T&GWU's Central Bus Conference, uncertain about the future and concerned about service cuts and OMO conversions, called for a one day stoppage on 1st January. The London Transport Joint Committee, an unofficial body linking bus and Underground workers, associated itself with this call. Following a meeting of T&GWU General Secretary Jack Jones and officers of the London Bus Section with the Minister of Transport to discuss deterioration of the bus service and working conditions, a meeting with LT Chairman Sir Richard Way was arranged for 7th January. The unofficial LT Joint Committee recognised that the Underground would not strike on 1st January and the bus strike decision was withdrawn. But the Conservative GLC continued with service cuts and fare increases.[3]

In 1971 a new bonus scheme was introduced for bus crews under which each driver and conductor received an individual bonus payment related to the actual amount of fares collected on their bus. The Report notes (P13) that adverse effects of staff shortages were kept to a minimum by the working of voluntary overtime and rest days by bus crews, as had been the practice for decades past. Some improvements were made: "From June 1970 all buses on route 74 have been controlled by direct radio contact and the system is to be extended to buses on routes 30 and 76".

In September 1970 a three day Industrial Relations Conference was held at Reading University including members of the LT Executive, full time officials from 11 Trade Unions, and staff representatives (the report does not say how these representatives were selected). The aim was "to improve the understanding of problems jointly facing management and staff" (P21). Finally, the 1970 Report acknowledges that: "Assaults on staff...on the Underground and late night buses continued to cause great concern and led staff at some garages unofficially to withdraw services on a number of occasions". So much for the supposed joys of OMO.

The 1971 Annual Report records "a fall in the number of resignations from the Executive's service...but the shortage is still fairly severe...LT must maintain, by the pay, conditions and security which it offers, a competitive position in the London labour market" (P12). It says "the general employment situation, together with substantial increases paid from April, kept recruitment buoyant and led to an overall reduction of over 30% in the number of staff resignations compared with 1970". The 'general employment situation' is a reference to the fact that unemployment had topped 1 million for the first time since the war. It is also noted that intimidation and harassment of staff continued to cause concern.

On page 13 it is recognised that the concerns about fare collection equipment have turned into real problems: "In spite of extensive trials by manufacturers and other bus operators...it has proved extremely difficult to find a simple, reliable and quick method of collecting fares from passengers boarding one man buses...Reliability... was so poor that on certain routes the equipment was taken out of use and passengers had to pay the driver". The Report of a Government working group which included the Trade Unions said: "The importance of persuading passengers to either offer the exact money for the fare or to purchase a ticket before entering the bus cannot be overstressed if OMO is to cope with high-density routes". It did not do any good to blame passengers for the failure of fare collection equipment or for the failure of the management to provide sufficient incentives or opportunities to encourage prepayment of fares. And despite clear evidence of these failures LT pressed on with the programme of One Person Operation of buses regardless.

On equal pay the Report has a particularly interesting entry on P24: "The Executive has applied equal pay for equal work to the majority of its staff for a considerable number of years. Having regard to the Equal Pay Act of 1970 the Executive's intention is to extend this principle to all groups of staff by 1973".

It also notes that a new superannuation fund for salaried staff was introduced on 1st January 1971 and from 1st September further supplementation of pensions for retired staff was introduced.

The 1972 Annual Report records that the shortage of bus operating staff became worse, with a 12% shortage of drivers and 9% shortage of conductors. It notes that the problem was not only pay but the unpopularity of shift and weekend work and the price of housing in London. (P5)

The GLC asked for the programme of OMO to be reviewed and said that OMO buses should not be used on the more intensively used routes. They deferred consideration of flat and zonal fares (we are not privy to the reason for this apparently bizarre deferral) but encouraged the use of prepaid and season tickets, although no practical measures were proposed.

Substantial increases in pay are recorded, amounting to 12.5% for rail grades.

The 1974 Report continues the depressing trend of problems identified but not dealt with. Shortages of staff in all areas – road, rail and engineering - are again highlighted (P4). There were further improvements in pay, especially for socially inconvenient and unpopular times. There is a call for the agreement of the Trade Unions to greater flexibility in the use of labour, "including the employment of women in grades hitherto restricted to men. Agreement has now been reached with staff representatives to the employment of women as bus drivers" it says (P5).

It also notes that "future requirements for skilled craftsmen are likely to be affected by an abnormally high rate of retirement due to the average age of the present labour force in this grade". This makes management's refusal to entertain the NUR's claim for promotion from semi-skilled grades to craftsman, detailed in chapter 16, all the more short sighted. "The Executive is planning to build a new Apprentice Training Centre adjoining Acton Works" (P26). Also, "improvements in pension provision for both salaried and wages staff were agreed".

Bagwell notes that 1974 was "the grimmest year for public transport in postwar London, 15% of bus and 18% of train services were cancelled, mainly for this reason".

In 1956 LT had sent a recruitment official and a medical officer (!) to Barbados and 70 stationmen, 50 men and 20 women bus conductors were immediately enrolled. In the following years 10,000 more followed, encouraged by an interest free loan to cover the cost of the fare. Bagwell says: "every effort was made to ensure that the West Indians settled in to their new environment with the minimum of difficulty. An 'Information Booklet for Intending Emigrants to Britain', giving tips about the British way of life, was issued in the West Indies...It was fortunate from the viewpoint of good race relations that advancement, at least in the railway operating department, went solely by seniority. It would be idle to deny that there were occasions of friction, or that some white staff tolerated rather than welcomed the newcomers...Management recruited coloured labour without first consulting the Unions on their views...some NUR branch members became alarmed. In December 1959 Rickmansworth branch wrote to General Secretary Sidney Greene complaining about the LTE's method of recruitment". The NUR Executive responded in June 1960: "we have considered the information submitted by our LTE Sectional Councils and are unable to find any adverse effects on our members. We therefore recommend that this matter should not be pursued". A social survey of the LTE workforce asked a lengthman member of the NUR whether he had experienced hostility on the part of white staff to the employment of coloured workers. He replied: "Yes, there has been hostility, but on the transport you have so much backing from the Union they can't do much".[4]

My personal experience on the Underground in the early 1970's was that there was considerable racism from the older generation of white workers and a minority of local Union representatives. The seniority system ensured that discrimination in promotion and higher grade working was kept to a minimum, but it was not until the Anti Nazi League campaign against the Fascist National Front in 1977-8, and its railway component Rail Against the Nazis, that discrimination and distrust at the social level was dealt with by staff themselves, especially younger people. Social and sporting activities organised by LT and the Unions played an important part in bringing people from different backgrounds together.

Following the takeover of LT by the GLC, management tried to 'cut the cord' which had linked the rates of pay on the Underground and British Railways and its predecessors for 50 years, with a view to reducing the LT motorman's rate below that of a BR driver. This linkage was enshrined in Wages Board decision No3 of 2nd March 1955, which states that the Underground motorman's rate of pay shall not fall below that of the British Rail driver. But the manpower crisis of 1973-4 made 'imperative substantial improvements in rates of pay and conditions of service', in Bagwell's words. A short commercial boom from September 1972 to September 1973 was particularly marked in the London area and saw unemployment in London and the South east fall from 2.1% to 1.4%, while the number of unfilled vacancies rose from 99,200 to 202,200. There was also a striking rise in property prices often making it impossible for recruits to find accommodation near railway and bus depots at prices or rents they could afford.

R.M.Robbins (he of the History of London Transport), for the LTE, wrote to the Unions on 9th January 1973 submitting general proposals for a restructuring of pay and for improvements in working conditions. But by the time the Railway Negotiating Committee met to discuss it on 9th April the Conservative Government's Phase 2 incomes policy was in operation, which limited pay increases to £1 a week plus 4% of the current paybill to be shared between members of a given work group. But when LTE proposed that the greater part of this 4% should be allocated to those groups with the greatest labour shortages the TSSA, in particular, were concerned about the consequent disturbance of pay relativities. Unions were also concerned about any departure from the link to BR rates of pay.[5]

But as the staffing situation worsened LTE in June 1973 withdrew 8% of its train services, except on the Victoria and Central lines. Representations from NUR General Secretary Sidney Greene to the GLC stressed the seriousness of the problem. On 3rd July 1973 the GLC wrote to the LTE requesting that it should submit to the Council "a detailed and urgent review of LT's overall staff position indicating in particular a. how bad the shortage is in the various departments b. what additional steps the LTE are taking to improve the position and c. what are the ways in which, in the LTE's view, the Council could give further help in this sphere". That really laid it on the line. It is noteworthy that Labour had taken control of the GLC at the recent elections. The 1974 Annual Report states that the GLC recognised "that the cost of providing an acceptable public transport system in London must be borne by the public in one way or another, if not as fare payers then as ratepayers and taxpayers" (P5). This policy change, before Ken Livingstone came on the scene, was of crucial importance but the 'ratepayers' were to have something to say about it, as we shall see.

The situation on the Underground had really reached crisis proportions, with LTE Chief Industrial Relations Officer John Cope reporting to Sid Greene that the unfilled vacancy rate for guards was 7.8%, for railmen 17.6% and for Station Foremen no less than 19.8%. LTE's board member Jim Mortimer liaised closely with the NUR and on 31st July 1973 a nine point plan was presented to the Unions. This aimed to improve earnings to a level sufficient to secure an adequate labour force, the enhancement of pensions to a level comparable with those in other public sector employments, recognition by special premium payments for work done at socially inconvenient times, established staff status, namely that given to salaried staff to be

Jill Viner, the first woman bus driver, in the cab of an 'RT' type bus, 1974

given to all grades after five years' service, improved holiday entitlements, improved travel facilities, expansion of staff housing and mortgages, bonuses for staff finding recruits, and crucially greater flexibility of labour including employment of women in areas until then restricted to men. The first woman bus driver (Jill Viner) started in 1974 and the first woman inspector not long after. The Underground had to wait until 1978 for its first woman train driver (Hannah Dadds).[6]

The Nine Point Plan was well received by the Unions and staff, but LTE Chairman Sir Richard Way refers to it as "our so-called nine-point plan" (no capitals) and says "it is more accurately described as a rolling programme". Estimating the cost at £35 million Sir Richard tells GLC Leader Sir Reg Goodwin in a confidential letter dated 4th October 1973 "the Council's control over what we are doing will be exercised through its approval of that budget; it cannot take the form of debate followed by approval or amendment of the "plan" as though it were a costed capital project." An interesting insight into relations between the LTE and GLC. This is why he discouraged the use of the term 'nine point plan'. He says in his letter: "What I would urge is that we should as far as possible no longer talk about a plan, but that you should accept in principle that we have a programme for improving pay and conditions of service which we shall implement as and when Government legislation permits and negotiations with the unions have led to agreements". He also insists that the GLC's role is "not to become involved in the management details of how to operate the services".

The nine points were:
1. Earnings throughout LT should be at a level which will secure the recruitment and maintenance of an adequate labour force.
2. Pensions should be fully comparable with others in the public sector generally.
3. Work done at socially inconvenient times outside normal factory hours should be recognised by special premium payments.
4. There should be 'established' staff status, similar to that of salaried staff, after five years' service.
5. Holiday entitlement should be improved where necessary to bring it into line with general industrial practice.
6. There should be new travel concessions for the families of all LT staff, including unrestricted free travel for the wives of staff throughout the LT system.
7. Staff housing and mortgage arrangements should be extended.
8. There should be bonuses for staff who find satisfactory recruits in certain areas of shortage.
9. There should be greater flexibility in the use of labour, including the employment of women in grades now restricted to men.

However, in a letter to Ralph Bennett dated 1st August 1973 the Minister of Transport says: "Thank you for writing...about staff shortages in London Transport. It is most helpful to have your clear statement of the situation, and I am making good use of this in discussion with my Ministerial colleagues...I am however bound to say that in present economic circumstances I see little prospect of a general solution to your problems through the full implementation of your package deal". This despite the Government having handed over control of LT to the GLC.

It is significant that it was not until the staffing crisis hit the Underground hard and the GLC gave LTE a mighty shove that such a comprehensive plan was put forward. Years of similar problems on the buses had given rise only to One Person Operation and calls for more overtime. Indeed, LTE had tried to improve bus services by lowering the qualifications needed for trainee bus drivers, increasing thereby the proportion of applicants accepted for training from 33% in 1970 to 42% in 1973. Many of those rejected were referred to the Underground for employment. 400 Council houses were made available for staff near depots and by 1975 it was reported that three quarters of these were occupied by bus or train crews and their families.[7]

The 1974 Annual Report notes that not until the end of Stage Three of the Government's pay code in July 1974 could the major improvements in staff pay and conditions be implemented. A reversal in the trend of recruitment then took place. "The effect of the improvements was dramatic", it says, "the status of the London busman and Underground workers was lifted to something approaching that which they had once enjoyed" (P4). "Directly after the main improvements were announced the number of new recruits doubled". The 1975 Report could note that staff wastage was "at a low rate" and "losses of scheduled mileage on buses and trains through staff shortages , which had reached levels of 15% and 18% respectively in the worst period of 1974, were down to 6% and 2% by the end of 1975".[8] The Report also notes that a Measured Incentive Scheme had started for many staff in engineering areas. Supposedly scientific work study, with a stopwatch, would record 'unmotivated' times; the incentive of a bonus would encourage faster work. In practice, the staff shortage meant that in most areas no staff were lost and workers got paid more for doing much the same as they had done before, so the Unions did not raise any objections to the scheme and wages were increased significantly without transgressing any Government limitations.

In these days of attacks on final salary pension schemes it is important to remind ourselves that back in 1974 there was an acute labour shortage on LT and an urgent need to make working on LT more attractive at a time when Government pay policies restricted LT's ability to increase wages at a comparable rate to private employers. The wages grade pension scheme was made close to parity with the salaried grades scheme, but contributions by staff were also increased. After the improvements, members paid in 9.33% of their net pay and the employer 14%, a 40-60 ratio. The NUR also began to demand a levelling up of wages grade sick pay, working hours and holidays towards those enjoyed by salaried grades. Some progress was made, but salaried status was not to come until the Company Plan of 1992. Under the arrangements which came into force in 1979 salaried staff received 26 weeks full salary and 26 weeks reduced sick benefit after 5 years' service, while wages grades received three quarters of basic rate (itself often much less than actual earnings which included bonus and shift allowances), for 26 weeks only after 5 years' service.[9]

Unfortunately yet again LT's progress was thwarted by Government policy. This time the Labour Government, having kept wage increases on LT down in conformity with Phases 1-3 of the Social Contract with the Unions, which in itself undid all the staffing improvements under the Nine Point Plan, then tried to implement Phase 4 from 1st August 1978. This proposed to limit earnings increases to 5% when inflation between January 1977 and January 1978 had been 9.9%. Since 1975 the retail price index had risen by 60.5% and the NUR's research department calculated that rises of 17% for railmen up to 25.3% for top grade supervisors were needed to achieve comparability in real terms with the 1975 rates of pay. Once again, wage levels on LT had become too low to attract adequate staff to operate the budgeted service levels and the quality of the bus service in particular declined once more. It had also become acutely difficult to recruit sufficient maintenance staff. With slow delivery of new buses and reliability problems with many of them the problem was exacerbated. As soon as the problem of recruiting drivers and conductors began to be alleviated the shortage of serviceable buses prevented any improvement in the service to the public.

Bus services were also adversely affected by severe reliability problems with the single deckers which had been purchased for OMO conversions, and with the new double deckers as well, a problem which has been the subject of several books; the effect on labour relations was one of low morale. Most transport staff want to provide a decent service and they felt let down by their management providing unreliable buses, not to mention the passenger frustration at poor services which as the 'front line' the staff had to deal with.

Female bus inspector and bus driver, 1975

Then in 1977 a GLC election saw the Conservatives come back into power. Their transport spokesman Richard Brew declared that the level of the Council's support to LT was "totally unacceptable". They reduced the fares relief grant from £62,725,000 to £50,600,000. To make matters worse LT had budgeted for a 5% pay increase, which they believed the TUC would accept, when the Unions had declared their opposition to Government pay policy and were not going to accept anything like it. The GLC gave LT permission to use funds from their general reserve and they offered a rise of 9% on 20th April 1979. The NUR met the Chairman of the LTE on 22nd May, and, significantly, met the other Unions on the following day. Their claim was for 17%. The NUR called a strike to start on 18th June, to allow plenty of time for further negotiations. Meetings took place at the Advisory Conciliation and Arbitration Service (one of the Labour Government's more useful ideas) on 12th and 14th June and it was agreed that an arbitration panel under the Chairmanship of Mr I. Buchanan would produce an award by 22nd June. On this basis the NUR agreed to postpone the strike. The award of an 11% increase plus consolidation of the existing £2 supplement and an adjustment of differentials for the higher paid satisfied the NUR and was backdated to 23rd April 1979. The Labour Government's pay policy was in tatters.

In the railway workshops the presence of the Craft Unions made the negotiating process more complicated than on the operating railway. Since April 1944 there had been a Joint Committee of Unions (JCU) with seven, later nine, representatives each of the NUR and the craft Unions. A difference of opinion on the application of the Government's pay guidelines effective 1st August 1976 led to the NUR withdrawing from the JCU. The Buchanan award of 1979 recognised that negotiations on workshop pay had been on an 'ad-hoc' basis and suggested that the NUR take the lead in bringing the other Unions together; discussions took place.[10]

Throughout the 1970s violence and vandalism on the Underground had been on the increase. In 1973 NUR branches had been demanding enclosed boxes for ticket collectors, who were the staff most vulnerable to attack, especially on late shifts. One of many incidents saw a woman ticket collector at Clapham Common station felled to the ground by a punch delivered by a young fare dodger on 5th March 1973. On the evening of 14th March 1980 at Neasden station 200 youths injured 25 people including a train driver and devastated station property. Between 1974 and 1979 207 guards and 76 motormen were assaulted and booking clerks had been injured by bricks or iron bars being thrown into booking offices. The NUR had an interview with Home Secretary William Whitelaw and Minister of Transport Norman Fowler on 2nd October 1979 but outbreaks of violence continued. On the District and Central lines there were unofficial stoppages after 10pm. Finally, the NUR EC called a one day stoppage for Saturday 19th March 1980 and instructed its members to close all LT stations at 10pm on Fridays and Saturdays 18/19th and 25/26th April. From a working conference with the Union LT promised more money for alarm systems, CCTV etc, and booking offices were made more secure. Bagwell presciently notes: "These security measures were undoubtedly necessary, but the lower figures for assaults in 1973 and 1974 when there was a GLC policy of static fares suggest that a more fundamental reform would be a substantial improvement in government support more in line with ...major cities overseas" [11].

In 1979 NUR General Secretary Sidney Weighell asked ASLE&F General Secretary Ray Buckton whether his Union would be willing to relinquish its right to organise employees on LT if the NUR ceased to recruit footplate staff on BR. The numbers involved were similar (about 1800). ASLE&F were unwilling to agree to this, and the NUR AGM also asserted its opposition, citing the NUR's principle of Industrial Trade Unionism and its consequent objective to organise all workers employed by BR and other transport undertakings [12].

The Conservative led GLC attempted to square the circle by making further cuts in services. Bus Plan '78 sought to reduce scheduled bus mileage from 211 million miles to 199 million miles and cut the staff establishment from 23,500 to 20,800. The irony was that to achieve this would actually mean the recruitment of extra staff as the staff shortage of 15% represented 3,600 drivers, operators and conductors in total. A joint 'Save Our Services' campaign was launched by the official Union leaders, principally the T&GWU and NUR. Lobbies of Parliament and the GLC were organised, but by October 1987 Charley Young, T&GWU Bus Section London District Secretary, complained that attendance had been very poor [13]. A motion to ban overtime in support of the campaign had been defeated and in June 1978 the London Bus Conference, having been less than enthusiastic about a proposal for lightning one hour strikes, accepted the Bus Plan, parts of which would be deferred until March 1979.

A deficit of £15 million was incurred in 1979 and further cuts were planned for 1980. The London Bus Section called a one hour strike on 3rd March 1980 but the response from T&GWU members was "less than 100%". Although the public often complain about service cuts it seems that they are generally not supportive of direct action to stop them and staff are rarely motivated to take action against cuts unless their own working conditions are directly challenged. This was an issue which was hotly debated by Trade Union activists at the time.

In 1981 management attempted to reduce scheduled bus mileage further to 193 million miles. When it was found that the actual performance exceeded this figure, recruitment, overtime and rest day working were all limited. The General Manager of LT Buses was reported to have told the T&GWU Bus Conference that there were too many staff on the books in relation to the budget despite the Section still being 14.4% short of establishment. Conference called for recruitment to continue at garages where staff shortages exceeded 20% [14].

The unpopularity of the Conservative administration at County Hall stemmed largely from the crisis in LT. Labour made great play of this in their campaign and gained control of the GLC in the election of May 1981, installing Ken Livingstone as leader. The cuts planned for that October were scrapped, recruitment increased, restrictions on overtime lifted and the budget revised upwards to allow an additional 5 million bus miles. Ken Livingstone and transport chairman Dave Wetzel recognised that without building additional lines there was little scope for additional mileage on the Underground and concentrated on improving bus services.

Following a process of public consultation, on 4th October 1981 the Fares Fair policy saw fares reduced by one third and a zonal fares system finally introduced. This latter, many years overdue, was in the long term to prove more significant for efficient operation than the cut in fares, which despite only returning them to their 1969 level in real terms, gained all the headlines. From a drop in passenger demand of 4.8% in the first 20 weeks of 1981 a dramatic turn round saw the number of passenger journeys increase by 10% and passenger mileage up by 12%. Chairman

Sir Peter Masefield stated in the Annual Report that: "for the first time in about 20 years the steady decline in the use by passengers of public transport was halted and reversed, in spite of the continuing growth in the ownership of private cars and declining population of the capital city". The level of subsidy rose to 54%, a similar level to Paris, Chicago and Copenhagen, and still considerably lower than Brussels, Stockholm, New York and Milan. But some ratepayers were unhappy.

On the grounds that their borough was not served by the Underground, Bromley Council brought a legal action and the Law Lords decreed on 17th December 1981 that Fares Fair was illegal and LT had a 'fiduciary duty' to break even. This was outrageous. As we saw earlier, the GLC in the Act of Parliament which established it had been given the "right and duty" to support public transport. LT duly announced a doubling of fares from March 1982 and a cut in services that would lead to the loss of an estimated 5,000 jobs over the following three years. At a joint TU meeting on 4th January 1982 it was decided that a campaign of protest be organised around six points, endorsed by the NUR in an EC decision of 21st January 1982.

a. The need for a campaign committee.
b. Leafleting the general public and every LT worker.
c. Organisation of a one day total stoppage.
d. Mass meetings of lay representatives.
e. Commitment to finance the campaign by the TU's concerned.
f. Full support to the meeting of the Campaign to Improve London Transport on 21st January.

On 17th February 1982 the NUR EC decided that: "LTE members are instructed to take industrial action jointly with other Unions opposing the increased fares and reductions in services and their effects on our members. To include non-collection of fares and a 24 hour withdrawal of labour on dates to be agreed with other Unions", and on 19th February the EC adopts the recommendation of the TU Defence Committee that the date for withdrawal of labour be 10th March, from midnight to midnight. Under the rules of their Union TSSA members could not take part in the strike but many supported it on an individual basis and not a single train or bus moved in London [15]. The introduction of revised timetables was delayed from 21st March to 21st June. On 24th June the NUR recommends that members not co-operate with any reductions in services or staffing cuts or station closures etc, nor agree to consultation taking place at Sectional Council level in the Conciliation machinery.

Members who refused to co-operate included 32 signal staff who refused to install new programme machine rolls for the reduced schedules. They were suspended and other members stopped work in support. ASLE&F called a strike, then called it off. The NUR EC resolved that: "having failed to gain firm assurances from LT that they would immediately reinstate our members who were suspended between 18-23rd June...this NEC instructs all our members on LT to withdraw their labour immediately". At this point the NUR did not ask the Bus Section for support. A special bus conference which was to have discussed the call for an indefinite strike jointly with the Underground was cancelled. Did the leadership take fright? Wandsworth garage pulled all its buses off the road to discuss possible action and the following Monday 9 garages were on unofficial strike. LT had proposed to cut 785 buses. Following negotiations they agreed to reduce this total by 115 and that was enough to get the

GLC leader Horace Cutler (wearing bow tie holding pneumatic drill) and LT Chairman Ralph Bennett 1978

WE ASK

Why should the greatest capital city in the world have a lower level of subsidy than most Scandinavian and Europe cities? Even in the home of private enterprise, the United States, they give bigger subsidies to many of their major cities' transport services. No other Cities services cater for 5.5 million passenger journies each day.

WHAT YOU CAN DO TO HELP

1 Hold on tight to your Union, for while your industry is under attack the Government is also legislating to attack your Trade Union, so it becomes that much harder for you to defend your job.

2 Support your Union's policies. Attend your Branch meetings. Whether you are Operating, Engineering or Catering members, it is your struggle, so join in.

3 Ensure that every bus or tube that can be operated runs **but do not compromise safety to achieve this end.**

4 Hold an enquiry into every bus or train that does not operate.

5 Make every endeavour to see that the best possible service is operated. Every bus or train that does not operate is a nail in the coffin of your industry and your job, so pressurise management to achieve maximum efficiency to complement your own efforts.

6 Support campaigns and demonstrations to defend your union, your industry and your job.

7 Discuss and debate this leaflet and its implications with your mates at work, your family, but most of all your passengers and point the finger of blame where it rightly belongs.

EFFECTS ON WAGES

On top of all the misery, the workers are now expected to pay for the Law Lords' decision by a reduction in their living standards. Since December, the 7% in London Transport Budget for Wages has now been cut to 5%.

As you can see, we are in for a rough ride ... so

HOLD ON TIGHT!

Published on behalf of: T&GWU, NUR, ASLEF, TSSA, ASBSBSW, ASTMS, AUEW, BTOG, EEPTU, EPEA, FTAT, GMWU, NSMM, NUSMW, UCATT
Printed by The College Hill Press Ltd (TU), London EC4

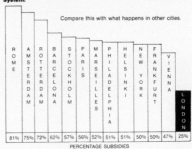

LONDON TRANSPORT WORKERS
UNDER ATTACK

HOLD ON TIGHT
TO YOUR SERVICES, YOUR JOBS
YOUR INDUSTRY

London Transport Workers Under Attack
so
HOLD ON TIGHT

In 1980 because of financial limits imposed on London Transport by the Tory GLC, the Management were forced to plan a reduction in the services. We faced a possible loss of jobs, cuts in many services, an increase in One Man Bus Operation and the elimination of thirteen routes, together with the proposed closure of the Epping–Ongar line and reductions in station manning. This was to become effective in 1981.

The loss of jobs was not going to be just Bus and Train crews but also the support grades, maintenance and engineering staff, workers at Acton, Chiswick and Aldenham workshops, supervisory grades and catering workers were threatened. The Workshops were being looked at as potential areas where work could be contracted out. The District and Divisional organisations lend themselves to this. Thousands of jobs were going to be placed in jeopardy.

1981 saw the introduction of what we termed the 'unfair fare' – the 25p minimum fare policy imposed on London Transport by the Tory GLC.

The Trade Unions are proud of their achievements for London Transport Workers, both for operating and engineering grades, especially against the backcloth of negotiating while the Tories were in control at County Hall.

Arising from the joint Union's campaign and the election of Labour to County Hall, the thirteen condemned routes were saved and the cuts in services and closures were never implemented. The OMO conversions were prevented and as a consequence we held on to jobs that were to be lost both among operating and engineering members. Indeed, the recruitment centre was put into top gear and 1,200 new staff employed.

The new Labour GLC ended the 25p fare on the Buses. They had promised a 25% reduction and a fares freeze for four years. They introduced a 10p minimum bus fare, with a 20p zonal fare and a 5p flat fare for children. The cost, in line with their election pledge, was charged to the rates. This was what Londoners had voted for and the promise was kept.

All over the world, large cities have cut fares to reduce congestion and improve the environment.

The London public knew that their rates would have to be increased to meet the cost of reducing fares. What they did not know was that the Government, in a display of political spite, would withdraw the existing £90 million fare subsidy as a penalty on Londoners for voting for Labour and for cheaper fares.

The policy of subsidising fares from the rates was opposed in the Courts by Bromley Borough Council, finally going to the Law Lords, who ruled that the GLC had acted illegally.

The Law Lords' ruling means that the cheap fare policy must be ended. The industry must now abandon the policy that improved the services and attracted 11% more bus and 7% more tube passengers per day. The

industry has been told to turn its back on the progressive method of financing Public Transport used throughout the world and revert to the perpetual decline of the last thirty years.

Fares must now rise by 100% to a new unprecedented height with a 40p zonal fare. It will mean a loss of approximately 30% of our passengers. Routes will be withdrawn or cut back and jobs either lost or earnings reduced, or both. For the first time, compulsory redundancies are a distinct possibility on London Transport.

There is a simple way of understanding this:
Cuts in Bus and Tube Services
= Loss of Duties which
= Loss of Jobs
Loss of Rota Duties
= Less Buses and Tubes which
= Loss of Jobs for Engineering and Workshop Staff
Loss of Drivers, Conductors, Train-men plus Engineering and Workshop Staff
= Loss of jobs for supervisory grades

All this means less job security and promotion prospects for all London Transport workers.

Higher fares will drive our passengers away leading to reduced services and more assaults on staff, it will also mean more cars and greater road congestion; it will mean less money to make the necessary improvements and will reduce earnings . . .

What a way to operate the World's greatest Public Transport System.

Compare this with what happens in other cities.

ROME	AMSTERDAM	ROTTERDAM	BARCELONA	STOCKHOLM	PARIS	MARSEILLES	PHILADELPHIA	HEW YORK	NEW YORK	FRANKFURT	VIENNA	LONDON
81%	75%	72%	62%	57%	56%	52%	51%	51%	50%	50%	47%	25%

PERCENTAGE SUBSIDIES

Hold on Tight! – pamphlet issued by the London Transport Trade Union Defence Committee

London Transport

55 Broadway London SW1H 0BD

Telephone 01-222 5600

John C. F. Cameron

8th March 1982

Your ref. MLT/28/5

S. Weighell, Esq.,
General Secretary,
National Union of Railwaymen,
Unity House,
Euston Road,
London. NW1 2BL.

Dear Mr. Weighell,

LTE DAY OF ACTION - 10th MARCH 1982

I have your letter of 5th March 1982, which we discussed this
morning, in which you confirm the point made by your
representative at our meeting here last Friday. The Executive
notes that you are instructing your members to take strike
action on 10th March on account of the cuts in services and
staff about which you have been advised.

We are therefore telling managers in London Transport that
certain trade unions, including your own, are of the view that
this industrial action is in furtherance of a trade dispute,
contrary to our earlier assumption.

Yours sincerely,

John C. F. Cameron

STOP THE INCREASES — FARE FIGHT 2

We are not alone

Fare Fight is not alone! Working alongside us in
the campaign to prevent the destruction of
London's transport are a host of other bodies —
large and small, national and local. (And public
support for our objectives is growing.) There
are definite signs that the Government is feeling
the pressure, which will be intensified in the
run-up to the planned fares increase on March 21st
with protest action starting in earnest on March
1st, and further activity planned.

Parallel campaigns are being run by the GLC
itself, the unions, and users' groups. There are
particular groupings representing all shades of
political opinion, and all kinds of approaches
to political action.

At Westminster, encouraged by the first vote
on the Private Members Bill introduced by
Douglas Jay, London Labour MPs are still
hopeful of forcing the Government to accept
legislation to restore the full rights of the GLC
and other councils to subsidise public transport
in support of progressive transport policies.

If the law is not changed by March 21st however,
amongst those favouring direct action are the
group of GLC councillors leading the "Can't
Pay, Won't Pay" campaign, who are seeking
to give a lead to those who plan to refuse to
pay the doubled LT fares. Already it is clear
that the London Transport trade unions will
not be acting as policemen in the implementation
of the new fares scales.

Not true.

Outside London the threat to local pro-public
transport policies which has come in the wake
of the Law Lords' ruling on London Transport
has led to local action groups in most of the
main conurbations.

In South Yorkshire in particular, the most
progressive of Britains' transport authorities,
where fares have been frozen for 7 years —
cold shivers have been sent down the spine of
local supporters when those hostile to the
successful policy began to search for ways
to challenge it in the courts as had been
done in London. 1200% increases in fares
now have to be considered.

But a first indication of a setback in the
euphoric hounding of local authority subsidy
policies since the Law Lords' judgement in
London came when the High Court upheld
the Merseyside County Council policy on
fares in the face of a legal challenge. But
the case could still run into difficulties at
the Appeal Court and House of Lords stages.

Representing all six metropolitan counties,
as well as the GLC and Strathclyde Regional
Council in Scotland, the Association of
Metropolitan Authorities Public Passenger
Transport Committee has agreed to support
representations to the Secretary of State for
Transport across the whole field of transport
policy — now in a shambles.

For not only has the local authorities' right
to subsidise local transport been undermined,
but at the same time they face cutbacks in
transport supplementary grant from Central
Government, unfavourable transfer of rate
support grant away from urban areas, and
the phasing out of the bus grants introduced
to assist with the purchase of new vehicles.

Even the State-owned National Bus Company,
which primarily operates services outside the
main conurbations, is under financial pressure
from the Government with proposals for the
privatisation of its profitable coach operations,
and severe pressure exerted on it by its
capital debt liabilities.

Meanwhile in London all the London Transport
unions covering both manual and white collar
staff are joining forces for the first time with
their campaign to safeguard services and jobs.

A mass meeting of union representatives, shop
stewards and branch secretaries across all 15
unions was held at the TUC on the 17th
February, and plans have been announced
for action to fight back. There will be a one
day protest strike on March 10th and other
selective protest action. Activities will be
co-ordinated with Fare Fight's own plans,
the first of which, our demonstration on
March 1st, is outlined in this newsletter.

Letter from LT Chairman John Cameron
to NUR General Secretary Sidney
Weighell, March 1982

161

London Bus Conference, by a 36-27 vote, to accept the cuts[16]. Divisions between well organised garages like Wandsworth and others led to the T&GWU not calling any official action. Fuller notes that some lay representatives had warned that if the London Bus Section did not vigorously fight the cuts an even greater attack would follow; sadly, this proved to be the case[17].

The Employment Act which came into force on 1st December 1982 stated that to be lawful an industrial dispute must concern only wages and conditions of employment ie strikes which could be considered political would not be lawful. There were voices which sought to take on the Government on this policy, but TU leaderships were very wary of transgressing the law. So instead a major public campaign was organised. LT Chairman Sir Peter Masefield himself called for a 20% fares cut held for at least 12 months (LT News 223, 23rd July 1982) Public meetings were held all over London, supported by the GLC, but the protests were not supported by industrial action on the buses, which according to Fuller was now regarded with 'cynicism' by busworkers.

The campaign was also divided by the fatally flawed 'Can't Pay – Won't Pay' initiative. Superficially attractive, the idea was to encourage passengers, as individuals, to pay the old fare instead of the new one. Apart from the difficulty of organising individual passengers to challenge the new fares, it alienated bus conductors, one person operators and rail ticket collectors whose job it was to collect the fares laid down even if they disagreed with them. Any refusal to accept less than the full fare laid them open to disciplinary action, and any action by their fellow workers to support them was most unlikely to happen. The decision on fares had effectively been taken at the national political level as a result of the Law Lords decision and any industrial action against it would have to be organised on that basis, not around individual cases. The 1982 struggle against the service cuts was indeed a missed opportunity. The 1983 Transport Act gave the Secretary of State for Transport an influential say in setting the level of subsidy for transport undertakings, including LT. The proposal to reconstitute LT yet again as London Regional Transport and divorce it from the GLC appeared in a Government White Paper later in 1983.

GLC Transport Chief Dave Wetzel campaigns for lower fares, 1981

In the NUR, when the AGM (Annual Conference) is in session the EC is stood down, so on 25th June 1982 the issue was referred to the AGM. On 28th June it was reported to AGM delegates that LT, on 24th June, had proposed to refer the matter to a Joint Working Party with recommendations to be made before 23rd July. They would be prepared to reinstate the former timetables provided there was a return to normal working, with no victimisation. The AGM sought an assurance that LT would withdraw the revised work schedules indefinitely. On 29th June the AGM suspended the strike action despite impassioned pleas not to do so by the LT delegates, and staff returned to work at 0001 hours on 30th June pending a meeting at ACAS. At ACAS LT agreed to reinstate the former timetables immediately pending a meeting of the RNC (Railway Negotiating Committee).

On 23rd September 1982 LT proposed less serious service cuts affecting only the Metropolitan, District and Piccadilly lines and, crucially, insisted on linking service cuts with pay and conditions. In August the issue had been referred to the Wages Board (arbitration), which on 21st October proposed:

1. A 7% pay increase (same as the buses)
2. One extra day annual leave
3. Reduction in the working week from 39 to 38 hours.
4. Abolition of the railman grade (assimilated into leading railman grade) and restoration of differentials.

The Hainault - Woodford service was withdrawn on Sundays and Monday – Saturday evenings and the Epping – Ongar and New Cross Gate services were reduced to peak hours only. The EC blamed the cutbacks on the Conservative Government and local authorities (Essex County Council in particular). The service changes were finally accepted by a Special General Meeting of the NUR on the basis that more peak hour trains than currently were scheduled which would require the recruitment of more staff. No further changes were proposed for 1983.

Thus by linking the issue of service cuts to staff conditions the NUR was able to reduce the impact of those cuts, but management trumped this by linking them to pay and conditions. The T&GWU unfortunately was hamstrung by internal divisions and was unable to make similar links despite heroic struggles in some areas. Co-ordination between rail and bus Unions had been at best sporadic. On 23rd September 1983 The NUR EC noted that the LT Defence Committee needed a more formal structure. An LT TU Council was proposed with a policy committee of 5 T&GWU, 3 NUR, 1 ASLE&F, 1 ACTSS (Clerical), 1 TSSA, 2 Joint Trades (Craft), 1 Building Trades and 1 ASTMS (Scientific, Technical and Managerial Staffs). This cumbersome structure had little effect.

Straws had been in the wind since the 1980 Transport Act which deregulated express bus and coach services. Despite complacency on the part of senior management, LT found that some longer distance commuters, particularly on the Metropolitan line, had transferred to coaches with a noticeable effect on season ticket sales and journeys to and from main line stations. The revenue loss was of the order of £1 million and increased traffic congestion in the central area was also noted.

LT's response to the Bromley challenge to the GLC's Fares Fair policy was, in the words of the 1981 Annual Report, that it "raised fundamental issues which require urgent solution. Without that solution not only is the level of service which can be provided seriously in jeopardy but also the lack of stability of policy towards public transport undermines the strenuous efforts being made within LT to improve efficiency, reliability and productivity of the system" (P5). "The solutions lie in the political field". "The doubling of fares was duly implemented and accepted with regret both by LT and the travelling public". Commercial revenue "increased by £156 million (£206 million on a full year basis – 40% up) but passenger numbers are down by 14% – the largest instant decrease in traffic ever" (P6). An initial agreement for an 8% pay increase on the buses was "well below the rate of inflation". But on the railways the threat of an official strike led to an extra 3% from August being awarded, which was subsequently applied to the buses. Agreement was made to a further 1 hour reduction in the working week on the buses to 38 hours from 1st January 1983, introduced "at minimal cost".

This train of events illustrates the changing relationship between the bus and rail Unions and their members. Historically, from the days of the LGOC and the Railway Conciliation Scheme of 1921, the bus staff and their Union had been far more militant than the rail side, albeit with mixed results. But after the disaster of the 1958 bus strike, bus staff and the T&GWU lost impetus as staff shortages dominated the agenda and services were cut again and again, while rail staff suffered less cuts and the new young leftist representatives began to gain leadership positions in the rail Unions.

The 1981 Report also records the highly significant establishment of a new suburban-wide flat fare zone (costing 25p) which led to faster boarding times on OPO buses and a reduction in fraudulent travel. Four zones were created to cover the whole GLC area. Integrated fares reduced the financial penalty of changing modes or buses. Assaults on staff fell by 10% as a result. The high level of unemployment made recruitment and retention of staff "less difficult". A 39 hour week was to be introduced on the Underground. Staff productivity rose as passenger numbers increased, and then fell again as passenger numbers fell following the Bromley decision and the fares rise.

The GLC's response to the Bromley decision was to develop the 'Balanced Plan', carefully designed not to fall foul of accusations of supposedly 'unfair' subsidies. The 1982 Report notes that it was designed to bring about "integrated, efficient and economic transport facilities and services" for which the GLC has responsibility under the Transport (London) Act 1969. Fares were to be 'restructured' leading to an overall reduction of 25%. This time the High Court "favoured the GLC's case" and the reduction of fares was implemented on 22nd May 1983. The expected deficit turned into a small surplus. The three year plan proposed a further increase in OPO of buses to 65% by 1987. This would lead to more job losses and the T&GWU's London Bus Committee asked the GLC to instruct LT to postpone its conversion plan on the basis that it would result in a less satisfactory service to the public (questionable now that the zonal fare structure was in place), and increase unemployment (which was true but was primarily the responsibility of central Government).

In the circumstances the 'Balanced Plan' was the best the GLC and LT could do. Travel cards were also introduced at this time, another major step forward in convenience and economy for passengers which led to a steady increase in passenger numbers. The concept of marginal cost pricing was introduced which led directly to the introduction of free passes for pensioners. The idea is that in the off-peak hours buses and trains have plenty of spare capacity, so it makes economic sense to fill those spaces, at little or no cost, with passengers who can be encouraged to travel by reducing the cost to them to nothing, or at least considerably less than the full fare. The marginal cost is negligible so the fare can be low in the off peak, as long as the peak hour passenger continues to pay the full fare.

In the 1982 Report we learn that the total number of employees fell again from 59,700 to 58,100 by not replacing staff who left and early retirement. Bus staff wastage and recruitment were at a very low level due to the economic recession and reduction in services. Rest day and overtime working were substantially reduced. In fact the new lower service levels created a small surplus of conductors and garage engineering staff, who were invited to apply for voluntary severance. 7% pay increases were agreed with the TU's and joint standing committees were established to review working practices and agreements with the object of reducing costs and increasing income, the benefits to be shared with staff.

Strikes on the Underground had caused a loss of £9 million. Restoration of pay relativities for certain staff was dependent on further improvements in productivity.

Productivity improvements at Acton Works, Rail depots and in the Works and Buildings Department "to bring costs into line with competitive prices for similar work" outside are reported. Further efforts to improve productivity in station manning (note terminology), engineering activities and administration are reported and they note that modern trains and equipment are designed to reduce the maintenance required, reducing the work at Acton Works.

Net income from Property was £7 million and from Advertising £5.3 million.

The 1983 Annual Report records that buses and trains ran more miles than budgeted. The May fares reduction, the launch of travelcards and improved reliability led to a "marked increase in the number of passengers carried. Many motorists switched to the Underground for work journeys leading to reduced traffic congestion".

It notes that female workers all receive the same pay and conditions as their male counterparts. Efforts were made to find alternative employment with protection of earnings for disabled staff, for instance those no longer able to meet the high standards of eyesight required. One of the less publicised effects of privatisation of so-called peripheral activities was to greatly reduce the opportunities for alternative employment.

"Well established collective bargaining and consultative machineries have been fully utilised" for consultation with staff, we are told, and the reduction in the requirement for conductors following OPO had been dealt with "in accordance with long standing agreement with the TU".

There was a surplus after grant of £36 million. What could possibly go wrong?

Dark clouds were on the horizon. The proposal to reconstitute LT as LRT, divorce it from the GLC, and have it report to the Secretary of State, gave rise to "debate and controversy" according to the 1983 report. In addition, the Act required that "all activities that could appropriately be undertaken by outside contractors...will be tested against the cost of buying in...(LT is to be) reorganised into self contained profit centres able to tender for internal contracts against outside competition, including building, computing, and other professional services" (P3).

These proposals generated widespread opposition. "Campaign groups sprouted all over London" says Ken Fuller. "CAPITAL, an organisation uniting the transport Unions with the campaign groups and largely funded by the GLC...gained the support of some 2,000 such organisations and individuals". A week of events culminated in 'Transport Day' on Monday 26th March 1983 when half a million leaflets were distributed at bus stops and Underground stations. Two days later there was a one day strike called by the LT TU Council.[18]

But all this activity was to no avail. An ideologically motivated Government was determined to introduce market relations and privatise anything it could. It was not open to political arguments about the overall contribution of LT to London life and business, let alone the concerns of LT staff. It is very noticeable that the 1983 Annual Report is the first not to have a section devoted to 'staff'. At various points in the report management bemoan the unsettling effects of policy changes from the GLC but nowhere do they recognise that these abrupt changes also unsettled staff, leading to low morale at times of cuts and retrenchment. Divisions arose between those who considered politics is none of our business – just hunker down and weather the storm, and those who saw that the only way they could influence affairs that concerned their jobs and conditions was to get their Unions to fight. These concerns found expression largely in the continuing struggles over OPO on both buses and trains. The paternalist culture that had guided management right from the days of the Combine through the LPTB and nationalisation was in the process of being replaced by a hard nosed confrontational profit oriented managerial approach which would inevitably lead to more industrial unrest. For instance, in 1988 Denis Tunnicliffe, newly appointed managing director of London Underground Limited (note the change in terminology) addressing TU leaders (I was there), said 'You are under-managed' and set about appointing large numbers of new managers, replacing the previous structure of engineers and managers with operating experience. LT changed from a service oriented organisation to a financially driven one.

The 1983 Annual Report goes on to say that productivity had been reduced by the changes to the working week and holidays but that bus performance had been helped by an increase in OPO. The sale of travelcards at newsagents and shops (opposed unsuccessfully by the Unions on the grounds of loss of booking office jobs) had led to greater convenience of ticket purchase, but none of the savings accrued to the staff. Travelcards had replaced most Underground season tickets and bus passes. OPO had been further extended to cover 50% of the bus fleet but the unsuitability of existing buses for OPO was recognised.

Report Extra of 1983 says that 'supporting activities (had been) reorganised into internal profit centres so that costs can be compared with those of outside suppliers to ensure cost effectiveness', which sounds quite inoffensive. What it does not say is that the Croydon Food Production Centre, which since 1950 had supplied all the canteens, was closed in July 1983 and direct delivery to the 138 canteens from local suppliers was introduced. A study by the Greater London Industrial Archaeology Society (supplement to Newsletter 90, February 1984), tells us that the Centre's remit had been to 'ensure quality, consistency and portion control'. Home sales from canteens of sausages, tea bags, Welsh rarebit, cakes, Xmas puddings, and other items produced at Croydon had been very popular. 106 production staff, 25 clerical staff and 15 van drivers lost their jobs. The Unions did nothing to defend them. We also learn that 'Property and LT Advertising made worthwhile contributions to the cost of providing public transport'.

Making sausages at the London Transport Croydon Food Production Centre.

Equal opportunities to all employees regardless of race, sex, colour, or religion were to be provided. Policies conforming to the Law involved a positive programme of action to avoid any discrimination, we are told. "A number of measures to ensure a greater role in management by women and members of ethnic minorities are being considered'. Some ethnic minority members of the NUR in my experience felt that the Union should help them in their efforts to achieve promotion to managerial jobs. But some in the Union felt it was not the Union's responsibility to help people become managers who may then be on the 'other side of the table' from the Union. Following the explosion in the number of managers, recruiting managers into the Union became a controversial issue. Eventually it was accepted that many of these managers were keen to have Union support and were not necessarily 'on the other side'.

In 1984 the London Transport Executive ceased to exist. The new London Regional Transport was established on 29th June 1984 and would continue the policy of no real increases in fares. Passenger business was up by 21% on the Underground and 7% on the buses. Travelcards were successful. Thus ended the period of municipal control of LT. Despite unsettling changes of policy occasioned by changes of political control and legal judgements, the period of stagnation from 1948 to 1970 was ended by a series of well thought out initiatives introduced by Labour administrations at County Hall. This is not to be politically partisan. Chief among them was the recognition that LT's contribution to London's economy could not be measured simply on a profit and loss basis. The realisation that by marginal cost pricing spare capacity could usefully be utilised was important, as was the determination to break the cycle of constant fare increases, especially by the innovative Fares Fair scheme and the well thought out Balanced Plan. The belated and necessary introduction of zonal fares and the Travelcard to encourage use of public transport and make OPO on buses workable was a vital factor. All this occurred at the cost of widespread and eventually total introduction of OPO on buses and trains. By the time of the GLC's abolition on 31st March 1986 (the Government had cancelled the election due in 1985) OPO had become an established fact of life on the buses, though there was to be more controversy on the Underground. No-one now can imagine trains with guards and buses with conductors (Boris bus notwithstanding).

CHAPTER EIGHTEEN

DISCONTENT ON THE UNDERGROUND

LONDON TRANSPORT TRADE UNION COUNCIL

Sub-Committee

25 September 1987

Dear Colleague,

I am writing to ask you to attend a meeting of the above Committee on Tuesday, 29 September at Unity House, Euston Road starting at 4.30pm.

I would appreciate if you could attend , because the sacking of all the builders and Bright's statements on privatisation present us with problems and opportunities.

I hope to see you all and look forward to hearing your reports.

Yours fraternally,

KEVIN HALPIN
Chairman

Need for LTTUC conference on privatisation of whole of LRT
fares Increase
lowering of standards of cleaning etc.
contracting — worsening of wages + conditions.
Proposed ban on food + drink.

Letter from Kevin Halpin of the LT Trade Union Council regarding sacking of builders, September 1987

As we saw at the end of Chapter 15, the steady progress towards One Person Operation on the Underground had been interrupted by the NUR's decision to have second thoughts on the desirability of losing guard's jobs in the light of the increase in unemployment. This was also a reflection of a general increase in militancy as a younger generation became active in both the NUR and ASLE&F who were less willing to put up with management actions they disapproved of and less patient with the glacial pace of negotiations in the Conciliation machinery.

A dispute arose on British Railways over the issue of flexible rostering for train drivers and this had an echo on the Underground. As the 'History of ASLE&F' expresses it, "The British Railways Board (BRB) embarked on a strategy to split the two Unions on the issue of flexible rostering. It resolved to delay the second instalment of a 3% pay rise until the Union agreed in principle to variable start and finish times for work rosters. The BRB and LTE were also using their commitment to reduce the working week by an hour to propose that the time be shaved off existing turns as part of a more flexible arrangement rather than an extra day off every 8 weeks... The ASLE&F representatives informed the BRB once and for all that they could not accept flexible rostering, that the issue was separate from the pay increase and should not be a pretext for withholding the 3%...ASLE&F would not give up the fixed 8 hour day and had no intention of allowing single drivers to work beyond that." [1]

On 23rd December 1981 ASLE&F General Secretary Ray Buckton learned that, following a 'secret' lunch with Sir Peter Parker and other BRB Directors, NUR General Secretary Sidney Weighell had persuaded the NUR Executive to agree to flexible rostering. From the end of December into 1982 ASLE&F organised 17 days of industrial action involving 48 hour strikes and bans on overtime and Sunday working. On 10th February 1982 a Committee of Inquiry chaired by Lord McCarthy recommended that ASLE&F and the BRB discuss productivity within the Machinery of Negotiation. If they did this and called off the industrial action the 3% would be paid in advance of any new productivity arrangements. But the flexible rostering issue had not gone away. A decision by the Railway Staff National Tribunal (No. 7 of 7th May 1982) to throw out the principle of the 8 hour day and accept flexible rostering was rejected by ASLE&F.

An NUR Guards and Shunters conference then also rejected flexible rostering despite their EC's support of it. Finally, as the BRB said there would be no pay rise in 1982 until flexible rostering was introduced, the NUR called a 48 hour strike for 28th June. ASLE&F, unwilling as ever to co-ordinate action with the NUR, struck from Sunday 4th July. Prime Minister Margaret Thatcher appealed to ASLE&F members to "respond to the spirit of the Falklands" and ignore their Union's call but the strike was solid. The 8 hour day had been achieved in 1919 and would not be given up. Even Labour Party leader Michael Foot supported the strike, something not seen before or since. NUR General Secretary Weighell condemned it amid controversial scenes at the Union's AGM at Plymouth (I was there).

The TUC got involved and, in the absence of ASLE&F representatives, agreed with the BRB at ACAS to the delayed introduction of flexible rostering if ASLE&F would call off its action. Failure to do so would result in the expulsion of ASLE&F from the TUC.[2] The threat by BRB management to dismiss strikers, strike breakers among ASLE&F's membership, and lack of support from other Unions in the TUC led eventually to acceptance of flexible rostering.[3]

– Protection of Employment) circumvented. The TUPE Regulations of 1981 state "employees have the legal right to transfer to the new employer on their existing terms and conditions of employment except pensions". But transgressions incur a lengthy claim process and if no-one transfers of course there is no-one to claim. And as the RMT pointed out, contracts can be changed within 90 days anyway.

At Hounslow, a completely new subsidiary was started on a greenfield site leaving existing staff unaffected at first. At Norbiton, with no redundancy on offer and the Court case lost a series of strikes took place. But in the end wages and conditions were worse than before, because to keep decent pay and conditions would lead to routes being awarded to the private sector, who paid low basic rates and imposed longer hours if staff were to earn a living wage. This was the dilemma the T&GWU faced.

As part of the London Forest bid management insisted that "all existing agreements procedures and practices are cancelled". Reductions in pay would amount to £45-50 a week and the fixed anniversary date for pay rises would be abolished. Leyton garage would close. But the T&GWU knew that the other companies competing for the routes were paying better than Forest proposed, and they decided to 'play the market'. A strike ballot was planned for 14th June 1991. Despite the Company threatening dismissal for staff taking part in any industrial action the vote for a strike at the 4 garages was 690 – 20, on a turnout of over 70%, covering both operating and engineering staff. The T&GWU then raised a number of questions about the bidding process with the Office of Fair Trading without success, and a 1 day strike was called for Thursday 20th June. But management threatened legal action unless the strike was called off – apparently the ballot paper was 'defective'. Talks took place but little progress was made. The Union would not accept a reduction in wages estimated at 16% and a further ballot was organised for 28th June. Following further talks, the Company rejigged the package to guarantee current earnings but increase hours by 20% to a 48 hour week with a maximum spreadover of 14 hours. Separate ballots at Walthamstow and the other 3 garages (to satisfy legal requirements over slightly different issues at Walthamstow) gave similar results – up to 97% voted yes to strike action.

On 1st July 1991 London Forest gave notice of termination of contracts of employment to all the Walthamstow drivers, trying to scare them into accepting on an individual basis the new terms which the Union had rejected. The T&GWU took legal advice, which said that staff who were dismissed 'may' have a claim for unfair dismissal, which advice was worse than useless.

The T&GWU's 'unconventional tactic' was to ensure that the contracts were re-awarded to the competitor companies. An end to tendering, they said, was not possible by strike action but could only be achieved by a "mass political campaign". 20 years later we have yet to see such a campaign. The strike started on 10th July and was very well organised. T&GWU members at other garages (West Ham in particular) demanded to join the strike and members at Stamford Hill curtailed route 253 at Clapton Pond in solidarity, but the T&GWU actively dissuaded non- Forest branches from taking action. Why? First, it would have been unlawful. But also the T&GWU actually thought it did not matter as they believed they could turn the division of LBL into subsidiaries to their advantage.[9] Activists in the rail Unions, following events closely, found this approach a little odd and developed different tactics.

The Miners Strike of 1984-5 was supported by a large number of LT workers, especially on the rail side as it was well known that railway staff were next on Prime Minister Thatcher's list after the miners, but sympathetic strike action would have been illegal. A pay rise of 4.9% on BR set the norm for LT. PM Thatcher had intervened personally to tell BR to reach an agreement because "it was vital that we keep the rail Unions working" [4].

After protracted delay to the spread of OPO the 1983 pay offer was made conditional on Union commitment to implementing OPO.[5] The Hammersmith & City and Circle (H&C&C) lines were converted on 26th March 1984 but the proposed extension of OPO to the East London line on 20th May 1985 proved controversial. There was unease following the H&C&C conversion. Some still opposed OPO on principle. As the principle had already been conceded the NUR decided to try to make the conditions for Train Operators less onerous by reducing the length of 'wheel turning time' before a break was taken and increasing the length of breaks.

The NUR EC minutes of 18th April 1985 note that nomination forms had been sent out to drivers on the East London line asking them whether or not they wished to take up a Train Operator's post. The EC "instruct our members not to take part in the introduction of OPO on any line until advised by the EC" and "inform LUL that if they impose OPO without our agreement they will be in conflict with this Union". LUL (London Underground Limited) had been formed as a subsidiary of LRT on 1st April 1985, along with London Buses Ltd and Bus Engineering Ltd. On 25th April 1985 the rail federation (NUR and ASLE&F, now on better terms since the departure of Weighell and election of Jimmy Knapp as NUR General Secretary), met Sectional Council No3 (the negotiating body for traincrew) and agreed on the principle of 2 hours maximum driving time and a 45 minute break. How this would be achieved was to be discussed further and LUL were to be informed "that there be no extension of OPO until agreement is reached with the Unions (note plural) on conditions for those concerned".

On 16th May 1985 discussions at the federation centred on the need to limit driving time to a maximum of 3 hours continuous and 5 hours in aggregate with a 45 minute meal break. They also sought to achieve a shorter working week, additional annual leave and the abolition of split turns to create additional Train Operator posts and cushion the effect of OPO on staff. These discussions had not been finalised before LT completed their training programme and decided to implement OPO on the East London line from 20th May "in preference to withdrawing the OPO related payments" as they said in a barely veiled threat. The NUR EC decided to "instruct all our members, with the exception of those employed in Acton Works, to withdraw their labour from the finish of traffic on Sunday 19th May 1985." Preparations for pickets and the organisation of the strike were made but there is no record of any official approach to ASLE&F and they did not take a decision to strike. Their representative on the East London line assured the NUR's London Transport District Council that he would take his members out on unofficial strike in support of the NUR but this did not materialise (I chaired that meeting).

On 17th May LT went to the High Court under the provisions of the 1984 Trade union Act. The Union was not represented.

20th May 1985. The NUR EC minutes note that informal discussions with London Regional Transport (LRT) took place on Sunday 19th May and that members are instructed "to resume normal working from their next booking on time". The strike had failed. I stood on a picket line at Ealing Common Depot and watched trains running almost as normal and reflected on the lure of extra money for a train operator's job versus the better conditions that might have been achieved for that job.

The Rail Federation Council "recommended that Sectional Council No3 should agree to the timetable for the District and Metropolitan (main) lines and that we immediately enter negotiations at the national level to pursue the question of conditions of service and other related items for the operation of OPO". In August 1985 they note that joint discussions have commenced at SC3 level and the programme for the introduction of OPO on the District is October/November 1985 and on the Metropolitan October 1986. Conditions of service were to be discussed at the Railway Negotiating Committee.

OPO was introduced on the District line on 4th November 1985 and on the Metropolitan (main) on 20th September 1986. Before the Railway Inspectorate would agree to OPO on the deep tube lines there had to be effective train radio in operation and a device to inform the controller if the deadman's handle had not been operated in a period of five minutes to ensure that if the driver was incapacitated the line controller would be automatically alerted. This was demonstrated to the Unions in December 1985 [6]. Then OPO was brought in on the Piccadilly line on 31st August 1987, the Jubilee line on 29th March 1988 (the original proposals for Automatic Train Operation were not implemented due to lack of finance for resignalling and suitable rolling stock not being available), and the Bakerloo line on 20th November 1989. As drivers moved to these lines with the Train Operator rate of pay a severe shortage of drivers on the remaining crew operated lines (Central and Northern) developed, so from October 1988 all drivers received the Train Operator's rate of pay. But still all was not well.

WARNING !

ONE PERSON OPERATION CAN
SERIOUSLY DAMAGE YOUR HEALTH . . .

**IT'S COMING TO THE METROPOLITAN
LINE IN OCTOBER 1986**

When the guards are done away with on your line how safe will the old 'Met' be?

London Regional Transport, despite public protest, plans to introduce one person operated trains this year on the Metropolitan main line and on the Piccadilly line in 1987/8.

One Person Operation has already caused problems for passengers and staff on the underground:

- more passengers getting caught in doors;
- more people, especially women, feeling that it's no longer safe to travel on the underground in the evenings;
- lack of staff like guards on hand to help out;
- more stress for train drivers doing two jobs — driving trains and operating doors.

WORKING ON LONDON TRANSPORT

I didn't know that I was being discriminated against. Do you?

Since June 1984, London Regional Transport has been promising to establish itself as an equal opportunities employer. Eight months later there is still *NO* published policy on equal opportunities! As a major employer of black people, London Regional Transport has a duty to make sure that its policies and employment practices do not discriminate against black workers or any workers for that matter—women for example.

"An Asian guard, after several years as a guard, wanted to train as a driver. He failed his test with an Area Manager, but later reapplied and passed, went to the training school, passed out as a driver there and then went for his last driving test with an Area Manager. He failed this test! And you know—it was the same Area Manager who had failed him on the first test."

LT tube driver

If you are black, you can get a job in a canteen or as a cleaner or working on a station or as a bus conductor—mostly manual jobs. The other jobs on London Regional Transport are reserved for whites only. *Are we being categorised???!!!!*

Leaflet opposing introduction of OPO on the Metropolitan Line 1986 and leaflet opposing racial discrimination 1984

1989 – THE SUMMER OF DISCONTENT

In 1987 LUL decided to reorganise station staffing with a view to reducing costs by merging many duties, especially operating roles and ticket office duties. New technology with automatic gates would enable staff numbers to be reduced. They also sought to abolish the long established principle of promotion on the basis of seniority. This system was not 'buggins turn'. It was still necessary for staff to undergo training and pass tests to prove that they were qualified for a higher grade job, but after this process the senior person who had passed would get the job. This ensured that management could not use favouritism to promote their 'blue eyed boys'. Management were particularly keen to be able to 'fast track' their chosen candidates for higher management positions. Many, though not all, managers were also of the racist view that white staff would not take instructions from ethnic minority staff who might be promoted above them. The large influx of staff who had been recruited from the West Indies in the 50's and 60's had patiently waited their turn for promotion under the seniority system, and just as many of them were reaching the top of the list where they might finally have access to the higher grades they were to be denied promotion. This was not acceptable and both the NUR and TSSA pledged to defend the rights of ethnic minority staff and the seniority system that gave them some protection from racist practices.

In August 1987 the NUR and TSSA agreed to participate in a working party to discuss the changes. It took some time for management to realise that with NUR and TSSA opposition to the core of their proposals (abolition of seniority and merging of station and booking office staff) there was no room for compromise. The working party dragged on. Finally, on 16th December 1988 the NUR EC decided to ballot all NUR members on the Underground for strike action on the issues of 'Organisational Change' (primarily 'Action Stations'), unsatisfactory attendance policy, and competitive tendering. The issues were chosen so as to build the greatest unity and include all members. LT then offered further talks on Organisational Change and on 12th January 1989 the EC suspended the strike ballot until 3rd April. No progress was made and the station staffing issue was eventually referred to the Wages Board (top level of the Machinery of Negotiation – compulsory arbitration in all but name) which, in Decision No 124 of 17.02.89. called on the NUR to re-enter negotiations and agree to a pilot scheme in the Harrow area with a parallel appointments system not based on seniority. The NUR EC decided not to resume negotiations unless the seniority issue was resolved first.

The pace of events was accelerating rapidly. In a provocative action on 13th January 1989 the first automatic UTS (Underground Ticketing System) gates were put into operation at Green Park station without the agreement of the Sectional Councils concerned. Management were 'unavailable' for an early meeting on the issue, which did not take place until 27th February. This kind of arrogant action by management infuriated station staff, who had been accustomed to the paternalist style of old where staff representatives were fully involved in all changes.

The NUR ballot was to go ahead over two weeks from 3rd April 1989. On 22nd March. as the NUR EC member for LT I met TSSA officials to co-ordinate action, and a number of meetings with ASLE&F representatives were also held. On 19th April the NUR ballot result was announced – a 7-1 vote in favour of strike action on a 60.9% turnout. An official meeting with ASLE&F and TSSA was to be arranged.

172

On 25th April the NUR called an all-out stoppage from Monday 8th May. ASLE&F did not ballot or call a strike.

The TSSA is a Union that seeks at all times to avoid industrial action and very rarely have they even considered it. But so serious were the issues and so determined to steamroller their new scheme through were LT management, with their new American inspired tactics, that the TSSA, unable to persuade management to drop their scheme, asked their members not to apply for advertised positions in the trial in the Harrow area and organised a strike ballot. On a 53.1% turnout 548 voted yes and 313 no. An indefinite strike of booking clerks and supervisor members was called to coincide with the NUR action on 8th May [7].

But LUL secured an injunction against the NUR making the strike illegal so the TSSA called their strike off. Mr Justice Simon Brown in the High Court had granted an injunction banning the 8th May strike on the grounds that not all the questions on the ballot paper applied to all the members. It had only recently become law that ballots had to be held before strikes could take place and there was no precedent as to how to proceed. I wrote the ballot questions myself with the intention of making it clear to the members what they were voting on but this did not suit the 'learned' judge. The NUR EC reluctantly cancelled the 8th May strike but instituted a strike ballot on BR. The NUR sought (unsuccessfully) to get the injunction overturned.

The Evening Standard had reported on 28th April 1989 that London bus staff were to be balloted and on 11th May said that the buses were set to strike from Monday 15th May Feelings were running high over LUL's legal 'chicanery'. On 15th May bus staff were offered a 7.6% pay increase.

Following long and acrimonious discussions at the RNC the NUR decided to re-ballot from 18th May to 7th June. Learning as we went along, this time the issues were spelt out in an accompanying letter and the question on the ballot paper was simply "Do you agree to take strike action". This is the format that continues to the present day.

The ballot on BR would run from 30th May to 5th June. On 12th May the NUR agreed to participate in a study into stress and strain for OPO train drivers. An overtime ban on BR Southern Region starts and results in the cancellation of 68 of the scheduled 539 trains.

On 16th May LT further inflame the situation by threatening to impose the station staffing trial in the Harrow area.

On 19th May the T&GWU decide to ballot dockers for strike action over deregulation, which means a return to the hated casual labour system of old.

On 25th May another failure to agree is recorded at the RNC but the Evening Standard reports that LUL are to 'give ground' on Action Stations. But what LUL actually do is attempt to bypass the Unions by addressing their 'improved' offer direct to staff through their new 'Centurion' managers (their term, not mine).

A claim for an improved rate of pay for Train Operators (T/Ops), who operate trains without guards, had been going round and round in the serpentine Whitley style Machinery of Negotiation for at least five years. Talks got bogged down, but following the NUR's failed strike of 20th May 1985 officials were reluctant to press for any action. A rank and file movement for more pay was initiated around the end of January 1989 by discontented local officials of ASLEF and grew rapidly, quickly involving NUR members as well.

Train drivers were already among the best paid workers on the underground, and some lower paid members (especially in the NUR) resented the fact that Train drivers wanted to further increase their differential. Nevertheless, it was true that OPO did impose greatly increased stress on staff in a highly responsible job and that this problem needed dealing with. Some of the initiators of this unofficial movement wanted to build a new union independent of both NUR and ASLEF with themselves in charge. Some saw it as a means of securing the re-election of the ASLEF District Secretary, who was greatly involved behind the scenes. Some, probably most, saw it as a chance to shake up two Unions that had perhaps become somewhat bureaucratic and complacent. It was certainly a chance to punish a management that since the defeat of the Miners' strike had changed from the paternalist style of old to what was in the view of many an arrogant, aggressive managerial style under Managing Director Denis Tunnicliffe.

Certainly, the first unofficial strike, on Weds 5th April, came as a great surprise to the leadership of the NUR and its NEC member. It had been called at an unofficial mass meeting of Drivers and Guards at Friends Meeting House in Euston which had formulated a demand for a rise of £64.85 a week and £23,000 in back pay. This had been calculated as 50% of the savings management made by doing away with the guard.

One of the most important features of the unofficial strikes was that they were able to circumnavigate the restrictive effects of the Conservative government's anti-strike legislation by not having identifiable leaders, keeping the date secret so as not to give management advance notice and time to prepare, and relying on the direct democracy of mass meetings to build solidarity. London Transport threatened an injunction, the Unions condemned the action, but the strikes continued.

Picketing

Possibly a unique feature, in contradistinction to the Miners' strike, was the insistence of the co-ordinators leading the action that there should be no pickets at all. Partly this was so no leading individuals could be identified and victimised, and partly to foster the solidarity of a group who claimed they had no need of pickets. Indeed, when official strikes were organised later that summer, we found on both BR and the Underground that the anger and resentment of the members of both Unions was so great that the pickets we organised had little or nothing to do.

One day strikes

The previous practice on the rare occasions when the Unions had called official strikes had been to call out the whole membership indefinitely to achieve maximum impact. The experience of the Miners, defeated after a year of privation and hardship, led militants to examine other tactics, particularly one day stoppages that could be repeated almost indefinitely without causing unacceptable loss of wages to the members. Such tactics, especially if imposed without warning, created chaos on the railways, especially in commuter areas like London. Union leaderships opposed this at first because it took a lot more work to organise and placed power in the hands of local leaders and the members, but they soon came to see the advantages. There were to be six unofficial one day strikes.

Official strikes

Some in the NUR opposed the unofficial strikes and any intervention by the Union in the unofficial mass meetings on the understandable grounds that all they were out for was higher differentials for staff who were already relatively well paid. The NUR was losing members to ASLEF over this issue and stood in danger of losing its influence among the industrially powerful traincrew, who really did have a grievance over the way OPO had been brought in. NUR members had already become part of the unofficial movement and there really was no option but to get involved. When NEC members of both Unions were invited to address the mass meetings on 4th May I accepted on behalf of the NUR and ASLEF's Bob Harris also accepted. The task now for the NUR was to make the strikes official and stop the loss of members to ASLEF. The NUR was also in dispute over station staff and other changes.

A ballot of all members, including traincrew, had been ruled illegal by the courts in January 1989. The result of the re-ballot on this issue (4,362 yes, 1,009 no) was announced on 12th June at the same time as the 'Yes' vote to industrial action by the traincrew over OPO pay (1,264 yes, 116 no). A T&GWU busworkers ballot resulted in a 5-1 yes vote.

On 8th June 2,000 dockers defy a court ban and strike against the abolition of the Dock Labour board. On 9th June a proposed bus strike is suspended to allow talks to take place. Unofficial strikes at Croydon and Thornton Heath bus garages were organised to coincide with the 6th unofficial Underground strike on 16th June.

An official strike of all NUR members on the Underground and British Rail, and T&GWU organised bus workers, took place on 21st June. This put the NUR firmly and officially back in the driving seat. ASLEF had decided to ballot their members but had not yet completed their ballot. Many ASLEF members unofficially supported the NUR walkout, showing more sense than some of their leaders. The LRT Chairman described the activists as 'ungodly'. LUL had made an 11th hour offer to abandon Action Stations but this came too late to affect the strike plans. 20,000 bus workers also took unofficial action after their delegates had rejected an 8.3% pay offer. The Law Lords lift the injunction preventing the T&GWU from organising a national dock strike. (Amazing what a transport strike can achieve).

BR impose a 7% pay rise when the cost of living in London is reported to have risen by 16%. The NUR note that nothing has happened with the review of OPO agreed to back in 1984 and again requested at the beginning of this year.

The NUR called two more official strikes for 28th June and 5th July. To their eternal shame, the unofficial co-ordinators called on their supporters to work on the 28th June NUR strike day, a call which was ignored by all traincrew. This was the ultimate test of the unofficial strike leadership and they failed it dismally. On 3rd July ASLEF finally announced their ballot result, a 13-1 yes vote, and the 5th July strike was another success. On 5th July the T&GWU recommend bus staff to accept an 8.6% increase. On 6th July ASLE&F announce an 8-1 majority vote for an overtime ban on BR and on 7th July BR offer an 8.5% pay rise. On 12th July there was an official strike by both Railway Unions on both BR and LT. But on 11th July the Evening Standard had reported that the Dock strike had been split by an offer of up to £35,000 redundancy payments. Starting on 17th July a pay strike by bus garage engineering staff keeps one third of buses off the road. On 3rd August bus crews finally settle for a 9.1% increase but the engineering staff strike is not called off until 4th August.

At the RNC on 1st August LUL finally unequivocally and totally "formally abandoned" their cherished 'Action Stations' scheme. The Personnel Director is heard to tell his managers 'whichever one of you can run backwards the fastest keeps his job'. That rarest of birds in TU negotiating history, a total victory for the Unions, has been achieved.

LT Management

It took six more official strikes (the last one on 2nd August) ie 14 one day strikes in all before an arrogant but ultimately weak management offered through ACAS a deal that was acceptable to the Unions' negotiators. They "accepted that the claim for a review of OPO and the Train Operators' rate of pay is well founded", recognised that OPO had seriously increased the responsibilities of Train Operators "to an extent not hitherto envisaged" and that the extra pay was to be without strings. Some of the unofficial co-ordinators wanted to trade off some of the T/Ops' conditions for more money, but the NUR was having none of that.

With OPO allowances made enhanceable the total increase for Train Operators was calculated as £51 per week. The claim had been for £64. Guards received an increase of £7 per week. The offer was made on the strict condition that the planned 10th August strike was called off and with the threat that any unofficial strikers would be sacked. There was to be no opportunity to place the offer before a mass meeting for approval or otherwise by the members, which I had promised to do before agreeing anything – it was take it or leave it. The ASLE&F EC member and I decided that the risks of losing all that had been achieved were too great and we took it, knowing that this would make our continuing as EC members untenable. So it proved. I resigned from the NUR EC and Bob Harris was later obliged to leave the ASLE&F EC.

Charmed life

Once the unofficial strikes had got under way it was clear that Management knew the identities of the leading co-ordinators. Management said they would not discipline them for fear of making martyrs of them. There may have been a morsel of truth in that, though it only demonstrated their weakness. But it is interesting to speculate as to what degree management was featherbedding the potential leaders of a new sweetheart union to undermine both official unions. It was notable that when the settlement was offered at ACAS management made it clear that any unofficial action against a settlement would result in dismissal of those involved, yet this was never threatened while the unofficial leaders were calling strikes. An unofficial strike against the deal was indeed called on 10th August but only a small minority supported it and a mass meeting on 14th August decided to stop the protests in light of management's threats of dismissal. By January 1990 the Train Operator's rate of pay was £17,300.

Evening Standard

It is also clear that the Evening Standard newspaper knew the identities of the unofficial co-ordinators but chose not to publish them, although it published plenty of information about the mass meetings and strikes. In fact, instead of its usual anti-union and anti-strike stance it often seemed surprisingly well-disposed towards the unofficial leadership. Did they know something we didn't? Was this a ruse to undermine the official unions? If so it backfired spectacularly.

Subsequently the Central and Northern lines became One Person Operated, the very last guard working on the Northern line on 27th January 2000. LUL had achieved their objective of 100% OPO on the Underground but at considerably greater cost than they had anticipated as Train Operators finally obtained a decent rate of pay. The radical changes to station staffing had been withdrawn completely. The Unions on the Underground were strengthened as a result of the Summer of Discontent and the T&GWU on the buses had shown it was still a force to be reckoned with. For the first and only time strikes had been co-ordinated with the Underground, buses and British Rail all taking action simultaneously which greatly strengthened their position. The Underground workers and their Unions were clearly now in a leading role, reversing the decades old dominance of the Central bus section.

But the first moves towards privatisation had been set in motion and this was to radically affect labour relations both on the buses and the Underground. The issue of competitive tendering had been on the NUR ballot in December 1988 but had unfortunately been overshadowed by the battles over OPO pay and station staffing.

Underground ticket collector, 1970s

CHAPTER NINETEEN

NATIONALISATION AND PRIVATISATION

The December 1984 cover of the union journal Busworker Monthly featuring Margaret Thatcher, stabbing a bus worker in the back, and leading members of her cabinet.

In 1983 London Transport celebrated the 50th Anniversary of its establishment as a public body in 1933. The Government cannot have been unaware of this fact when they published a White Paper "Public transport in London" in June that year which paved the way for privatisation. The GLC and transport Unions organised a campaign against this called 'Capital Transport' (no relation to the publisher of this book). There was a lobby of Parliament on 17th January 1984. The TUC and local government Unions organised a 'democracy week' between 26-29th March to defend the GLC, which was to be abolished. A day of action was organised on 28th March when all buses and trains came to a halt [1]. But the LRT Act received Royal Assent on 26th June 1984. It gave the Secretary of State for Transport control of LT and required that "all activities that could appropriately be undertaken by outside contractors, such as maintenance and support services, will be tested against the cost of buying in...(LT is to be) reorganised into self contained profit centres able to tender for internal contracts against outside competition, including building, computing and other professional services", as the 1983 Annual Report puts it on P3. The GLC election scheduled for 1985 was cancelled and the GLC and other Metropolitan Counties were abolished from 31st March 1986. So once again LT was nationalised, this time as London Regional Transport (LRT).

The Employment Act of 1982 had made illegal any industrial action which could be construed as political. Labour Party leaders, especially transport spokesman John Prescott, promised that privatisation would be reversed when they regained power, and these two factors led to a muted response to the LRT Act from transport union leaders. Many activists remained sceptical but any large scale industrial action was effectively ruled out.

GLC support for the extension of OPO on the Underground had not improved the credibility of the GLC with the rail Unions and the GLC's opposition to OPO on the buses had been limited to the farcical and ineffective "can't pay won't pay" campaign. LT's 1983 Annual Report refers coyly to "Debate and Controversy" over the LRT Bill, but significantly it is the first Report not to have a separate section devoted to 'staff'. It notes that sale of Travelcards at newsagents, opposed by the Unions on the grounds of loss of booking office staff, had increased the ease and convenience of ticket purchase. The highly successful Travelcards had replaced most Underground season tickets and bus passes. OPO on the buses had extended to 53% of the fleet although the unsuitability of existing buses is noted. Productivity on the buses had improved by 4% helped by the increase in OPO.

Female workers now all received the same pay and conditions as their male counterparts.

In 1984 the Report tells us that passenger business was up by 21% on the Underground and 7% on the buses.

From 1st April 1985 LRT established three subsidiary companies – London Buses Ltd (LBL), Bus Engineering Ltd (BEL), and London Underground Ltd (LUL). The 1985 Report says there was consultation both of "employee representatives at all levels" and the public. The response from the Unions was muted. Change of company name or organisation in itself was neither here nor there, but the implications were severe. The Secretary of State set the objectives of the new Companies, which included the requirement to "involve the private sector in the provision of services where that is more efficient, and to make better use of public assets, including the sale of assets which are no longer required" (1985 Report P5). There were no consultations, let alone negotiations, on this, the meat of the changes. Union leaders again asked us to rely on the Labour Party to reverse it all. Bus support activities were to be tendered with "at least 10% of bus engineering requirements to be placed with outside suppliers". LRT policy was that "where agreement can be reached on achieving viability within a reasonable timescale, the activity should be retained in house in its new cost-effective form". Bus OPO, now more practicable through use of passes and Travelcards, had increased to 58% "to meet competition for routes in the tendering process". The only good news was that 150 Youth Training Scheme places had been established, 25 for railway operations, 45 for young engineers and 80 office positions, though this did not compare well with the number of youth trainee positions available in the 1960's and 1970's.

In July 1984 The Government produced another White Paper, entitled just "Buses", which proposed to deregulate the bus industry so that anyone could run a bus on any route without co-ordination with other operators or local authorities. The National Bus Company (NBC) would be divided into small units which would be offered for sale to the private sector. The T&GWU and TSSA again lobbied against the Bill without success, with the important exception that London was exempted from deregulation. The Act became operative from 26th October 1986 and rapidly led to the break up of London Country Bus Services, the old LT Country Area [2].

The 1985/6 Report, covering the period to 31st March 1986, notes a reduction in unit costs of 4.6% overall as a result of further conversions of buses and trains to OPO and improved productivity in engineering services. Staff reductions were achieved by natural wastage, redeployment and voluntary severance. On the buses "Major changes (were sought) to the formerly centralised machineries for negotiating with the TU's so as to ensure that future arrangements for consultation match the separate business identities" – another opportunity for building unity which the T&GWU seems to have missed. The report says "Involvement of employees in matters relating to their working environment and the future development of the organisation was encouraged". 67% of buses were now OPO. A further 8% of bus mileage was tendered out – of 56 routes, 26 were won by LBL, 20 by NBC Companies and 8 by private operators. An activist in the T&GWU at the time tells me that the Union never got involved in the campaign against privatisation and did not address the issue. Local Empires with bureaucratic interests got involved in issues like facility time payments for Union representatives but walked away from the main issue. They asked for protection under the TUPE Regulations but these provided no long term security as the price of winning contracts was precisely to reduce pay and conditions. They even failed to organise a campaign to stay in the LT Pension Fund, which would have been a unifying issue. Transfer of routes to Union organised NBC Companies seems not to have troubled the officials at all. Wallace notes that as a result of privatisation many bus workers have seen their conditions of service worsened, their working day lengthened and pension prospects dashed [3]. The Annual Report even says on P15 that "London Buses staff showed much goodwill and effort and there was no serious disruption to services". That must have hurt activists who were trying to defend wages and conditions.

In catering productivity savings were identified prior to competitive tendering in 1986-7. Computer services were privatised on 30th June 1986.

LUL put a small amount of work and various support services out to tender but front line operations were not affected. Following successful trials at Vauxhall the (privately sourced) Underground (automatic) Ticketing System was given the go-ahead. Reorganised as an independent business, LT Builders recorded a significant financial loss.

In the 1986/7 Report we learn that the Business Services Department including Computer Services had been "transferred" to CAP (UK) Ltd. in May 1987 ie privatised. CAP then also "acquired" LT's 32% holding in Data Networks plc. The report says that "agreement was reached with the TU's to test the market for catering services at 4 bus garages and 2 railway depots". The Unions at this time clearly saw no possibility of a fight against 'marketisation' and privatisation. In LT Builders employment fell by half to 487 as work was given to outside contractors. The contracts, painting, concrete casting and joinery shops were closed.

An additional 9% of bus mileage was put out to tender. A drive to reduce 'unit costs' on the buses in order to win tenders led to unspecified industrial relations problems which affected bus operating performance. We know that some well organised bus garages were ready to take action to defend their conditions, and several did just that, which makes the failure of the T&GWU to take up these issues and generalise them all the more shocking. To win tenders LBL (the in house operator at this time) had to become 'competitive' which meant attacking staff conditions. The only possible way for the T&GWU to fulfil its duty to defend its members' conditions would have been to organise fleet-wide action to circumvent one group of staff competing against another. Did they fear concerted action being branded political and therefore illegal? The NUR was to find a way round this difficulty by calling industrial action around the effects of privatisation on its members' terms and conditions, not a difficult policy to implement.

The NUR learned a lot from the campaign to keep Acton Works open. Heavy overhaul of trains every 4-5 years had been carried out at Acton Works for many years. A 1983 management study into its future had concluded that overhaul of trains should be transferred to the individual train depots where it could be done "very cheaply and at substantially lower cost than having this work done by contract" ie privatised. In 1984 these measures were agreed with the TU's who had to accept the transfer of work and drastic reduction of the workforce at Acton Works as the lesser evil to privatisation. New trains would not have a 4-5 year overhaul as part of their maintenance schedule at all, but would have a half-life refurbishment, to be the subject of further negotiations as to whether this would be carried out 'in house' or by an outside contractor. It turned out to be almost entirely the latter. A new Equipment Overhaul Shop would be built at Acton, to which some of the former Acton Works staff could transfer. A Depot Engineering Support Unit was built adjacent to the nearby Ealing Common Depot to assist with train overhauls and heavy work in the changeover period. This building is now the Acton Depot of the London Transport Museum and houses its reserve collection. Also, after a long fight by the NUR, rail access into the site was maintained so that whole trains as well as components could be worked on. Train overhaul at Acton Works ceased in 1985 as the work was transferred to the various depots. The new Railway Equipment Works (REW) was built on the site of the former lifting shop and opened in 1989 with 450 staff, mostly former workers at Acton Works. It overhauls various items of train equipment (compressors, motor alternators, control gear,) which cannot be bought 'off the shelf'. Attempts to sell it off to the private sector as an individual entity failed. It was attached to the Sub Surface Lines package and taken over by Metronet, and when Metronet collapsed brought back in to LUL. It currently employs about 250 permanent staff with additional agency staff brought in as and when the workload requires.

Power generation was also examined and it was decided that LT's own power generating stations would be closed by about 1990, after which all supplies would come from the not yet privatised London Electricity Board. Lots Road power station closed on 21st October 2002, though the former LCC tram power station at Greenwich was kept as a standby.

Aldenham bus overhaul works, near Elstree, had a staff of 1,800 when it opened in 1956. The loss of the Country Area in 1970 had reduced its efficiency, and the modern rear-engined buses were not suited to its highly efficient modular flow-line system of overhaul. In fact so poor were the modern buses that they often did not last long enough to warrant a 4-5 year overhaul anyway. In November 1985 LBL changed the maintenance schedule for its newer vehicles removing the need for a major works overhaul every 4 years and undertaking more extensive servicing in its own garages. This removed a large volume of work from Aldenham. BEL closed Aldenham in November 1986 and the remaining overhauls of traditional type buses were transferred to Chiswick works in West London. BEL was sold off in January 1988.

The 1987/8 Report records that 63 more bus routes were tendered along with more unspecified Underground 'activities'. In January 1988 the Risk Management Services Department was sold off. "Commercial viability" had not been achieved in LRT Builders and it was closed down in November 1987 A vigorous campaign by the NUR achieved opportunities for individual members of staff who were willing and able to apply for jobs elsewhere within LUL, but could not stop the closure. The Report states on P22 that "understandings have been reached with the TU's on handling necessary change", their code word for Government imposed tendering and privatisation. It says "pay settlements for 1989 again incorporated measures to reduce labour costs and improve utilisation of staff" and "the success in winning LRT area based (bus) tenders required fundamental changes in the pay and conditions of the staff concerned" ie cuts. At Norbiton bus garage in a challenge by the Union over cuts in pay and conditions the High Court found that the Company had acted "lawfully" despite the TUPE regulations. "A number of stoppages of work still occurred before the matter was settled satisfactorily" says the Report on P23. No satisfaction for the staff.

The Report tells us that unit costs had again been reduced, by 5% on the Underground and 6.2% on the buses due to continually increasing passenger numbers and long term savings from competitive tendering. Far from any of these savings making their way into staff pay packets we are told that tendered bus routes cost per mile was 22% lower than before due, we must assume, to lower wages and worse conditions. Assaults on staff were down, however, and were less frequent on driver only buses, where safety screens had been introduced. The total number of staff fell by 8.9% to 47,291. Staff costs were now 61% of total costs. On P13 the report says "Employees have been involved in discussion relating to their working environment and the future development of the organisation". As a member of staff and Union representative at the time I must say that I did not notice any of this – I wonder which chosen employees they spoke to. Competitive tendering of bus routes and bus and rail engineering activities continued. Two new subsidiary bus companies at Stanwell and Orpington "are operated with a pay and conditions structure which is more in line with that of other bus operators...enabling LBL to compete more effectively with outside competition" says the report, but "operating performance was affected by industrial relations problems arising from the cumulative effects of the drive to reduce unit costs and to become competitive". Clearly some bus staff were fighting back, but their Union was not organising a fleet-wide response. The 1986 pay settlement, the report notes, included "agreements to improve quality and reduce costs".

Terms such as 'productivity improvements' and 'reduction in unit costs' abound in the Reports and are often a way of saying 'cuts'. Maintenance standards were continuously cut on both buses and Underground and this was to contribute to the tragedy of the Kings Cross fire of 18th November 1987. This is usually blamed on a cigarette end being dropped on an escalator, but of course there had to be something there for the fag end to set fire to. Since the first escalator was installed at Earl's Court in 1911 millions of cigarette ends must have been dropped on escalators, but it was the build up of dirt and grease under the escalator at Kings Cross as a result of maintenance cuts that underlay those tragic events when 31 lives were lost. Actions arising from the Fennell Report into the disaster included greater concentration on the cleaning of escalators, removal of wooden components and improved training for

T&GWU London District Secretary Oli Jackson with banner, 1989

staff. The cleaning issue is conveniently ignored in most reports. In January 1987 the NUR had had a successful ballot for industrial action over the issue of competitive tendering and the impact of the new ticketing systems (see Chapter 18), but the strike was suspended when LUL agreed to negotiate.

The Docklands Light Railway (DLR) opened on 30th July 1987. The Annual Report makes no mention of staffing issues. Despite the presence among the initial staff of many members of the NUR and a small number of ASLE&F members DLR Management did a 'sweetheart' deal with the Electrical, Electronic, Telecommunications and Plumbing Union (EETPU) along similar lines to the deal which excluded the Printing Unions from the new newspaper printworks at Wapping. The EETPU actually had no members on the DLR. A 1987 ballot of the 101 staff then employed produced a vote of 44-11 in favour of a Union but recognition was not granted because this did not amount to a majority of the staff as a whole. Following a vigorous campaign of recruitment by the NUR a further vote was called which produced a 92% yes vote for TU recognition (representing two thirds of all staff). Management would only recognise a single Union and as by far the largest Union at the DLR the NUR took over the 'franchise' [4]. The 1990-1 Report to Employees says that staff numbers on the DLR were 348 and would increase to 465 when the Bank extension opened.

In 1987/8 42 more bus routes were tendered, including the first high frequency central London route, the 24. It was this privatisation which brought one of the 'unintended consequences' of privatisation to the attention of 'the powers that be'. The private operators used their own livery, which did not matter to the high-ups when it was out in the suburbs. But the London Tourist Board complained that tourists expected London buses to be red, and so did many MP's who could now see the green, orange and grey buses of the Grey Green Company passing the Houses of Parliament. Regulations were rapidly changed so that when routes were re-tendered it became a requirement that the buses should be at least 90% red whoever owned them. LRT retained the commercial risk of the routes and kept the fare revenue. The private operators were paid a fee by LRT to run buses to pre-determined schedules. The prospect of deregulation for London buses has, says the Report, "important implications", but so far no-one has managed to create in London the chaotic free for all that exists in other parts of the country. At this time 106 routes were under contract representing 18% of mileage and, they say, substantial savings were being made.

In 1989 LBL bus operations were split into 12 subsidiary companies, clearly a precursor to privatisation. The 1989 pay round was the last to be negotiated on a fleet wide basis, and the success achieved by linking the whole bus fleet with the Underground staff dispute shows what the potential still was and how much the T&GWU was about to lose (see Chapter 18). In future pay and conditions would be the responsibility of the 12 subsidiary companies, as foreshadowed in the LT Annual Report.

An idea of how the T&GWU responded to this challenge can be found in Ken Fuller's book. He starts by pointing out that if the private operators win profitable inner London routes LRT's ability to cross subsidise uneconomic but socially necessary routes in the suburbs would be compromised. This may have been a concern to the GLC and the passengers but it seems a strange place for a TU to start a campaign given what we had already seen of the ineffectiveness of the "can't pay won't pay" campaign and Parliamentary lobbying. The GLC was shortly to be abolished. He correctly identifies the main danger to bus workers as the division into several different companies "as a result of which their negotiating strength would be weakened, in a competitive race to become 'economic' there is a clear danger of service cuts and thus job losses. Finally, LRT is already indicating that it will be using the threat of competition in an attempt to introduce wage differentials between inner and outer London garages". He points out that LRT's 3 year plan could entail 6,000 job losses and further extension of OPO with 100% OPO planned for the 1990's. The subsidy of £192 million in 1984-5 would be cut to £95 million by 1987-8, the Minister told LRT. Yet there were no proposals for any fleet-wide action while it was still possible. The only action the London Bus Conference decided on was to continue to accept disabled persons bus passes from 9am when the London Boroughs Association decided they would only fund them from 9.30am. Ken concludes that this symbolised the scope for a joint campaign "backed up when necessary by the industrial strength of the London Bus Section and other LRT workers". Unfortunately this remained symbolic as the scope for action on this basis proved to be extremely limited and the Union took no effective action at all. That there was a mood for action among some sections of the workforce was clear, but many others had much more limited horizons and would only act when their immediate interests were at stake. As we will see in the story of the London Forest District dispute in 1991, by the time that happened it was probably too late [5]. The 36-27 vote at a special London Bus Conference on 23rd July 1982 to accept service cuts was more symbolic of the 'mood' of busworkers than Ken Fuller's thoughtful analysis, correct conclusions and high hopes in 1985 [6]. The failure of the T&GWU to deal with the division of LBL into 12 separate companies proved catastrophic.

The London Forest strike of 1991.
In June 1991 London Forest, one of the LBL subsidiaries, was awarded the contract for 11 routes in the Walthamstow area based on a low tender. Ash Grove (Hackney), Clapton, Walthamstow and Leyton garages were included in the company. The tender required new personal contracts for staff (getting around TUPE Regulations) with an increase in the working week of 20%, and cuts in holiday leave and sick pay. A strike of the 1,200 workers began in July and lasted 19 days but LBL used their position above the individual companies to pass the routes on to other LBL subsidiaries or private companies. Eventually Ash Grove and Walthamstow garages closed leading to job losses and displacement of staff and London Forest collapsed [7]. Once again the lesson of the need to organise on a fleet wide basis was demonstrated. Why were other groups of London busworkers actively dissuaded by the Union from taking industrial action?

Unconventional tactics were used by the T&GWU. Their District Officer at the time of the dispute, Ken Fuller, says (P261) that it was always obvious that route tendering was going to be a recipe for cutting wages and worsening conditions within LBL. While at first LBL bid on a basis of existing wages and conditions, they lost a significant number of routes to the private sector. Then they bid for routes at Potters Bar and Hounslow garages on the basis of 'dramatically' reduced wages and conditions. At Potters Bar the redundancy trap was used – given the choice of the new reduced terms and conditions or a generous redundancy package the vast majority of staff opted for voluntary severance. Thus was TUPE (Transfer of Undertakings

When LBL got other private operators to provide buses on the strike hit routes the T&GWU did not treat it as strike breaking as their strike was against London Forest only, though when some T&GWU members refused to operate these services the Union welcomed what they called 'gestures of support'. Calls at a T&GWU Conference of LBL delegates for industrial support for the Forest strikers were met by the strange argument that secondary action, as well as being illegal, would "shift the spotlight from the London Forest strikers and reduce the capacity for fund raising" [10], a bureaucratic nonsense if ever there was one.

Talks resumed on 17th July with the strike still solid. On Tuesday 23rd July LRT's Tendered Bus Unit recognised that due to Union resistance to worsening of pay and conditions London Forest would be unable to operate the Walthamstow contracts, which were then re-awarded to the Citybus, County Bus and Thamesway companies. The T&GWU claimed victory and a march from Leyton to Walthamstow ended the dispute. The T&GWU again committed itself to a political campaign to defeat tendering and the plans to deregulate London's bus services. Every Walthamstow striker would have either a job to go to or severance payments, which was better than nothing but far from a complete victory. The agreement reached provided that:

a. Ongoing attempts would be made to arrive at a formula for the future discussion of tenders.

b. The provisions of the LBL voluntary redundancy scheme would apply to all surplus engineering staff who could not be accommodated by transfers.

c. Attempts would be made to accommodate all surplus staff by means of transfers to other London Forest garages and other LBL garages.

d. Drivers who had signed to indicate their acceptance of the proposed new wages and conditions at Walthamstow would have the possibility of leaving under the terms of the voluntary redundancy package. The T&GWU was of the view that this should apply to all staff and had written into the document its intention to pursue this through legal channels.

[11] Thin gruel. And there was a failure to generalise across the fleet what had been achieved.

Despite the absence of redundancy payments if no jobs could be found for the 160 Walthamstow drivers who, at the request of the T&GWU, had not signed the new contracts, there was a return to work on 29th July. Management at Walthamstow rubbed salt into the wound by granting the 12 strike breakers a week's paid leave and then allowed no overtime or rest day working at the garage.

On 3rd September the Company agreed a pay increase of 3% at Ash Grove and Clapton garages, and on 16th September London Forest announced that the company would cease to exist from 22nd November 1991. Leyton garage would remain open and pass to the East London LBL company while Ash Grove would close instead and Clapton would pass to the Leaside company. Walthamstow would close and its routes operated from Capital Citybus's new depot at Northumberland Park, where the T&GWU sought recognition. They paid more than Forest had proposed, but still less than before the tendering. Eventually, all surplus staff were slotted into vacancies, albeit at different garages.

The 1988-9 Annual report states that in the 11 bus companies plus London Coaches set up as LBL subsidiaries on 1st April 1989 "improved staff communications are helping to develop a teamwork culture which in turn is helping to raise morale".

Grey-Green Volvo single decker No. 855 on route 20. Note 'London Transport Service' sticker in windscreen

This would be laughable if it were not so tragic. The 1989-90 Report says that LBL had secured only 60% of routes put out to tender. Recruitment had also been decentralised. The 1990-1 Report notes that a Government consultation paper contains a plan for deregulation and privatisation of LBL. The subsidiary companies now negotiated their own pay and conditions and further "cost savings" were achieved by re-tendering of routes.

Privatisation

Another Government consultation document "A bus strategy for London" was issued on 11th March 1991. It proposed to privatise the LBL bus subsidiaries and their 50 garages and deregulate London's bus routes. Public money was spent to update the fleet. While LRT Chairman Sir Wilfred Newton was disappointed that the Government did not in fact deregulate the buses, some senior LT officers warned that chaos would result if the Government went ahead [12]. In October 1993 a campaign sponsored by the T&GWU, TSSA, the London Region Passenger Committee and private bus operator Grey Green, and supported by leading Conservative MP Robert Adley, convinced the Government not to deregulate in London. But they reiterated that privatisation would take place in 1994 and instead of tendering companies being given a fixed price to operate London bus routes with LRT receiving all revenue, operators would have to bid for the minimum subsidy from LRT that they considered necessary to make the service viable. The 10 Companies, owning 4,600 buses operating 75% of the network were sold to private companies or management buyouts for a total of £220 million. London Transport now no longer operated buses but retained the statutory duty to ensure that the private companies provided a 'suitable' level of quality and service, establishing LT Buses on 1st April 1995 for this purpose in place of LBL. Wallace notes that "under the new regime the overwhelming majority of employees experienced a worsening of their conditions of service" [13].

LT Catering produced 30,000 meals a day at 77 outlets with approximately 500 staff. LRT decided in November 1992 to withdraw from in-house catering and this was implemented in March 1993. Gardner Merchant took over the 28 Underground canteens. 70% of the staff were offered jobs and 25% took them up. Contracts for bus canteens were awarded by each subsidiary and went to Sovereign, Sutcliffe, Gardner Merchant, CCG, Compass, T&M and AGM. The canteen at 55 Broadway was taken over by ARA and all existing staff there were offered jobs (LT News 29th April 1993).

There was a plan to privatise the Central Line but this was thwarted by technical problems, or the cost of solving them. British Rail Engineering Ltd (the about to be privatised former Derby Works) was awarded a contract for new trains (report in 25th July 1991 LT News) and Westinghouse Brake & Signal Co. received a contract for a new moving-block signalling system and automatic operation of trains. Unfortunately for LUL this did not work effectively and had to be abandoned. And when the new trains began to arrive in 1992 it was quickly realised that they were unreliable and expensive to maintain. So the privatisation plan was quietly shelved and the still nationalised LUL had to shoulder the cost of making good an expensive mistake. Private companies, we learned, are highly risk averse and will only take on contracts if the profits are guaranteed and investments have been made in advance by the public sector at taxpayers' expense. No more has been heard of Underground lines being privatised.

Also in 1991, Cleaning Services won the contract for cleaning of 8,000 bus stop flags on competitive tender and had a contract with LT Advertising for cleaning bus shelters.

In LT News No 402 30th January 1992 we learn that Streatham bus garage was to close on 13th March following loss of 3 routes in the tendering process. Its other routes are to be transferred to other garages. A 'reduction' of 100 drivers, 50 engineering and 50 management, supervisory and administrative jobs resulted. Redeployment of staff, 'natural' wastage and voluntary redundancy were used to deal with the 'surplus' employees.

Privatisation continued apace. Staff who were privatised had benefitted from Union representation and the pay, if not good, was generally better than similar jobs outside along with a staff pass and pension provision which would not be available in the private sector. LT ceased to be a bus operator. Cleaning on the Underground was about to be privatised under the Company Plan (see Chapter 20) and the horrors of PFI (Private Finance Initiative) and PPP (Public Private Partnership) were about to be let loose.

CHAPTER TWENTY

THE LUL COMPANY PLAN AND THE PRIVATE FINANCE INITIATIVE

New dawn or false dawn? The cover of the Company Plan

The changes set in train by the formation of LRT in 1984 also had a major impact on the Underground. As we have seen, the old corporate paternalism of the Combine with its emphasis on service to the public was swept away and replaced by a financially driven aggressive management style with many more managers. The privatisation agenda was driven forward relentlessly, but in a different form to that on the buses. The European Union, in a Directive of 29th July 1991, had imposed on railways a split between operations and infrastructure which was designed to introduce an internal market to encourage privatisation. This idea was enthusiastically embraced by British governments of both political hues, although other governments in the EU were able to circumvent the worst aspects by more or less ingenious methods. Following the Central Line fiasco the operating side would be left alone, but the infrastructure was seen as ripe for privatisation. The Company Plan of 1992 pulled all these ideas together.

It was presented to the Unions on 26th November 1991. "In return for financing a major programme of capital expenditure on the Underground in preparation for privatisation the Government expected LUL to deliver wage productivity gains" as Griffiths puts it. Staffing cuts of 19%, amounting to 5,000 redundancies were proposed, saving £150 million per year by 1996. LUL staff numbers would fall from 21,000 to 16,000 and total LRT staffing would fall to 42,700. ASLE&F members voted 74% to oppose the Plan, demanding no compulsory redundancies, no worsening of conditions and that safety remain the top priority.[1] However, LT News 401 of 19th December 1991 says that voluntary severance packages were offered with a lump sum of up to 90 weeks' pay – a highly attractive offer for staff with long service. An augmented pension package for those aged 55-59 years with at least 5 years member-ship of the pension fund was offered. The Railway Negotiating Committee (RNC) met on 8th January 1992 to discuss the Plan. The key features were:

- An end to the seniority system for covers and promotion
- Station grades to be reduced to two with new rosters
- Cleaning Services to be closed with contracts to be placed externally
- Train maintenance job 'demarcation' to be ended with the merger of workshop and conciliation staff into teams of 8-12 with mixed skills
- Promotion to skilled grades from lower grades to be permitted
- Depot shunters abolished – train maintenance staff to do their own shunting
- Train maintenance on one line to go out to competitive tender
- Signals productivity to be improved by 15% with multi skilling and better supervision (more managers). Booking on to be at the work site to save travel-ling time
- Train crew productivity to be increased by flexible rostering and changed booking on procedures, preparation of trains for service to be done by depot staff instead of train crew
- The paid meal break for operating staff to be replaced by an unpaid break
- Acton, Lillie Bridge and Ealing Common workshops to be merged with most cuts falling on Lillie bridge
- DLR ownership to be transferred to the London Docklands Development Corporation following direction from the Secretary of State
- The Machinery of Negotiation to be changed to reflect the merger of shops and conciliation – the end of the 1921 Staff Councils Scheme.

The new structure to be:

> Wages Board
> Central Negotiating Committee
> Directors Committees for passenger services and engineering
> 10 Line and 4 Functional Committees for each business centre
> Local Committees

- All staff to become salaried - equal status at last, the end of hourly pay and all bonuses – the salary to incorporate all unsocial hours payments, Sunday enhancements and London Weighting. All overtime to be paid at time plus one quarter. All staff to be paid four weekly by direct credit – staff to open their own bank accounts. The abolition of timekeepers.
- Changes to pay relativities which reduced the pay of senior booking clerks and some senior rolling stock staff in particular (my grade, Leading Carriage Examiner Callpoint, was abolished and I lost £5,000 per year, for instance), but increased the pay of others, effectively dividing the workforce.

The TSSA balloted its members on LUL who overwhelmingly rejected the proposals. LUL refused to go to ACAS (Advisory Conciliation and Arbitration Service) for mediation and reaffirmed their policy of avoiding compulsory redundancy and using voluntary severance, providing the Unions co-operated. Any industrial action would result in withdrawal of the voluntary severance offer and compulsory redundancy with much less favourable statutory rates of payment. They also threatened to withdraw paybill deduction of Union dues from any Union that took industrial action. This did happen with the RMT; paybill deductions (known as check-off) were a commercial arrangement, with the Union paying management for the service. Fortunately for the RMT withdrawal of checkoff coincided with the change from cash pay to direct credit, so members who did not have bank accounts rapidly had to open one. The RMT had a very difficult time during the transition, losing a lot of dues income, but eventually managed to get all its members signed up to pay their Union dues by direct debit. The TSSA, normally a moderate Union that avoided industrial action, balloted its members and received a 77% vote for strike action, albeit on a 39% turnout, noting that this was an indictment of LUL's management style. TSSA members were advised not to sign new contracts – all staff had been told that they would have to re-apply for their own jobs, and on 16th November 1991 employees were threatened that refusal to sign would lead to dismissal.[2]

The EC of the RMT (National Union of Rail Maritime and Transport workers, formed in 1990 following the merger of the NUR and the National Union of Seamen) on 2nd March 1992 noted it had received support from representatives for the EC's instruction to them not to participate in any consultation or negotiation on the Company Plan, but recognised that management had started to implement the Plan piecemeal anyway, particularly in the rolling stock depots. A failure to agree the new Machinery of Negotiation at the RNC led to a decision on 13th April to ballot RMT members for strike action. The result, announced on 7th May 1992, was 69% yes and 30% no on a 65% turnout. The RMT sought a meeting with the other railway Unions and decided to 'educate' the general public that the Plan was a "detrimental step".

Talks commenced on 5th June and, on the 18th, management proposed to terminate the Machinery of Negotiation. Sectional Councils could continue to deal with uncompleted matters (given the glacial pace this took some time) but no new items would be accepted. All new items would be referred to the new CNC (Central Negotiating Committee) on an ad-hoc basis. The RMT sought the views of its branches and met the other TU's. On 21st July 1992. they accepted the new Machinery, which provided Functional Committees for Trains, Stations, Train Maintenance, Signals and Permanent Way, with lay representatives at Levels 1 and 2. The Unions gained concessions on the Company Plan and it was agreed in principle in August, but by 27th October there were still some outstanding issues with it. LUL refused to go to the Wages Board (arbitration) and proposed to implement the Plan on 1st November without agreement. The RMT balloted again and the result, announced on 17th November 1992, was 74% yes, 24% no on a 55% turnout. Following discussions at ACAS a joint statement agreed to working parties being convened and reference to the Wages Board if no agreement was reached – the strike was called off. Members who stood to receive large voluntary severance payments were, of course, opposed to a strike, and this internal opposition weakened the RMT's position. Finally, on 3rd March 1993, the new Machinery, including representation for administrative staff, was accepted. But the industrial strife was not finished.

On 21st May 1993, LUL gave formal notice that the existing RNC (Conciliation) and JNC (Workshops) machineries would end after 11th June and 11th August respectively. The Union Head Office officials were very defensive about the Staff Councils scheme, which as we have seen was a comfortable environment for them. But the scheme had long been discredited among the lay representatives and the membership and Union officials were forced to accept that no-one was going to take action to defend it.

In the mid 1970s the Sectional Council representatives for traincrew (No 3) and station staff (No 4) had been granted full time release from work as the members they represented were spread out all over the Underground system and all did shift work. The representatives were given offices at 55 Broadway. Sectional Councils No 2 (booking office staff) and No 6 (operating supervisors) had similar arrangements. The advantages of having staff representatives on hand to deal immediately with industrial relations issues that arose and to represent staff at Disciplinary Boards were appreciated by management as much as by the rep's, but the downside for the Unions was that the rep's could, and sometimes did, become almost part of management. Under the terms of the Staff Councils scheme, as analysed in detail in chapters 3 and 5, rep's were not officially Trade Union rep's and could not be forced to carry out TU policy, although the Unions did their best to ensure that they did and would deselect those who stepped too far out of line. It could be a comfortable life for those rep's who allowed themselves to be drawn in by management. Certainly, by the end of the scheme many staff were highly dissatisfied with the system, especially if they had rep's who rarely if ever visited their workplace.

On the engineering Sectional Councils (No 5 Engineering supervisors, No 7 Signal Engineering, No 8 Permanent Way and No 9 Mechanical Engineering wages grades, mostly rolling stock) only the Chairman and Secretary had full time release and no office accommodation was provided. The other rep's had to apply to their manager for time off as and when it was necessary. I was a rep on Sectional council No 9 from 1975 to 1993, other than my spell on the NUR National Executive in 1988-9. Almost all the people I represented worked shifts, as I did myself, and were spread out over myriad work locations and shift patterns. Some were grouped in depots, some worked in small groups or alone at outstations and sidings, some were on permanent nights. Keeping in contact with them and giving report backs on negotiations was a logistical nightmare. Management were unwilling to grant time off with pay unless there was a meeting with management scheduled. Even then it could be difficult especially if I was on nights. But with support from the NUR/RMT meetings would be cancelled if rep's such as myself were not granted release with pay. We would say 'if you're not willing to release the rep. from night duty you will have to defer the meeting until he's on days'. In particular, at first if release from night shift was granted it would only be for one night. Imagine the effect on your metabolism (which takes 48 hours to adjust from days to nights and back again just like jet lag), not to mention the dangers of tired staff working in a safety critical environment. It took decades of struggle to achieve 2 nights off to allow sufficient rest and recovery time (meetings were always called during the day of course as management never worked nights). Management from a workshop background were particularly inconsiderate in this respect. In the workshops shop stewards were always in the depot on permanent day work and could easily temporarily drop whatever work they were doing to deal with staff issues or attend meetings.

The nature of my work as a carriage examiner and later a train technician was such that even if I was on days I could not just drop it to do TU duties for part of a shift as we were subject to and responsible for the timetable. Supervisors and Duty managers made it very clear to higher management that if I was granted release for rep's duties it had to be for a whole shift so they could arrange for other staff to cover my work. If I was on a rest day when required to do rep's duties it could be difficult to get a deferred rest day (we worked at least one weekend in two and had rest days during the week to compensate).

Many of the maintenance staff on the Underground regard themselves as the forgotten army, hidden away in remote locations and often on night shift. None more so than the Pump Staff who maintain the pumps that operate 7/24 to keep the Underground from flooding. So important is their job that they are always exempted from any strikes that are called. So it is doubly important that their often hazardous work locations are visited periodically by Union Health and Safety rep's as the management never go near them; I have done my share of visits to pump sites, fans, lift and escalator machine rooms and the like, often at night.

The new machinery eased these problems by allowing a greater number of rep's, but it is not always easy to find members who are prepared to become rep's as the amount of disruption to personal life and inroads on your own spare time is considerable. Union meetings, for instance, are not usually eligible for paid time off. Not everybody is willing to stick their head above the parapet and stand up for their fellow workers.

With nearly all conciliation staff working shifts to provide 7/24 coverage changes to shift patterns are always a sensitive issue. Our trains do not run at night so that much of the maintenance work on track, signals and rolling stock can be done during the shut down period. Some train crew and station staff also work night shifts so that the crew who bring in the last trains (up to 0130 or so) are there to put the first ones into service from 0430. Similarly, the staff who close the stations at night are there to open them in time for the first trains in the morning. When I started in the rolling stock depots staff worked either 2 shifts (days and nights) or 3 shifts (nights

– lates – early). A major issue was that the 3 shift staff never had a Saturday rest day and worked 2 Sundays out of every 3 as part of their rostered week. When I was first elected to Sectional Council in 1975 this was the first issue members wanted dealt with. A colleague and I developed a radically different shift pattern using 4 shifts to give a built in rest week and this pattern continues to this day at some depots. Other depots have elected to have 2 long 12 hour shifts per day – it is important to allow people to choose shift patterns that suit them, although obviously this has to be done collectively as everyone in any particular depot has to work the same pattern.

The other big issue when I was first elected was that there was no minimum rest period between shifts laid down – you could 'double back' with as little as 6.5 hours rest (including travel time to and from home). We found that the Victoria line had an agreement for a minimum 7 hour break between shifts so started off by negotiating for this Victoria line agreement to be extended to all depots. Then we gradually over a period of many years got the minimum break extended until we achieved 12 hours, which we considered a reasonable time for travelling and rest (sleep). Then the European Union (EU) came out with the working hours directive which said that the minimum rest period should be 11 hours. LU management immediately tried to reduce our agreed 12 hour period to 11 hours. It took a great deal of tough talking to prevent them from taking away our hard-won conditions. Brussels had laid down a minimum figure, not a maximum.

As previously mentioned, before the Company Plan promotion and higher grade cover was on the basis of suitability with seniority (not purely seniority as has sometimes been claimed). Those applying for promotion had in some cases to undertake training and pass a test and in all cases go before an interview panel to ensure their ability, or suitability, to do the job they had applied for. This was no formality. Applicants were entitled to have a TU rep. on the panel to ensure fair play. I sat on many promotion panels and it was very tedious, because as a TU rep. you were not allowed to participate or contribute – you just sat and observed to ensure there was no favouritism or discrimination. Those who passed the panel would then be offered the job in order of their seniority in their existing grade. With the Company Plan all this was swept away and cases of favouritism and discrimination re-appeared. There was an upsurge in claims of racial discrimination in particular and measures had then to be taken to set up committees and commissions to deal with this.

The RMT did manage to extract a commitment from management to negotiate the Company Plan through the existing Machineries. Early meetings of the RNC, JNC, RWWS (Workshop Supervisors) and RWWSJNC took place, followed by local discussions. The industrial action was suspended by RMT and TSSA, and ASLE&F called off its planned ballot. An increase in pay and London weighting of 4.5% was accepted. The new machinery of negotiation started to function.

In 1993 LUL and BR imposed unannounced drug and alcohol testing for all staff. Those who failed would be dismissed and were liable to custodial court sentences. The Unions had never condoned drug taking or excessive alcohol consumption but these measures were considered to be too harsh. Industrial action on BR was proposed for 5th March 1993. The EC of the RMT decided not to ballot LUL members. LUL stated that the testing was non-negotiable under the Government's Transport and Works Act, though this was arguable. The policy remains in force.

The RMT then sought an urgent meeting with LUL on job loss, the threat of compulsory redundancy and, crucially, utilisation of private contractors. Finally, on 23rd February 1994 a ballot was called over voluntary redundancy and increased use of private contractors. On 11th March LUL offered further talks. On 14th April the ballot result of 63% yes 36% no on a low turnout led to further meetings after which LUL gave an undertaking of no compulsory redundancy and to treat competitive tendering as a negotiable item, to be listed at the CNC (Central Negotiating Committee).

The 1992-3 Annual Report says that the train maintenance depot put out to tender (Stonebridge Park) had been won by the in-house team. It was noticeable that many local managers were opposed to privatisation and worked hard to keep work in house. Some even joined the RMT! Increased performance, as the Report puts it, following the Company Plan, had led to the reduction of staff by 2,200 "without industrial relations problems". This is stretching the truth somewhat. The massive disruption and unrest I have recorded above apparently did not qualify as an industrial relations 'problem' because no strikes actually took place.

LT News 437 of 15th December 1994 reports that a deal worth £400 million had been signed for new Northern Line trains. Since its founding in 1933 LT had been barred from building its own trains so supply of new stock from private manufacturers (usually Metro Cammell in Birmingham) had been the norm for many years. But this contract was different in two ways. To start with, it was the first large

Trainee Train Operator at Golders Green Depot, 2002

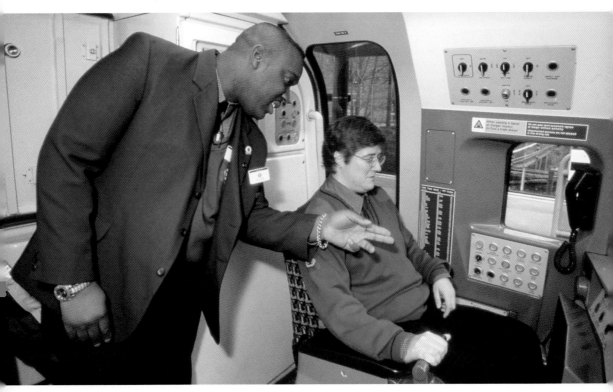

scale use of the Private Finance Initiative (PFI). This idea was conceived by the Conservative Government in the forlorn hope that if private finance could be utilised for public infrastructure projects the risk would be transferred from the public to the private sector and the cost would not count against the Public Sector Borrowing Requirement (PSBR) which was restricted by EU rules. They were wrong on both counts. The private sector charge ruinously high rates of interest and profit levels to take on the risk, yet opt out and demand Government money when unforeseen costs arise (as with the Channel Tunnel for instance). And the EU eventually ruled that if the project was for a public enterprise then the cost would after all count against the PSBR whether or not it was financed privately. Similar projects in the NHS and education sector have saddled those services with crippling debts. Second, the deal won by GEC-Alsthom was of the then fashionable all in Design-Build-Operate-Maintain type, so train maintenance at Golders Green and Morden depots would be privatised, including train cleaning. The 20 year train service contract would also cover specialised trackside equipment, depot plant, CCTV etc.

The RMT EC looked at the proposal on 27th April 1994. The positive side was that the stock would be built at the former BR Works at Derby, which although now privatised was still Union organised with many RMT members. But they set a policy that maintenance should be by LUL members and a ballot was set for 28th September 1994 to keep maintenance in-house. On 1st November LUL stated that they could only commission new stock under the Government's PFI and under their catchy but insulting 'happy to stay – happy to go' policy TUPE would apply to the pay and conditions of staff transferred. Faced with the threat of privatisation of what it considered a 'mainstream' railway activity the RMT made a crucial change of policy.

Previously public campaigns and promises by Labour Party leaders had failed to prevent privatisation or restrict the worsening of pay and conditions. Cleaning Services, mainly stations and other buildings, and train cleaning, had been privatised under the 1992 Company Plan. Local RMT representatives campaigned hard for the retention of cleaning in-house but were told by management that the cost under the private company would be half what they were paying for the in-house service. As almost 100% of the cost of cleaning is wages it followed that wages were going to be halved. Almost none of the existing staff chose to transfer to the private company under these conditions. TUPE was not applied and the RMT did not pursue it. The RMT found that industrially powerful groups like train drivers and signallers were not willing to take action to defend their less fortunate colleagues in cleaning, canteens or other areas.

Having lost these privatisation battles local representatives in the RMT, and in the T&GWU at some garages, were unwilling to accept pleas from Labour Party figures to wait for a Labour Government, or the platitudes of full time Trade Union officials who followed that line. They could see that the issue for a Union was to defend the wages and conditions of their members here and now whether privatised or not. One of the problems for full-time officials was the difficulty of negotiating with a plethora of small companies when they had been accustomed to a small number of meetings with one big nationalised employer. After many internal battles the RMT began to adjust to this reality, helped greatly by the ousting of General Secretary Sidney Weighell in 1982 for falsifying the Union's vote at the Labour Party conference, and his replacement by the left wing Jimmy Knapp. From a highly bureaucratic, centralised, top-down Union the NUR changed into a much more flexible member-led organisation which was better able to respond to the new situation, with local representatives taking a more prominent role. Gradually, with considerable difficulty and much hard work the Union was able to gain recognition at some of the private companies, as it had on the DLR, and improve wages and conditions, a process which continues with the RMT.

The difficulty for the T&GWU, as Ken Fuller implies, was that the entire new structure on the buses needed to be challenged head-on while they still had fleet wide pay negotiations and organisation. Having not engaged then they had a lot of difficulty adjusting to the new privatised world they found themselves in. Divisions proved fatal despite some heroic fights like London Forest in 1991. A very senior member of bus management who was involved in the whole privatisation process, whose name I am not at liberty to reveal, told me that management were surprised at the lack of fight from the T&GWU. He said that although the T&GWU could not have stopped the privatisation process they could have made a fight over pensions and gained a much better deal overall. Their organisation, he said, was good but they were let down by internal divisions, and their full-time officers did not seem to be comfortable negotiating with 12 separate companies. Overall, management thought that the T&GWU 'rolled over'. Hard words, but telling.

So, on 15th March 1995 the RMT took the crucial step of pledging to defend every job and condition of service, whoever the employer, and to secure from LUL and GEC-Alsthom an agreement that if any members are deemed surplus by GEC-Alsthom they are to be unconditionally re-employed by LUL. On the 'make or buy' policy for outsourcing engineering and depot maintenance functions, on 9th May 1995 the RMT EC laid down a policy to "seek an agreement with LUL that guaranteed the jobs of all our members whether the work transferred out of LUL or not". The fight would be not against privatisation as such but to defend members from the effects of privatisation and try to pin responsibility on LUL. The Northern Line privatisation issue was then linked in to this overall company-wide policy. On 13th June 1995 it was decided to ballot all LUL members on job security. By a 4 – 1 yes vote engineering members voted to strike against 'make or buy' and they struck on 27th July, while an overall one day strike took place on 3rd August and another was called for 8th August. Note that learning from experience, not least that of the miners' year long strike, the policy was for one day stoppages to cause maximum effectiveness at minimum cost to the members.

On 26th July 1995 the RMT re-balloted on job security and pay and conditions of service, with a 6% pay claim added. Further meetings with management took place following similar votes at Railtrack and BR. LUL offered 2.75%. Ann Burfutt, director of Human Resources, said nurses had got 3%, teachers 2.7% and civil servants 2.5%. On 17th August 1995 the RMT announced another successful ballot result and strikes were called for 25th August, 1st September and 4th September. On 24th August 1995 the RMT declined to go to ACAS due to management's "total failure to address our claim and their intransigence". The key issues were: paid meal breaks, abolished under the Company Plan, banking up of the reduction in the working week to give increased leisure time, job security in the face of privatisation, replacement of full time by part time jobs, the self financing cut in hours, the break up of collective bargaining and its replacement by personal contracts.

The 27th July 1995 LT News reports that Court action had prevented a strike by ASLE&F on the grounds that their ballot said there should be no industrial action if there was an improved pay offer and LUL had upped their offer to 3%. The RMT withdrew its strike action and on 'make or buy' the company reiterated assurances on job security. The 28th September issue of LT News says that ASLE&F and TSSA accepted the 3% pay offer. The RMT had held 3 one day strikes but LT News says around 60% of the service operated. A further 48 hour strike from 1200 noon on 20th September was called. But this had to be suspended as a Court injunction claimed that new members who had joined since the ballot could not be called upon to strike. The RMT EC on 22nd September 1995 "note the decision of the Court and reluctantly comply with the order". The injunction was later overturned by the Court of Appeal as the members had joined in full knowledge that a strike was to take place, and in many cases because they wanted to strike.

Yet another successful ballot result was recorded on 24th October 1995 and a 3 day strike called for 7-8-9th November, rescinded on 13th November.

Finally, the 23rd November 1995. issue of LT News reports that the 5 month dispute had ended with the RMT settling for 3% and improved conditions regarding job security. It says it was "agreed to protect staff outsourced on the Northern Line contract by a scheme which will give them additional payments to the statutory minimum should they be made redundant by their new employers". "A register has been set up for outsourced staff who might be displaced allowing them to be considered for LUL posts along with redeployed staff". LT News 449 of 18th December 1995 says 178 staff at Golders Green and Morden depots had moved to GEC-Alsthom in a £400m deal under the 1981 TUPE Regulations on 26th November 1995. The staff remain in the RMT, in the same branch as their colleagues in other LUL depots, following another internal row in the RMT, whose full time officers had thought it more convenient to transfer them into the branch at Derby.

Other privatisation projects
Meanwhile, LT News 440 of 23rd March 1995 had reported that under 'make or buy' the ICC Company had taken over LUL's technical services department with 30 staff transferred. And on 22nd June 1995 No 443 reports that bids had been invited for the new Railway Equipment Workshop at Acton.

The 1993-4 Annual Report notes that total permanent staff numbers are now down to 34,921, a reduction of 9,000 over 4 years following privatisation of London Buses. Medical Services, payrolls, property valuation, and staff training were all put out to tender, with the closure of the highly effective White City railway training centre soon to follow.

Further PFI projects were undertaken. The biggest was the almost 10 mile long Jubilee Line extension to Docklands. Olympia & York, the property company that developed Canary Wharf, was supposed to contribute £400 million but became insolvent and eventually only paid 5% of the bill. The project was put on hold for 18 months while alternative financing was sought. Various technical difficulties caused expensive delays, especially the 'moving block' signalling system that was developed by the Westinghouse Company. This had already failed on the Central Line and had to be abandoned. You might have thought that the Company would take responsibility for this failure, but under Government pressure LUL picked up the tab rather than suing Westinghouse. If they had been put out of business 3,000 jobs would have been lost at their factory in Chippenham, Wiltshire. The eventual cost when the line opened in 1999 was nearly double the original estimate. LUL managers complained of communication difficulties with contractors and lack of information, problems which were to dog other PFI projects. Labour relations, of course, became the responsibility of the contractors and managers were no longer able to directly control or supervise staff. Union negotiators noticed that without the unlimited resources of Government behind them, private companies could be more amenable to reaching settlements and any disputes were quickly settled without recourse to industrial action.

The control room at Lots Road Generating Station in 1997

The next PFI was for Power Supply. A 30 year contract worth £1 billion was awarded to Seeboard Powerlink, private successor to the South Eastern Electricity Board in 1998 and LUL's generating station at Lots Road in Chelsea was closed. Subsequently EDF (Electricite de France, owned by the French Government) bought up the company, leading to jibes that our power generation was privatised by the British Government and nationalised by the French Government. But LUL found it was cheaper to re-nationalise it themselves and exercised its option to terminate the contract in 2013 after 15 years. It estimated that the initial cost would be more than offset by significant savings in future years. The staff, members of the engineering Union AUEW, now part of UNITE, and the RMT, had to cope with considerable upheaval and changes in working practices. The principle of getting back into a unified LUL was welcomed, but the practicalities of working for a private company were not all bad as long as they retained their strong Union organisation.

Also in 1998 the new 'Prestige' smartcard ticketing system was built by the Transys Consortium. The £1 billion 17 year PFI contact was again terminated early, resulting in considerable savings. The operational and managerial convenience of having these functions in-house generates great savings while the profits and other payments levied by private contractors do not have to be paid. Another large PFI contract was let in 1999 for the new 'Connect' integrated train radio system, valued at £475 million. Various other smaller PFI's were also entered into.[3]

The 1993-4 Annual Report says that at the beginning of the year there was some industrial unrest following the introduction of revised bus operating staff pay rates and conditions of service.

On 1st April 1994 LT Buses was created to procure safe reliable and efficient services for passengers says LT News. "LBL continues to exist to manage the subsidiary companies until they are sold". The Tendered Bus Division joins LT Buses and 20 'surplus' bus garages are to be sold. The successful and profitable LT Advertising was incorporated as a separate subsidiary in November 1993 in preparation for it to be sold.

The 1994-5 Report continues the same refrain. LT Advertising was sold to the American TDI Company for a cool £100 million. The 10 remaining bus operating companies were sold and now ran services under contract to LRT. Centrewest, East London, Selkent and Leaside were sold in September 1994, Metroline, London Central and London Northern in October 1994 and South London Buses in January 1995. LT News 443 of 22nd June 1995 tells us that Victoria bus garage has been sold off as "surplus to requirements" and the proceeds from sale of 20 bus garages were expected to be £45-50 million. The 26th October issue tells us that a shortage of bus drivers had forced the London General Company to recruit from Plymouth, Devon – nothing to do with pay cuts, then? The Report says that an operating profit of £40 million had been achieved with no requirement for revenue grant from the Government and wage costs were below those for the previous year.

If you thought you may need to rest and recover from all the bad news, the 25th May 1985 LT News reports that the Fonthill Convalescent Hotel in Torquay, owned by the Transport Benevolent Fund, was to close as it was under-used and loss-making. 16 jobs were lost.

CHAPTER TWENTY-ONE

THE PUBLIC PRIVATE PARTNERSHIP

Natural light maximised at Canary Wharf station

When the Labour party returned to Government in 1997 the commitments to re-nationalisation of public services like transport had been abandoned along with Clause Four of the Party's constitution, removed in April 1995. But it was clear that the PFI was an expensive mistake that needed to be dealt with. So the idea of the Public Private Partnership was cooked up. The theory was that the private sector would provide the money and the public sector (the Government) would determine the policies. Unfortunately in the real world finance always determines policy and the price of bringing in private finance remained very high, with long term contracts, high rates of interest, and complex but expensive financial dealings. If Government could understand them at all it was powerless to control them for fear of bringing the entire financial edifice crashing down. In practice the PPP was no different from the PFI. Transaction costs arising from the need to have a structure for administering relations between the different companies and sectors which resulted from the marketisation of what had been a unified, collective organisation, were enormous even before any legal disputes broke out, and were not factored in to the costs. With the disappearance of an overall cohesive management structure the client side, which was supposed to set overall policy, enforce standards and control costs, became severely weakened. The structure has been described as one where those with responsibility have no power and those with power have no responsibility. Many managers who disagreed with the policy left, and many others joined the private contractors.

The partial privatisation of the Underground under the PPP was announced in early 1998 by the same John Prescott who, as an MP sponsored by the RMT, had earlier promised the re-nationalisation of the parts of the railway privatised by the Conservatives. Operation and the freehold of the infrastructure would remain with LUL while maintenance, renewal and investment would pass to the private sector. The rail unions had campaigned unsuccessfully against the privatisation of BR in 1992-3. The 'Employment' laws prohibited industrial action for what the Courts deemed to be 'political' ends, and action against privatisation was considered to be political. So just as in the fight against the PFI the RMT decided to focus its campaign on the specific job implications of privatisation under the PPP. In 1998 the RMT, this time without the support of the other rail Unions, balloted its members for action on 6 demands:

1. Staff to remain employees of LT.
2. Preservation of terms and conditions of employment.
3. Preservation of contracts with the current employer.
4. Opposition to splitting up current work.
5. Preservation of current disciplinary procedures.
6. Preservation of the machinery of negotiation.

Having won a 6 – 1 majority a 48 hour strike was called for June 1998. Despite the RMT going it alone, services on some lines were reduced to a third of the schedule and it was considered worthwhile to put up a fight against privatisation. A further 24 hour strike took place in July, but then action was put on hold in the hope that ASLE&F could be brought on board. John Prescott, a long-time member of the RMT and its predecessor the National Union of Seamen, left the Union when the RMT AGM passed a resolution demanding that sponsored MP's who did not oppose privatisation should have their sponsorship withdrawn.[1]

24 hour strikes called for New Year's Eve 1999 and 3/4th January 2000 were stopped when LUL won a High Court injunction banning them on the grounds that the time taken between negotiations and the calling of the strikes was too long (did they want us to strike over Xmas?). A new ballot was held and a 48 hour strike took place from 14th February 2000. But no progress was made against the PPP and in May the RMT held a referendum of its LUL members which showed overwhelming opposition to the PPP plan. Despite resistance from industry professionals who could see the pitfalls and excessive costs, and opposition from the travelling public, the PPP was pushed ahead.

Since the abolition of the GLC in 1986 London had been the only major city in the world without any overall administration or leadership, all functions being devolved to the 32 boroughs in a vicious and spiteful act of vengeance by Prime Minister Thatcher. The Labour Government, in the GLA Act of 1999, set up an elected assembly for London under a directly elected Mayor, who would have overall responsibility for transport in London through a new body called Transport for London (TfL). LRT was abolished and LT was back under municipal control. The former leader of the GLC, the left wing Ken Livingstone, stood for Mayor, and part of his platform was the rejection of privatisation of the Underground infrastructure. But despite a year-long battle with the Labour Government the PPP was still pushed through. In the first elections for the new 25 member Greater London Assembly (GLA) transport was a major issue. Conservative policy was for the full privatisation of LUL and they opposed the PPP on this basis. The Liberal Democrats called for the Underground to remain in public hands financed by a bond issue, like New York and some others. Livingstone and the London Labour Party opposed the PPP, not without serious rows inside the Labour Party which led to Livingstone standing as an independent and winning. Frank Dobson stood for Labour, supporting the PPP. Labour won 9 seats in the Assembly election, the Conservatives 9, Liberal Democrats 4 and Greens 3.

The Government then ruled that TfL, now controlled by Mayor Livingstone, could not take over from LRT until the PPP was in place as LUL still belonged to the Government despite being a subsidiary of TfL. Even the Evening Standard campaigned against the PPP. A Trade Union rally against PPP was chaired by noted transport journalist and campaigner Christian Wolmar. Mayor Livingstone announced an independent enquiry into the PPP chaired by Chief Executive of the Industrial Society Will Hutton, which concluded that PPP was poor value for money and would jeopardise public safety. But he did believe that PPP "offered the prospect of significant efficiency improvement". Livingstone then appointed former New York subway chief Bob Kiley as Commissioner of TfL. He produced another report on PPP which concluded that "the basic structure is fatally flawed", giving TfL little control over the privatised Infraco's (Infrastructure Companies) and no right to select a new contractor in order to remedy serious mistakes. Kiley and Livingstone now also supported the issuing of bonds as the most effective means of financing LT, just like the LPTB set up of 1933.

Months of meetings between John Prescott and Ken Livingstone then ensued to try to reach a compromise. All this time, of course, staff were expected to continue running the service in an atmosphere of great uncertainty. Central policy and financing was up in the air with no clear direction.[2]

In spring 2001 the RMT and ASLE&F called three one day strikes against the threat to jobs and safety which the PPP posed. The two Unions jointly tabled 4 demands:

1. Establishment of a joint body of employers and unions to oversee maintenance and safety.
2. No compulsory redundancies.
3. Staffing levels to be agreed by the unions.
4. Employees to remain on existing terms and conditions with their existing employer unless agreed otherwise.

TfL and LUL rejected the demands and the Unions balloted for strike action, the RMT gaining an 83% yes vote and ASLE&F 74%. TSSA and AEEU (Amalgamated Engineering and Electrical Union) chose not to ballot their members. But before the planned strikes were to take place the Government announced on 2nd February 2001 that the disagreements over the PPP had been resolved. Livingstone claimed that problems over safety had been settled and that the PPP could now be accepted. It was widely though inaccurately claimed that Prescott had climbed down. The Unions were not reassured.

The RMT ballot had received a massive 9 – 1 yes vote. LUL again took legal action, this time using rules brought in by the Labour Government requiring the Union to give full details of the exact work location of every member. On a railway, with constant movement of staff between jobs and locations through covering vacancies, transfers and promotions, this is difficult. Not all of the RMT's 7,500 members on the Underground remember to tell the Union when their work location changes, which may be only a short term change anyway. Some think the management tell the Union when staff move, which they do not.[3] Furious at the denial of their democratic vote and knowing that they had a great deal of support among Londoners the anger of RMT members turned to defiance. The Court injunction did not apply to ASLE&F, whose strike went ahead on 5th February 2001. Many thousands of RMT members struck unofficially, leading to 90% of trains being cancelled. RMT General Secretary Jimmy Knapp condemned the Court ruling, saying that it made it harder, not easier, to conduct a legal ballot. The Evening Standard admitted that many commuters were supportive of ASLE&F's action. Talks led to LUL agreeing the first demand, for a joint cross-company safety body. ASLE&F suspended the strikes planned for 12th and 19th February. The RMT lost its appeal against the court injunction and balloted its members again, this time securing an 11 – 1 yes vote. It called another strike for Thursday 19th March 2001.

Further talks between a new transport minister and Ken Livingstone were said to be progressing well. ASLE&F reached agreement with LUL and called off their strikes. Suddenly the talks became deadlocked. Commissioner Bob Kiley had very reasonably demanded the power to define capital investment priorities, approve Infraco work plans and budgets, direct changes in Infraco's work and directly control all maintenance activities that affect train movements (my job as Train Technician fell into this category). Prescott called these demands "wholly incompatible with the key risk transfer and performance management characteristics of the PPP".[4] The Government again decided to press ahead with the PPP. A furious Mayor Livingstone denounced the decision as "a show of contempt for the overwhelming views of London". TfL launched an application for Judicial Review of the PPP.

The RMT strike went ahead on 29th march 2001, supported unofficially by many ASLE&F members and LUL could only run 25 of their scheduled 500 trains. Negotiations started at ACAS where the TUC General Secretary John Monks and future General Secretary Brendan Barber intervened, presumably at the behest of the Labour Government, and tried to get the RMT to call off the strike planned for 3rd May. Four hours before it was due to start the RMT EC did call it off, but workplace representatives meeting a few days later opposed this decision and rejected LUL's inadequate offer. Two 24 hour strikes were called for Monday 4th and Wednesday 6th June 2001, just before a general election on 7th June. The Labour Government were furious. The Evening Standard denounced the action, characterising the demand for no compulsory redundancies as 'jobs for life'. No mention of TUPE was made.

Learning from their experience of the PFI LUL staff were determined to retain their TU organisation and fight against any cuts to wages and conditions. The RMT's opposition to the cuts and privatisation agenda of the Labour Government finally led to the Union's expulsion from the Labour Party in January 2004 as it refused to revoke a motion allowing branches to support some left wing candidates who were standing against Labour on a programme of no cuts.[5]

The PPP was implemented by dividing the Underground infrastructure into 3 Infrastructure companies - Infracos's – Jubilee Northern and Piccadilly Lines (JNP) in one, Bakerloo, Central and Victoria Lines (BCV) in another and Sub-Surface Lines (Metropolitan, District, Hammersmith & City & Circle, East London – SSL) in the third. LUL continued to operate trains, stations and signals., calling itself the 'Opsco' (Operating Company). It collected the fares and paid a fee – the 'Infrastructure Service Charge' – to the Infraco's, which would be leased to private companies. Chancellor Gordon Brown claimed that the private sector would bring "a wide range of managerial, commercial and creative skills to the provision of public services". But the 1997 LUL Annual Report argues cogently that it would "reduce the seamlessness of the network and increase the risk of things going wrong at interfaces". The Health & Safety Executive also cautioned that the potential loss of safety increased as the Underground's structure was subdivided.[6]

The effect on infrastructure staff was to reinforce their determination to maintain their strong Union organisation, now almost entirely the RMT in the areas of rolling stock (where I worked), signal engineering, permanent way (track) and lifts & escalators. The changes to grading introduced in the Company Plan of 1992 had grouped all non-skilled grades in rolling stock together as 'Train Maintainers' (TM) and all skilled grades as 'Advanced Train Maintainers' (ATM), with the possibility of promotion from TM to ATM. The Amalgamated Union of Engineering Workers were unable to prevent this, which took away their control over entry to the skilled grades, and they responded by starting a recruiting drive among the non-skilled TM grade. Unfortunately they posed as 'the Union that does not go on strike' as against the 'strike happy' RMT. This was a bit rich after their extended strike action to defend their rights back in 1969, and most staff could see that the RMT's strikes were their only means of defending themselves against the effects of the PPP. The AUEW's policy backfired spectacularly, with most skilled staff gradually joining the RMT, which up to then had respected the TUC's Bridlington rules and had not attempted to organise the skilled grades. The RMT also offered a specialised structure for LT with officers dealing solely with LT.

Shadow running of the Infraco's prior to privatisation began in September 1999. The 'Performance Specification' was lost customer hours, expressed as Notional Accumulated Customer Hours (NACH). This complex system rated every station according to how many 'customers' used it in the peaks and off-peaks, which was then multiplied by the number of minutes delay to provide a figure for the NACH. This was then allocated according to the cause of the delay, causing many disputes between departments, the Opsco and the Infraco responsible, which was then charged an 'abatement' fee which reduced the payment it received.

Passengers did not like being reduced to the status of 'customers' who were only as good as the fare they paid. This change was symptomatic of the shift from a service-based ethic to a financially driven commercial approach. Incidentally, the most expensive station on the entire system was Gloucester Road Eastbound in the morning peak hour because a delay there can lock up the entire District and Circle lines in both directions. It fell within my area of responsibility as Train Technician so I was involved in a lot of the disputes that took place.

All rolling stock staff were re-interviewed for their jobs at this time, under threat of dismissal if they refused. Craftsmen had to agree to become multi-skilled – any who disagreed were reduced to the TM grade. In most cases the interviews were a formality as most managers wanted to keep loyal and experienced staff. Enormous pressure was put on staff to minimise delays and shift responsibility to other areas, particularly the Opsco. My job as Train Technician was right at the interface between the Infraco and the Opsco. The situation became ridiculous when we were instructed to wear an Infraco high visibility jacket instead of one with the familiar LT logo by which passengers could identify us as members of staff. We were told not to become friendly with LUL staff, with whom we were working closely every shift. This was a crazy policy as a railway, like most work environments, relies on co-operation between different members of staff. They tried to place us in a confrontational position, which we resisted. As a Union representative I was singled out by a particularly vindictive manager and accused of not being loyal enough to Infraco SSL as I was in the same Union as some of the train drivers. For a while I was withdrawn from the callpoint to the depot, but they could not reduce my pay. Subsequently a less narrow minded senior manager reinstated me. Staff and managers spent a great deal of time discussing and arguing out the allocation of failures and delays. The cost of this process was estimated at £677,114 per year.[7]

Customer 'ambience' was the other key determinant of payments to the Infraco's. This was measured by 'mystery shoppers'. LUL retained the right to require refurbishments of stations, the cost of which was to cause massive problems once the Infraco's were privatised. The financial benchmarks were set at 5% below existing standards, an extremely generous financial offer to the companies which allowed services to the passengers to deteriorate.

The Government blunted Commissioner Kiley's opposition to PPP by appointing him Chairman of LT, which put him in charge of negotiating the PPP contracts. Mayor Livingstone now talked of helping the PPP along [8], and started denouncing senior LUL managers, several of whom left to take up lucrative appointments with the soon to be privatised Infraco's. The Government, in the form of the transport minister, ordered LUL to concede the so-called 'jobs for life' guarantee of no compulsory redundancies to avoid a strike just before the election. The negotiation of staffing levels, protection of terms and conditions and not transferring the Infraco's to private employers while the PPP was still under discussion between Government and Mayor were all conceded. Having achieved these assurances the RMT called off the strike but continued to campaign against the PPP.

Labour won the election. On 3rd July 2001 Commissioner Kiley told new transport minister Stephen Byers that he could not agree contractual terms with the bidders because "there is a yawning chasm between this convoluted 30 year privatisation and the single point accountability for investment and service delivery that the Underground's passengers deserve".[9] Two days later Byers told Parliament that he would now impose the PPP and the following day the Health & Safety Executive endorsed the PPP safety case. Byers then sacked Kiley as LT Chairman on 17th July 2001. Metronet and Tubelines were the 'preferred bidders' for the contracts. Metronet was a consortium of rolling stock manufacturer Bombardier (who had bought up Adtranz), Seeboard, Balfour Beatty, Thames Water and Atkins. Tubelines consisted of Amey, Bechtel and Jarvis, describing themselves as operational and project management organisations, along with French based rolling stock manufacturer Alsthom, who had acquired GEC.

Meanwhile, Livingstone's legal challenge to the PPP was ruled out, as was an application for judicial review. In October 2001, following the collapse of the privatised Railtrack, the PPP bidders 'persuaded' LUL that they should be liable for only 5% of their debts if anything went wrong. 5%! Byers agreed that the Government would underwrite 95% of their loans, guaranteeing up to £33.7 billion. The Infraco's then signed the PPP contracts on 8th May 2002. Expectations of work to be done had already been lowered – 61 station modernisations instead of 196, and less work on track, yet with still higher charges.

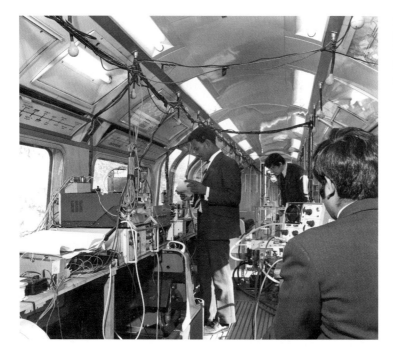

1967 Tube Stock used for testing Westcode brake for new rolling stock, 1971

The engineering side of LUL, the so-called infrastructure, was divided into three. To call rolling stock and attention to trains in service 'infrastructure' was stretching the term but it was included nevertheless. The sub-surface lines contract was won by Metronet, as was the BCV contract. The JNP contract, which included the already privatised Northern Line and Jubilee Line train maintenance contracts and the Emergency Response Unit (ERU) which provided cover for the whole of the Underground, was won by Tubelines. Concerns over the negative safety and engineering implications led to calls for more action, and following another 9 -1 vote the RMT again struck on 17th June 2002, again unofficially supported by many ASLE&F members. A further strike that Autumn by both Unions did not directly address the issue of PPP. The Tubelines contractors signed on 31st December 2002. following Government assurances that they would reimburse the Infraco's for any losses incurred from any delay caused by Ken Livingstone's legal challenges – yet another Government bribe using taxpayers' money to smooth the process of privatisation. The two Metronet contracts were signed on 5th April 2003.

In June 2003 the RMT decided on a threefold campaign. First, a political campaign for renationalisation, second a review of the membership and a plan to retain the member base in the privatised Infraco's, and third a campaign for pay rises, shorter hours, improved pensions and equal staff travel facilities across Metronet and Tubelines.

The fight put up by the Unions had not stopped privatisation but had ensured that the transfer did not adversely affect terms and conditions of staff. Experience with the Northern line train maintenance privatisation under the PFI had shown the effectiveness of keeping the privatised staff not only in the same Union but in the same branch. Their wages and conditions, with the notable exception of pensions, were kept in line with those of the still-nationalised staff on the other lines and when these in turn were privatised the companies were unable to worsen wages and conditions. A separate negotiating structure was put in place for each company which was very similar to that which had existed when we were still in LUL. It gave a greater degree of control to locally elected lay representatives as the Unions were unable to provide full time officers from head office for the large number of meetings at the many separate companies. This suited us very well as we had sufficient able local rep's and we could still call on the Union at Head office level if necessary.

The three consortia were given 30 year contracts during which they were expected to maintain and improve the infrastructure as well as providing trains for service and maintaining the 'ambience', which included cleanliness of trains and stations. The Tubelines contract was further complicated by the fact that it took under its wing the Northern Line train maintenance contract already privatised under the PFI and the Jubilee Line train maintenance also previously privately run under a separate PFI. Despite separate negotiating structures the RMT kept the members in the same branch and various struggles ensued to keep their wages and conditions broadly in line with those on the Piccadilly line and the Metronet contracts. The most difficult of these struggles was over pensions. After major battles by the RMT Infraco staff were allowed to remain in the LT Pension fund, albeit in a separate section. But immediately after privatisation Tubelines closed its section to new recruits and after a couple of years the LT Pension fund was closed to new entrants from Metronet. New staff were obliged to join the Tubelines or Metronet pension funds, whose benefits were inferior. Tubelines had been indemnified against pension cost rises in the first 7.5 year period of its contact and had its contribution to the LT Fund's deficit refunded in respect of staff employed at the transfer date. The RMT felt it had an obligation to existing members at time of transfer, but was not prepared to go into a battle to protect future employees who may or may not join the Union. This allowed two tiers of pension provision to be established which over time weakened the position of the members who could stay in the LT scheme. This division was controversial within the Union although the provision offered to new employees in the company schemes was still superior to what was available elsewhere. This was to remain a major bone of contention when Metronet was effectively re-nationalised in 2008 and Tubelines in 2010.

One of the major components of the Tubelines consortium, Amey plc, was acquired by the Spanish Ferrovial construction company as early in the contract as April 2003. A sub-contract to maintain communications systems on the Jubilee Line was awarded to the Marconi Co. and a contract to replace or refurbish 150 km of track, all work previously done in-house, went to Grantrail Ltd and Trackwork Ltd. Staff and managers in all three Infraco's noticed that bureaucracy and buck-passing increased greatly and the time taken to get faults fixed got longer. A surge in the number of breakdowns, points failures, track problems and missed reliability targets accompanied the companies' takeover in 2003. The House of Commons Transport Committee noted that despite benchmarks set at 5% below performance levels under LUL the companies' performance was 'abysmal' and they had 'no confidence' that the Infraco's would meet future targets. LUL rejected Tubelines plans for station enhancements as 'inadequate' and TfL complained that Infraco's were failing to invest in new equipment. New LUL Managing Director Tim O'Toole complained that he had very little power to do anything about it[10].

But it was the staff on the trains and platforms who were the butt of passengers' justified complaints and unjustified violent attacks. When you are the one wearing the orange hi-vi you are the target, as I found personally on many occasions. Complaints by Union representatives to management elicited the response that they were powerless to do anything about it – the companies kept a tight rein on finance at the very top level. Lack of clarity in the contracts as to who was responsible for repairs and other 'non-programmed' work led to delays and disagreements while staff just had to 'get on with it' and do the best they could. Problems particularly affected signal maintenance, track maintenance and 'ambience' ie cleanliness and graffiti removal. Sub-contact and agency staff were insufficiently trained and supervised, leading to frequent failures and delays. In my personal experience a project to refurbish and improve the air-operated train doors on the District Line led to frequent failures and delays. The weakened 'client side' had passed the work as 'satisfactory' despite obvious failings, so the sub-contractor who did the work escaped blame. Metronet permanent staff, inherited from and trained by LUL, had to completely redesign and rebuild the door operating mechanism.

Some agency staff were engaged on a 'self employed' basis with no sick pay or holidays. Protection Masters, responsible for the safety of people working on the track, were contracted out with in some cases dangerous levels of incompetence resulting, of which again I have personal experience. Delays also resulted from additional precautions taken by permanent Metronet or LUL managers to protect their staff from the consequences of these dangerous practices. Although management were loth to admit it, they knew that this could not go on, and the financial cost was high and rising. Staff discontent with the situation was also rising and sooner or later there was bound to come a crisis point.

Trains on the Central Line were still suffering from the serious mechanical problems with gearboxes and motor mountings which had scuppered the full privatisation of the line planned back in 1992. Under Metronet the frequent safety-critical inspections required to keep on top of these problems were being carried out by agency staff working long hours of overtime. The problem came to a head when a motor fell off causing a train to be derailed at Chancery Lane on 25th June 2003. It was fortunate that no-one was killed. The cost of the derailment, £40 million, was almost entirely borne by LUL with Infraco BCV, now owned by Metronet, responsible for just £100,000, having had an 'indemnity' at the point of transfer. The Central and Waterloo & City lines were suspended. Then a District Line train was derailed at Chiswick Park on 14th June as a result of a motor breaking loose due to failure of the 'Huck' bolts. Further derailments on the Piccadilly Line at Hammersmith on 17th October 2003 and on the Northern Line at Camden Town only two days later on 19th October, resulting in seven passenger injuries, were blamed by LUL on job cuts and use of sub-contractors. Track inspections had been reduced from every 24 hours to every 72 hours. The on-call senior project manager for the Hammersmith area was a consultant for a third party whom LUL had difficulty locating. The convoluted process for reporting defects was blamed by both RMT and ASLE&F for the failure to check reported defects in time, or in some cases at all. Repair gangs were obliged to do only the specific work that was on the 'job ticket', rather than look at the job as a whole and use their initiative to do what work was necessary as before. This was a 'work to rule' imposed by a financially driven management.

The RMT EC on 24th October 2003 noted: "It is clear that the contracting out of infrastructure maintenance to Metronet and Tubelines has created a crisis of confidence in the system." The RMT demanded, among other things, of LUL, Metronet and Tubelines assurances that:
- The standards that applied for infrastructure and maintenance prior to the transfer of the Infraco's, including 24 hour track inspections, will be restored straightaway and that where defects are found, immediate speed restrictions are put in place
- That the standards are not changed unless agreed with the TU at Company Council level
- That there are no staffing reductions unless agreed at Company Council...and that all...vacancies...be advertised and filled

The assurances were not received and a ballot for industrial action was organised. The results were:

for a strike 1,673 yes, 1342 no; for action short of a strike 2,427 yes, 577 no. On 20th November 2003 members were instructed to drive trains at a maximum speed of 25mph, to close congested stations, to work to rule and to ban overtime.

A working party was set up to review track patrolling, fault reporting and fixing. From 1st December the number of night track patrol staff was restored from one to two per section and on 11th December the RMT called off its proposed industrial action. Guess what? Nothing happened until yet another derailment on 11th May

2004 near White City on the Central Line. The points had been identified as potentially dangerous following the Camden Town derailment. Again the PPP contract exempted Metronet from fines and the H&SE (Health and Safety Executive) decided not to prosecute Metronet, so there was little incentive for them to fix problems [11]. Metronet staff showed they were not willing to have their wages and conditions threatened by striking against a 2.4% pay offer in Summer 2004, gaining 3.6% which was in line with what their LUL fellow workers had gained.

When Metronet ordered new rolling stock from Bombardier for the Sub-Surface and Victoria lines in 2003 it attempted to include maintenance of the Victoria line stock in the contract, which would have entailed transferring staff to Bombardier on inferior conditions. (TUPE protection was as good as useless as companies can change employment contracts with 90 days' notice). RMT resistance managed to put this idea off but then in 2005 Metronet proposed to transfer all its fleet maintenance staff to Bombardier. Although we already worked for a private company (Metronet) such a transfer could only have resulted in our further isolation from colleagues working for LUL and was resisted fiercely. The overwhelming majority of fleet staff were members of the RMT and in a ballot a large majority voted for strike action. Worried about the cost of any industrial action Metronet agreed not to outsource any current work to another company and that a proposed re-organisation would not cause any compulsory redundancies. They also dropped a plan to sell off the REW (Railway Equipment Works) at Acton following RMT resistance. But seeing a loss of potential profits Bombardier challenged the dispute settlement and in 2007 Metronet again tried to transfer staff to Bombardier.

Then in September 2005 tripcocks, which stop a train if it attempts to pass a signal at danger, began to fail on the Northern Line. The PFI maintenance contract with Alsthom was still in place operating as a sub-contract to the main Tubelines maintenance contract. ASLE&F and RMT insisted on a second person travelling in the cab with the driver to monitor operation of the tripcocks and LUL issued an 'Emergency Direction' requiring Tubelines to audit the work of Alsthom and rectify the faults. But the system failed again and ASLE&F and RMT announced a ballot for industrial action. The line was suspended for three days while every train's tripcock mechanism was checked. TfL Commissioner Bob Kiley demanded the termination of Alsthom plc's PFI contract and complained again that lines of authority were not clear under the PPP. LUL admitted that repairs had been more difficult because of the complex PFI and PPP contracts. LUL Chief Operating Officer Mike Brown wanted to put 'our' engineers in and bypass Tubelines where necessary [12]. LUL issued Tubelines with a 'Corrective Action Notice' in December 2006.

Maintenance staff, twice privatised, undermined by sub-contractors, pension provision cut and treated with contempt by management were expected to pick up the pieces.

TfL and re-elected Mayor Ken Livingstone planned to extend the East London Line north to Hackney and south to Herne Hill, but it was packaged up with the already privatised North London Line. The 157 staff could stay with LUL only by transferring to other lines when the East London Line closed in 2007. When the extended line was opened in 2010 it was privately owned and operated.

Despite frequent failures to maintain property or deliver upgrades on time Metronet and Tubelines continued to pocket large profits and bonuses. Frequent complaints and attempts at corrective action by TfL and LUL ran up against the appall-ingly one sided contracts that Government had foisted on them. Mayor Livingstone called Metronet a 'consortium of nightmares'. But the two Infraco's did not collapse. Metronet's refurbishment work at Putney Bridge station was described by District line General Manager Bob Thorogood as 'very disappointing and unacceptable'. Then another derailment on the Central Line between Mile End and Bethnal Green on 5th July 2007 was blamed on incomplete training, guidance and documentation for the gang which had left materials unsecured. The gang included employees of at least 6 different contractors, all with different policies and powers.

On 18th July 2007 Metronet said it could no longer afford to meet its obligations and called in the administrators. Despite having been effectively given a licence to print money it had paid out massive profits to its constituent companies and their shareholders. Then when even a little financial responsibility for its multiple failures came home to roost it went bust and left the publicly owned and financed TfL and LUL to pick up the tab. Mayor Livingstone was in no mood to bail out Metronet.

The station refurbishment projects had involved much more work than Metronet had planned for and the maintenance failings on trains and track had been expensive – LUL blamed Metronet for inefficiency but it was not that simple. A Metronet insider told Janine Booth that Metronet were obliged to pay their sub-contractors whether work was done satisfactorily or not on the expectation that, having a 95% indemnity against loss, they would always be bailed out by the publicly funded LUL ie the tax and fare payer [13]. Metronet froze recruitment and planned to axe 290 clerical posts and up to 200 temporary and agency jobs. RMT workplace representatives condemned Metronet for "poor project management, chaotic financial control and deskfilling". Having an effective Union behind them staff were not intimidated by Metronet threats of looming insolvency. We knew that their financial situation was precarious and reminded them of it frequently. Previous struggles under the private regime had given us confidence that we could defend ourselves. To be effective we knew we did not need the big battalions of the train drivers and signallers.

PPP supporters in the Government and the employers' organisation Confederation of British Industry (CBI) insisted that it was Metronet that had failed, not the PPP, and were seeking another company to take Metronet's place. Staff knew that the whole PPP set-up was rotten and were not prepared to tolerate more unsafe practices, more attempts to undermine working conditions. TfL stated that while the PPP was not the policy of their choice they thought it was not unworkable. Mayor Livingstone had abandoned his campaign against PPP. The PPP would not collapse of its own accord so we knew action had to be taken against Metronet, who were after all our employer. The Unions demanded no loss of pension rights, no job losses and no forced transfers to another employer (Bombardier were still hoping to take over train maintenance). Metronet Chief Executive Andrew Lezala, in an act of desperation, addressed mass meetings of staff, calling for loyalty to Metronet with the implicit threat of being transferred to Bombardier if Metronet collapsed. I was present in the mess room at Ealing Common Depot when he addressed us. He said if we went on strike the abatements they would have to pay LUL would bankrupt the company (already in administration). It took 3 seconds to sink in – a shout went up – OK, we'll go on strike. We made it clear that we wanted to return to LUL and that any sell-off to Bombardier would not be tolerated.

The RMT balloted its 2,700 members in Metronet – only 70 voted 'no'. TSSA and Unite (incorporating the former Engineering Union AUEEW) also balloted, indicating the strength of feeling. RMT and Unite called two three day strikes, the first starting on 3rd September 2007, the second a week later. Metronet offered some assurances on pensions, jobs and transfers and TSSA and Unite called off their action. But the RMT continued. London was shut down. LUL cancelled all services. They were aware of the safety implications of trying to keep lines open and the likely refusal of traincrew to work on safety grounds. Following a letter from the Mayor TfL agreed to secure Metronet staff's pensions in full and the Metronet administrators pledged no job losses or transfers during the period of administration. The strike was ended following negotiations in which I was involved. We had been handing in a petition at the Department of Transport in Marsham Street when General Secretary Bob Crow told us that Metronet had agreed to talks. I was one of a team of negotiators under a full-time officer immediately despatched to Holborn where the talks were to take place. The problem was there were no trains to get us there as we were on strike. We jumped on a bus which got stuck in traffic in Whitehall. Our officer asked the bus driver to radio his control, who informed him that the whole of central London was gridlocked. So we got off the bus and walked to Holborn, where in another interesting side effect of marketization the management team were waiting for us in a commercially let office suite. Metronet's Headquarters at Templar House, just round the corner, was apparently too expensive to hire. The team we met were from LUL, not Metronet, reflecting the realities of the situation. After nearly 9 hours of talks, without refreshments of any kind, they agreed our demands, the deal being described by the Evening Standard as 'gold plated'.

Yet, almost unbelievably, at a report back meeting a few days later some fleet workplace representatives accused us of selling out because there was no written guarantee that staff would not be transferred to Bombardier. The fact that the meeting had been with LUL management seemed evidence enough that we were to be taken back into LUL. Despite great efforts by the Government no private firms had come forward to take over from Metronet; perhaps they realised that now the reality of the PPP had been exposed rich pickings would no longer be forthcoming, especially with an effective Union ready to take action to defend its members.

Further battles ensued as Bombardier insisted it 'owned' some Metronet employees. Employees who had started since Metronet withdrew from the LT Pension Fund still did not have access to it or full travel passes. A backdated 0.75% pay increase was also still outstanding. A further 48 Hour strike from 28th April 2008 was necessary to win these final points.

It took until November 2007 for the Metronet administrators to finally announce that TfL was the only company interested in taking Metronet over. Metronet was still charging LUL a hefty price for the use of its staff. Its responsibilities were not finally transferred back to LUL until May 2008 and the transfer of its employees back to LUL was not made permanent until September 2009. The uncertainty did nothing to smooth the course of staff relations. Metronet tried to halve the frequency of signal maintenance and a one day strike on 5th February was necessary to stop them imposing new rosters which would have reduced signals staff's take home pay. In 2009 maintenance costs were cut by £60 million and a strike threat was needed to secure a pay rise. But eventually ex-Metronet staff did obtain full LT Pension and travel facilities and were re-integrated into the LUL negotiating machinery, although with woefully inadequate representation rights. An RMT pamphlet of 2013 says re-integration of Metronet into LUL saved £53 million in 2012-13.

One of the continuing casualties of the shambolic PPP scheme was, and remains, the Sub-Surface Lines resignalling scheme. The contract was placed with Westinghouse in April 2003 under the PPP. When LUL regained control the contract was cancelled on the grounds that it was over-priced. LUL decided to re-scope and re-tender and a new contract was awarded to Bombardier (!) in June 2011. Their Cityflo 650 Automatic Train Control system was said to be a 'proven product'. But by September 2013 it emerged that 'significant challenges' remained and the project was in serious trouble by November 2013. LUL decided that the only way work would be completed would be to find another contractor. So in January 2014 the contract is being put out to tender again, with Siemens or Thales the likely bidders. Westinghouse, owned since 1999 by Invensys, was acquired by ....Siemens in 2013 although the factory at Chippenham had previously been closed. (Information from 'Informed Sources' e-Preview February 2014).

Those who argued that Metronet was the problem and that the PPP was a good system claimed that the Tubelines contract was successful but the facts belied this. Although Tubelines avoided the spectacular collapse that ended Metronet, it was experiencing problems in delivering upgrades on time. A strike took place in 2008 to secure a pay deal. The Jubilee Line upgrade, due to be completed in March 2009 was not completed until well into 2010, at the cost of dozens of weekend closures and massive cost overruns. Tubelines was criticised for slowness in responding to problems. Its signalling contractor Thales, who had taken the project over from the failed Westinghouse system, had 'significantly underestimated' the scope and complexity of the project. Tubelines continued to demand more money from LUL – the Piccadilly line upgrade was at risk along with 75 station upgrades.

Eventually the 'Arbiter' ruled that LUL should pay Tubelines more but LUL's estimate of what it should pay was still £463 million short. Eventually independent arbitration dismissed Tubelines' claim as 'labyrinthine, artificial and unconvincing'. However, LUL would still have to fund the shortfall from its own budget. Having forced Metronet to the wall the same was not going to be allowed to happen with Tubelines. The Transport Minister refused to allow TfL to borrow more, expecting them to plug the gap by cutting back on planned upgrades. The arbiter did not coun-tenance bankrupting Tubelines, which would have brought it back into LUL free or at lower cost. On 7th May 2010, the day after the election, TfL paid £310 million to Bechtel Corp. and Amey plc to buy their shares in Tubelines. Conservative Mayor Boris Johnson said "the great advantage is we no longer have to accede to Tubelines' requirements" but activists pointed out that having paid a lot of taxpayers money to get them to take on the contract in the first place we were now paying them even more to get out of it.

But if Metronet had been eventually re-integrated back into LUL, Tubelines continued to be operated separately [14]. Pensions were a particular bone of contention that has still not been settled. The Northern Line train maintenance PFI continued, and staff who had joined the company had joined the Alsthom scheme, then the Alstom scheme (no 'h') when the company was re-structured. So far they have not been allowed to re-join the LUL scheme, of which some of their colleagues who were employed before the privatisation are still members. The separate Jubilee Line PFI was 'TUPE'd' across to Tubelines in 2012 and Jubilee Line staff are in either the Alstom or Tubelines schemes. Overall about 50% of Tubelines staff are in the Tubelines scheme and 50% in the LT scheme. Now that Tubelines is finally part of TfL again the RMT is trying to get all staff into the TfL pension scheme.

Cleaning staff unfortunately have not yet been brought back into LUL and remain employed by a variety of companies. But the RMT has worked hard to recruit cleaners and improve their wages and conditions. In 2007 part of Tubelines' attempts to save money involved it cutting the price it paid its cleaning sub-contractor ISS, which responded by announcing the loss of 200 jobs, but under pressure from the RMT and public opinion the threat was withdrawn. In June 2008 cleaners who were RMT members voted by 99% to strike for better wages, sick pay and holiday pay. The RMT called strikes on contracts held by ISS, Initial Transport Services, KS and GBM, winning a commitment to introduce the London Living Wage on what was then Metronet immediately and finally achieved on Tubelines in 2010. A resolution at the Fleet Maintenance branch of the RMT on 15th January 2014 concerning cleaners shows there is still much to do. It demands:

The end of contracting out, agencies and zero hours contracts.

Implementation of the London living Wage.

Improvements to pensions, sick pay, holidays and Union rights.

Power generation and distribution was brought back into LUL from UK Power Networks on 16th August 2013, saving more money, although supplies still have to be bought in as the Lots Road generating station will not be re-opened. The Greenwich reserve power station continues in LUL ownership.

In the canteens it is reported that dismissal of an RMT staff representative at the Sodexho company led to calls for a boycott of the canteens.

On the buses although the T&GWU, now part of Unite, has achieved recognition at the privatised bus companies wages and conditions vary from company to company and morale among staff is low.

In November 2012 2,000 bus drivers at Arriva North London voted to strike against the company's refusal to offer any pay increase. In 2013 a number of Drivers were sacked by Metroline for minor offences in an apparent attempt to get rid of long serving staff and replace them by lower paid new recruits following a Union agreement to new contracts which paid lower rates to new starters.

Attempts by the Union to achieve common wages and conditions across London are frustrated by the continuing tendering process. Individual routes, or sometimes small groups of routes, are tendered every five years with the possibility of a two year extension. Thus, 15-20% of the network is tendered each year. Quality Incentive Contracts are awarded to the company which wins the tender, which are supposed to encourage efficiency. The overall frequencies and routings are still regulated and determined by TfL through its London Buses subsidiary. Companies involved at present are Abellio (Dutch Railways), Arriva, CT Plus, Ensignbus, First, Go-Ahead, Metroline, RATP (Paris), Stagecoach, Sullivan, Transdev, Transit Systems (internet sources). These are not necessarily the fleet names which appear on the sides of the buses.

Rates of pay and conditions vary greatly. To the question 'how much does a bus driver earn?' there is no simple answer. An internet source says none of the major companies will give figures for an average pay week. Selective figures along the lines of 'can earn up to' are often given in job advertisements. The internet source gives the following useful summary based on the year 2009.

"Most of the operators have a minimum 38 hours guaranteed pay week. Each of the major operators in London pay different rates, for example my own company pay £13.25 an hour for a mid-week mid-day rate. This is further enhanced at weekends and after 9.30pm to £14.25. I get paid from sign-on to sign-off less one hour. So if I start at 6am and work until 3pm I work for 9 hours and get paid 8 hours. Other companies pay from sign-on to sign-off ie they include a paid meal relief, but this will mean a lower hourly rate. 'First' pays sign-on to sign-off but does not have any enhancements for weekend or evening work. London General only pay for 'driving time' so if your duty is scheduled to have a 1.5 hour break each day you would be paid for just that ie 7.5 hours on a 6am to 3pm.

"What makes it difficult to compare across the companies is the enhancements and meal relief payments in addition to the rotating shift pattern – I would get more money in my pay packet on a week of 'lates' than a week of 'earlies'. I have no way of knowing how many of the duties in your potential company have long spreadover duties for which you will not be paid, or how long the duties are in the companies that pay all the way through a duty.(Note that speadovers are still a major issue after all these decades). Arriva state that you can earn over £550 per week, but this would be working lates, long duties, including a weekend and probably working a rest day too.

"I earned £31,000 last year, this did not include rest days or overtime just following my rota (earlies, middles, lates). But I know people who earn £45,000; this means working 13 days out of 14 and as much overtime as you can get". Current Arriva pay rates are quoted as £35,000 to £45,000 pa.

However, an advertisement in my local newspaper for bus drivers at Heathrow Depot quotes a minimum of £400 per week, equivalent to only £20,000 pa. It says 'benefits include £10.50 per hour, 38 hour week, enhanced rates for Saturday/Sunday working, paid holidays, pension scheme, free bus and tube travel, free UK travel on Arriva buses'. (TGM Group advertisement in the Ealing Gazette April 4 2014). You would need to work an awful lot of overtime to get that up to a decent living wage considering the level of house prices and rents in London.

It is sometimes claimed that privatisation of the buses has increased efficiency and made bus operations profitable. This is a myth. Worsening pay and conditions for staff clearly improves the financial performance of companies, who make large profits, but Government figures show that these profits depend on a high level of Government subsidy. It has been clear since the 1960s that bus operation in London would not be possible without a subsidy, which repays itself many times over in the effective functioning of London's economy. Many Government spokespeople like to pretend that the company profits are achieved by efficiency rather than subsidy. Department for Transport statistics for 2012-3 show high and increasing levels of subsidy from central Government, including depreciation of capital:

Net public transport support (tendered or supported bus services) - £500 million
Concessionary travel   - £222m
Bus service operators grant   - £87m
Total subsidy   - £809m

This subsidy is set to reduce to £450 million in 2017-8 says GLA Transport Committee chair Caroline Pidgeon in a 2010 seminar 'the Future of London's buses'.

The TAS Transport Briefing of 4th July 2011 says that only 47% of the cost of the bus network was met from fares in 2009-10. The only year break-even was achieved was 1997-8 immediately following privatisation. This was done by depressing drivers' wages and 'pausing' investment in new vehicles during the privatisation process. LRT concluded that this was not a sustainable business model and attempts to break even were abandoned.

It is difficult for Unite to find local representatives on the buses, the unsung unpaid heroes without whom no Union can function effectively. The Union has a lot of work to do.

According to UNITE (the Union) in 2015 there are some 27,000 bus drivers in London working for some 18 bus companies. Pay rates vary from £9.30 per hour to £12.30 per hour. There are usually lower rates for the first year or more of employment so even on the same route drivers earn different rates of pay.

Having recruited a large majority of drivers in all the companies and won

Harrow Buses Volvo-Ailsa in 1988

recognition Unite lodged a claim for improvement of pay and conditions and an end to pay disparities across all 18 companies. However, Union complaints about the difficulty of negotiating with 18 separate companies unsurprisingly received short shrift from the Companies. Nevertheless, a strike across all the Companies, the first such since privatisation, was called on 5th February 2015 and received a high level of support from bus drivers. Independent social survey company MASS 1 recorded 66% of passengers supporting the Union's campaign.

Further strikes were called off as an 'Act of Goodwill' to allow talks to take place. And in August 2015 there the matter rests. No information on the progress of the talks has been made available. Bus driver activists are somewhat dispirited with the lack of progress and the momentum built up around the strike has dissipated. Most of the unpaid local representatives and activists who a Union relies on to communicate with and mobilise the members left the industry following privatisation. Competitive tendering of routes every five years leads to a continuing squeeze on pay and conditions.

The parallels with the struggles of railway workers in the 19th and early 20th centuries are striking (if I may use that word). The position of the railway workers was only attenuated by the requirements of the first world war.

NIGHT TUBE

London Mayor Boris Johnson announced that the Underground would run all night on Fridays and Saturdays from the night of 11/12th September 2015. This announcement closely followed his edict that almost all ticket offices would be closed. Taken together these two actions would have enormous consequences both for passengers and staff. The security and safety implications of exposing the remaining staff to often drunk and sometimes violent night time revellers need careful examination. The need to reschedule essential safety and maintenance work which can only be done when trains are not running in the tunnels seems not to have entered Mr Johnson's consciousness.

The Unions (ASLE&F, RMT, TSSA and Unite) took up all these issues with LUL management (the mayor having refused to talk to the Unions directly despite being responsible for these policy decisions). The Unions have never opposed the introduction of 'Night Tube' but have pointed out that the implications for staffing, safety and rosters take time to be resolved. But Mayor Johnson stuck rigidly to his implementation date of 12th September.

So the issue of 'Night Tube' is not a simple one. Several other issues are involved:

'Fit for the Future' – the name LUL give to their proposals to close nearly all ticket offices. This involves changes to job roles (in particular ticket office staff having to work in the open areas of the station), changes to staff rosters involving much more night and weekend work, staff being moved to other locations, reduction in staff numbers albeit with voluntary severance, and not least the provision of adequate protection for passengers possibly including an enhanced role for the British Transport Police.

The impact on infrastructure maintenance and renewal (track, signals, tunnels, trains, stations), much of which can only be done when trains are not running. Changes to maintenance schedules and staff rosters to allow 'Night Tube' have a major impact on staff and need to be treated sensitively, which can take time.

In addition, two other issues have become embroiled.

Train Preparation: Since the Company Plan of 1992 essential (and legally required) testing of safety and functional equipment on trains has been carried out by depot staff. This must be done at not more than 24 hourly intervals, normally at night when trains are not running. This was part of my job when I worked on the Underground. An issue has arisen over the attempted extension of the 24 hour period by management and the use of non-qualified agency staff to do the work. ASLE&F and RMT have referred the issue to the Office of the Rail Regulator who have launched an investigation. Meanwhile, ASLE&F have been threatened with legal proceedings for proposing industrial action on the issue.

The annual (or multi-year) pay claim: An offer of 1% plus £500 for 2015 and Retail Price Index (RPI) or 1% whichever is higher for 2016 and 2017, plus a £500 lump sum for all staff for night running, was made on 6th July 2015. LUL management demanded acceptance by 1830 the same day or the offer would be withdrawn. Just as in 1989, this ultimatum gave Union negotiators no time to consult let alone ballot their members. The RMT ballot had recorded a 91% yes vote for strike action and 96% for other industrial action (overtime ban). The days of TU Barons telling their members what to do are long gone. Members rightly insist that they should decide on major issues themselves. For Mayor Johnson to demand that the Unions put the latest offer to their members (BBC TV 6th August 2015) after this kind of behaviour by his management was insulting and inflammatory.

The offer was rejected by all four Unions and a 24 hour strike took place on 8th July. This is believed to be the first time all four Unions have struck together (the forerunners of Unite had not officially supported the 1989 strikes). A continuing overtime ban had a major impact.

On 30th June RMT General Secretary Mick Cash had asked LUL to delay the implementation of Night Tube planned for 10 weeks later to allow talks to continue and members to be consulted (LBC report). This plea was rejected by LUL. A further offer from LUL only re-packaged the offer of 6th July and did not change the situation. A further 24 hour stoppage started at 1830 hours on 5th August. All train services were cancelled by management on safety grounds and there was no attempt to run 'propaganda trains'.

Too late to stop the strike, although still refusing to talk directly to the Unions, Mayor Johnson helpfully indicated (BBC TV 3rd August 2015) that there may be some flexibility over the 12th September implementation date for 'Night Tube'. On this basis talks resumed following the strike and at the time of writing there is hope of a settlement.

Interestingly, the TSSA estimates that 'Night Tube' will not break even until 2033. Most Londoners will never use it and the level of support for its introduction appears to be limited. The RMT warns that it risks wrecking expensive infrastructure by interfering with maintenance work. Another consequence may be additional complete closures of sections of line so that the work can be carried out.

In hospitals and other areas where shift work is necessary and there is contact with the public it has proved increasingly difficult to recruit and retain skilled staff if wages and conditions are held down. Without adequate pay and conditions the transport sector risks facing the same problems.

CHRONOLOGY OF CHANGES OF CONTROL OF LONDON TRANSPORT

1933 LPTB	Government controlled, privately financed through bonds.
1948 LT Executive	Nationalised under BTC, Government financed
1963 LT Board	Nationalised, separated from BTC, Ministerial control
1970 LT Executive	Municipal control under Greater London Council
1984 LRT	Nationalised, Government financed, buses and trains separate subsidiaries
2000 TfL	Municipal control under London Mayor, Government financial control

I did not set out to write such a long book but I quickly realised that to set events since 1933 in context it was necessary to look back at the development of the buses, trams and trains, their Unions and the struggles they engaged in. As I did so a number of themes emerged:

- The strict separation of staff relations and Unions between the road and rail sides of LT, which continues to this day despite a short-lived attempt by some bus staff to change to the RMT.
- The changing fortunes of the two sides, the buses having been dominant for much of the period. I suggest that the change started with the new works programme of 1935-1948 which increased the importance of the Underground. This continued with the great loss of traffic after the war which affected the buses much more than the Underground. These changes had a gradual long term impact on labour relations and the relative strengths of the Unions.
- The impact of the municipal tramways and their staff, the significance of which has been underrated.
- The differing impact of privatisation on bus and rail. I would suggest that it was possible to privatise bus operations more easily than rail because of the relatively small capital inputs required which also allowed bus management to profit from it. The enormous sums required on the Underground led both PFI and PPP models to fail miserably and Underground management to be much less in favour of privatisation. The continuation of regulation of London's buses attenuated the negative impacts of privatisation.
- The differing ways in which the bus and rail Unions responded to privatisation and the challenges they faced.
- The continual changes in control and lack of long term consistent financing leading to extreme difficulty in long term planning and execution of large investment projects, and the lack of local input, let alone control, for long periods.
- The impact of the change from the paternalist corporate management style of the Combine and early years of LT, with its emphasis on service, to the aggressive, confrontational style that accompanied the change to financially driven management in the late 1980's.

Readers will draw their own conclusions.

Notes to Chapter 2

1. Bagwell, Dr Philip, The Railwaymen, Allen & Unwin 1963
2. Bagwell PP50 & 141
3. Bagwell P224
4. Bagwell P262
5. Bagwell P263/4
6. 1907 Royal Commission
7. Bagwell P268
8. Bagwell P268
9. Ken Coates, Notes towards a history of the T&GWU, chapter 10, unpublished
10. Bagwell P269
11. Bagwell P270
12. Bagwell P270
13. Bagwell P276
14. Bagwell P277
15. Bagwell P278
16. G.D.H.Cole A short history of the British working class movement, PP82 & 89,
17. Bagwell P277
18. Bagwell P282
19. Bagwell P284
20. Bagwell P285
21. Bagwell P286
22. Bagwell P283
23. Bagwell P295
24. Bagwell P299
25. Barker, T & Robbins, M, A History of London Transport, Vol 2, Allen & Unwin 1976, P137
26. Alcock, G.W., Fifty Years of Railway Trade Unionism, Co-operative Printing Society 1922, PP286-7
27. Barker & Robbins Vol 2 P139
28. Barker & Robbins Vol 2 P507
29. Barker, T & Robbins, M, A History of London Transport, Vol 1, Allen & Unwin 1963, PP274, 289
30. 1896 Booth Report, quoted in Barker & Robbins Vol 1 P289
31. 1890/91 Standing Committee, quoted in Barker & Robbins Vol 1 P289
32. Barker & Robbins Vol 1 P289
33. 1892 Royal Commission on Labour, quoted in Barker & Robbins Vol 1 P290
34. 1896 Booth report, quoted in Barker & Robbins Vol 1 P290
35. Fuller, Ken, Radical Aristocrats, Ishi Press 2011, P19
36. 1884/5 Royal Commission on Housing quoted in Barker & Robbins Vol 1 PP290
37. Barker & Robbins Vol 2, Allen & Unwin 1976, P320
38. Barker & Robbins Vol 1 P291
39. Barker & Robbins Vol 2 P315
40. Barker & Robbins Vol 2 P315
41. Barker & Robbins Vol 2 P316
42. Gordon, Alex, Unity is Strength, RMT 2012, P37
43. Gordon P55

Notes to Chapter 3

1. Barker & Robbins Vol 1 P25

2.   Barker & Robbins Vol 1 P31
3.   Fuller P25
4.   Barker & Robbins Vol 1 P39
5.   Barker & Robbins Vol 1 P61/2
6.   Barker & Robbins Vol 1 P50
7.   Barker & Robbins Vol 1 P60
8.   Barker & Robbins Vol1 P76
9.   Barker & Robbins Vol 1 P278
10.   Barker & Robbins Vol 1 P73
11.   Barker & Robbins Vol 1 P77
12.   Barker & Robbins Vol 1 P93
13.   Barker & Robbins Vol 1 P83
14.   Barker & Robbins Vol 1 P88
15.   Barker & Robbins Vol 1 P246
16.   Barker & Robbins Vol 1 P255 Quoting Herepath's Railway Journal 3rd March 1877
17.   Barker & Robbins Vol 1 P275
18.   Barker & Robbins Vol 1 P280
19.   Barker & Robbins Vol 1 P282
20.   Barker & Robbins Vol 1 P283
21.   Fuller P20
22.   Fuller P20
23.   Barker & Robbins Vol 1 P286/7
24.   Fuller P21 Quoting The Trade Unionist 6th June 1891
25.   Fuller P21 Quoting H.C.Moore Omnibuses & Cabs 1902
26.   Barker & Robbins Vol 1 P287/8
27.   Tramway Review No 232, December 2012
28.   Fuller PP24-25

Notes to Chapter 4
1.   Barker & Robbins Vol 1 PP187/8
2.   Barker & Robbins Vol 1 P190
3.   Barker & Robbins Vol 1 PP95, 192
4.   Barker & Robbins Vol 1 P269
5.   Barker & Robbins Vol 1 P270
6.   Barker & Robbins Vol 1 P282
7.   Barker & Robbins Vol 1 PP283/4
8.   Barker & Robbins Vol 1 P284
9.   Barker & Robbins Vol 1 P284 quoting Railway Times 20 June 1891
10.   Barker & Robbins Vol 1 P285
11.   ed. Terence Cooper The wheels used to talk to us – Stan Collins,a London tramway man
      remembers PP162/3
12.   Barker & Robbins Vol 2 P27
13.   Barker & Robbins Vol 2 PP88/9
14.   Barker & Robbins Vol 2 P97 quoting LCC Highways Committee 1896, 1897, 1898, 1899,
      1900.
15.   Barker & Robbins Vol 2 P97
16.   Barker & Robbins Vol 2 P99
17.   Barker & Robbins Vol 2 P189
18.   Barker & Robbins Vol 2 P153

Notes to Chapter 5
1.   Bagwell P539
2.   Bagwell P356
3.   Alcock P529
4.   Alcock P530
5.   Alcock P532
6.   Alcock P533
7.   Alcock P534

Notes to Chapter 6
1.   Bagwell P375
2.   Bagwell P396
3.   Bagwell P397
4.   Bagwell P398
5.   Gordon P58
6.   Gordon P60
7.   Gordon P61
8.   Bagwell P404
9.   Bagwell P404
10.   Bagwell P418
11.   Bagwell P410
12.   Bagwell P412
13.   Bagwell P412
14.   Bagwell P413
15.   Bagwell P380
17.   Bagwell P306
18.   Bagwell PP331, 334
19.   Bagwell P324
20.   Bagwell P426
21.   Bagwell P427
22.   Bagwell P429

Notes to Chapter 7
1.   Barker & Robbins Vol 1 P280
2.   Barker & Robbins Vol 1 P281
3.   Barker & Robbins Vol 2 P123
4.   Barker & Robbins Vol 1 P166
5.   Barker & Robbins Vol 1 P127
6.   Barker & Robbins Vol 1 P314
7.   Barker & Robbins Vol 2 P170 Quoting LGOC Board minutes 15.11.10.
8.   Barker & Robbins Vol 2 P189
9.   Fuller P26
10.   Fuller P26
11.   Fuller P32
12.   Barker & Robbins Vol2 P314
13.   Fuller P34
14.   Fuller P46
15.   Fuller P50/1
16.   Fuller P36
17.   Fuller P39

18. Fuller P40
19. Fuller P41 Quoting LVT Record 6th Dec 1916
20. Fuller P41
21. Fuller P42
22. Women workers in the first world war by Gail Braybon, Croom Helm 1981, PP80/1
23. Women Workers and the Trade Union Movement by Sarah Boston, Lawrence & Wishart 1987, PP122-3
24. Fuller PP43/4
25. Women in the Trade Unions by Barbara Drake, Virago 1984 (written in 1920), P149
26. Fuller P44
27. Fuller P37
28. Fuller P37

Notes to Chapter 8
1. ed. Cooper PP163-8
2. ed. Cooper PP166/7
3. ed. Cooper P167
4. Fuller P55
5. Fuller P73
6. Fuller PP74/5
7. Fuller PP75/6
8. Fuller PP76/7
9. Barker & Robbins Vol 2 P320

Notes to Chapter 9
1. Barker & Robbins Vol 2 P207
2. Barker & Robbins Vol 2 P214
3. Barker & Robbins Vol 2 P217
4. Barker & Robbins Vol 2 P219
5. Barker & Robbins Vol 2 P317
6. Barker & Robbins Vol 2 P318
7. Fuller PP58/9
8. Fuller P68
9. Fuller P80
10. Fuller P82
11. Fuller P65
12. H.A.Clegg, Labour Relations in London Transport, Basil Blackwell 1950 P15
13. Fuller PP82-84
14. Malcom Wallace, Single or Return, TSSA 1996, P176
15. Bagwell P413
16. Bagwell P419
17. Bagwell P422
18. Bagwell P434-7
19. Bagwell P443-4
20. Barker & Robbins Vol 2 P322
21. Bagwell P473
22. Wallace P190
23. Bagwell P474
24. ed. Cooper PP169/170
25. Fuller P86 quoting Phillips, the General Strike, London 1976 P333

26.   Fuller PP86/7
27.   Wallace P195
28.   Wallace P196
29   Wallace P200
30.   Fuller PP89/90
31.   Fuller PP93/4

Notes to Chapter 10
1.   Barker & Robbins Vol 2 P283
2.   Barker & Robbins Vol 2 PP233-240
3.   Barker & Robbins Vol 2 P284
4.   Barker & Robbins Vol 2 P271
5.   Barker & Robbins Vol 2 P272
6.   Wallace P237
7.   Barker & Robbins Vol2 P282
8.   Barker & Robbins Vol2 P286 and Clegg P10
9.   Bagwell P517
10.   Bagwell PP531-3
11.   Wallace P315
12.   Fuller PP134-140
13.   ed. Cooper P170
14.   Barker & Robbins Vol 2 P323

Notes to Chapter 11
1.   Fuller P112
2.   Barker & Robbins Vol 2 P326
3.   Clegg P72
4.   Glatter "London busmen – rise and fall of a rank and file movement" in International
      Socialism No 74 Jan 1975, P6
5.   Fuller PP114/5
6.   Fuller P115
7.   Fuller P115
8.   Glatter P7
9.   Fuller PP116/7
10.   Fuller PP117/8
11.   Glatter P7
12.   Glatter P7
13.   Fuller P123
14.   Clegg P106
15.   Fuller P123
16.   Glatter P8 and correspondence with Laurie Akehurst
17.   Clegg P106
18.   Glatter P8
19.   Clegg P121
20.   Fuller P140
21.   Fuller PP145. 147
22.   Fuller P149
23.   Fuller P151
24.   Fuller P138
25.   Fuller P151

26.   Fuller PP152/3
27.   Glatter PP10/11
28.   Barker & Robbins Vol 2 P327
29.   Fuller P156
30.   Ed Cooper P170
31.   Bagwell P553
32.   Bagwell PP562/3
33.   Bagwell P587

Notes to Chapter 12
1.   Ed. Cooper P104
2.   Wallace PP283/4
3.   Barker & Robbins Vol 2 PP307/8
4.   Ed. Cooper P110
5.   Ed. Cooper P112
6.   Clegg P77
7.   Clegg P95
8.   Fuller P184
9.   Fuller P177
10.   Fuller P183

Notes to Chapter 13
1.   Fuller PP187-8
2.   Barker & Robbins Vol 2 PP308-9
3.   Fuller P189
4.   Barker & Robbins Vol 2 P327
5.   Fuller P188
6.   Fuller P189
7.   Fuller P186
8.   Bagwell P601
9.   Barker & Robbins Vol 2 PP338, 352
10.   Barker & Robbins Vol 2 P352
11.   Clegg P95
12.   Women at Work on London's Transport, Tempus 2004, P126
13.   Barker & Robbins Vol 2 P351
14.   Ed. Cooper P114
15.   Fuller P190
16.   Fuller PP191-3
17.   Fuller PP193-8
18.   Fuller P202
19.   Fuller PP205-7
20.   Fuller PP205-6
21.   Wallace P316

Notes to Chapter 14
1.   Fuller P232
2.   Fuller P212
3.   Fuller P204
4.   Fuller P223
5.   Fuller P224

6. Fuller PP225-6
7. Fuller PP227-8
8. On and Off the Rails, Sir John Elliot, Allen & Unwin 1982
9. Barker & Robbins Vol 2 PP354, 357
10. Barker & Robbins Vol 2 P353
11. Fuller P226
12. Fuller PP226-9
13. Bagwell P654
14. Bagwell PP654-9

Notes to Chapter 15
1. Fuller P229
2. Fuller PP232-3
3. Fuller PP234-6
4. Barker & Robbins Vol 2 P355
5. Fuller PP211-2
6. Fuller PP214-7
7. Fuller P213
8. Bagwell Vol 2 P169
9. Bagwell Vol 2 P270
10. Bagwell Vol 2 P273
11. Bagwell Vol 2 P278
12. Bagwell Vol 2 PP273-4
13. Fuller P209
14. Bagwell Vol 2 PP288-291

Notes to Chapter 17
1. Bagwell Vol. 2 PP267-270
2. Bagwell Vol. 2 P270
3. Fuller P238
4. Bagwell Vol. 2 PP273-5
5. Bagwell Vol. 2 PP281-2
6. Women at Work on London's Transport, LT Museum Tempus, P126
7. Bagwell Vol 2 P283
8. Bagwell Vol 2 P285
9. Bagwell Vol 2 PP347-352
10. Bagwell Vol 2 PP286-8
11. Bagwell Vol 2 PP291-3
12. Bagwell Vol 2 PP370-1
13. Fuller P242
14. Fuller P243
15. Wallace P461
16. Fuller PP244-5
17. Fuller PP246-7
18. Fuller P247

Notes to Chapter 18
1. 'Driven by Ideals – a History of ASLE&F', Robert Griffiths, ASLE&F 2005, PP230-1
2. Griffiths P236
3. Griffiths P237

4.   Griffiths P241
5.   Rails Through the Clay, 2nd Edition, Croome & Jackson, Capital Transport 1993, P468
6.   Croome & Jackson PP420-1
7.   Wallace P468

Notes to Chapter 19
1.   Wallace P462
2.   Wallace P463
3.   Wallace P464
4.   Griffiths P248
5.   Fuller PP248-9
6.   Fuller P245
7.   Wallace P465
8.   Fuller P277
9.   Fuller P279
10.   Fuller P280
11.   Fuller P291
12.   Wallace P466
13.   Wallace P467

Notes to Chapter 20
1.   Griffiths PP256-7
2.   Wallace PP468-9
3.   Plundering London Underground, Janine Booth, Merlin Press 2013, PP12-17

Notes to Chapter 21
1.   Plundering London Underground by Janine Booth, Merlin Press 2013, PP33-34
2.   Booth, PP59-71 for a full description of this difficult period.
3.   Never on Our Knees by Mike Berlin, Pluto Press 2006, PP138-140
4.   Booth P75
5.   Berlin PP156-163
6.   Booth P23
7.   Booth P48
8.   Booth P78
9.   Booth P83
10.   Booth P96
11.   Booth P107
12.   Booth P121
13.   Booth PP134-137 for a full examination of the failings of the PPP
14.   Booth PP151-160

APPENDIX 1
THE 1911 ROYAL COMMISSION ON THE RAILWAY CONCILIATION AND ARBITRATION SCHEME OF 1907

The verbatim minutes of this extremely thorough enquiry were published by Her Majesty's Stationery Office in 1911 and amount to 788 pages of text. I have picked out some of the more interesting contributions, mostly from the Trade Union side.

PP1-17 J.E.Williams, General Secretary of the ASRS raises first the practical difficulties of finding arbitrators, and delays in the process. He complains of the insistence of the companies that the secretary of the Sectional Boards must be an employee of the company not an official of the Union. "In making the suggestion that the secretary for that one board should be outside the employment of the company I think I am only advocating what is generally accepted now as not only a reasonable procedure but a very beneficial procedure" (P7). "I do feel that it is the real kernel to the whole situation, and the men feel this also, in view of the fact that in the whole of the mining industry and in really the whole of the industries of this country that principle has been conceded to them" (P8). He wants all issues to be eligible for the scheme: "The scheme hitherto has only permitted the question of hours and rates of wages to be discussed. When I come to look at the schemes of arbitration and conciliation that are recorded in the Board of Trade publication I see that they are entitled to the recognition of their leaders in dealing with matters of general dispute" (P8). He wants a national board standing above the individual companies: "I feel sure that the work of this national board would be very small if the officials of the organisation were recognised and accepted in the deliberations of the other board; but in the event of large points of dispute arising which they may not be able to settle, then I suggest that there should be a national board instituted." He wants seats allocated to the three Unions in proportion to their membership, and notes that the UPSS is not part of the scheme. He claims "The right of the Unions to deal with all matters affecting the employees. I mean that they should correspond and so on" (P9). Chairman Sir David Harrel: "But there must always be a section that would not be satisfied with an award" – Williams: "I am decidedly of the opinion that we would have a large majority of the men exercising a reasonable disposition that would ensure the carrying out of the award. I think that the severe restrictions provide material for the more violent men to get adherents to their cause. I say if … there had been an avenue to consider the hundred and one other grievances that have largely contributed to this unrest, we should not have had the recent railway strike" (P12). Mr Henderson: "Am I correct in concluding that the whole object of your evidence today has been to point out the limitations of the 1907 scheme, with the sole idea of securing its amendment?" Williams: "Quite". (P12)

The membership of the ASRS was put at 100,000 – 46% of those eligible to join. They do not organise in the workshops. Between the Unions they have 75% of railwaymen organised. There are about 300,000 operating (traffic) staff in total.

Chairman, re election of sectional boards: "Then there should be no distinction drawn between Union men and non-Union men?" Williams: "No, there never has been so far. I wish the railway companies would draw that distinction and that they would only give these concessions to Union men, as Union men have of course obtained them". "How do you propose that the railwaymen's organisation should find representation on this board? They would have to take their chance in the ordinary way?". Williams: "Quite. Same as hitherto". At no point does he question the principle of the scheme.

PP17-27 Albert Fox, General Secretary ASLE&F. Claims to represent about 50% of drivers, firemen and loco cleaners. Insists on these grades having their own section in the scheme and that the companies must not add in other grades. Mentions issues that are not covered by the scheme, especially disciplinary punishments, lack of promotion in seniority, etc.

PP27-37 Thomas Lowth, General Secretary GRWU takes a completely different approach. Has 10,000 members in the traffic department, plus goods, permanent way and 10,000 in the workshops – the workshops were not included in the Conciliation scheme. "The men employed in the shops do not want to be included in the scheme of 1907 and those who are included want to get liberated from it". We want "The abolition of the Conciliation and Arbitration scheme of 1907, in consequence of its uselessness to meet the requirements of the employees on the railways, and its ineffectiveness in the joint administration of the awards and obtaining interpretation of same from the arbitrator". (P27) Chairman: "You observed that Mr Williams in giving his evidence as regards representation did not go directly for any Representation of his Union". Lowth: "I have definite instructions not to support anything by way of a new scheme that does not give full recognition of the railway Trade Unions in that scheme. Our experience is where we have recognition we have less trouble. With regard to the construction of the sectional boards and election of representatives we are not there and we have no influence. They are all employees on those boards right away to the central board ... we have in a marked degree lost the control that we had previous to that agreement (1907) and I respectfully suggest that we would regain that control by Trade Union recognition". This is a particularly significant point. When I was first elected to LT Sectional Council No9 in 1975 it was made clear by the TU side secretary that we were not bound by Union policy or under the control of NUR Head Office.

Chairman: "Take the North Eastern railway case ... where I understand the Trade Union representatives have been recognised". Answers from Tom Lowth show that he wanted to use recognition to give him and the Union power to call out staff on sympathy strikes to build a national movement or dispute on an issue rather than having it restricted to one company. Chairman: "You want to get rid of this conciliation board altogether" – "Yes". Chairman: "Mr Fox (ASLE&F) and Mr Williams (ASRS) have both suggested that there should be a method ... of settling these disputes by conciliation and arbitration – do you share this view?". Lowth "For preference no boards at all ... the alternative would be that if the Trade Unions and railway companies could not settle the difference between them" there should be a tribunal "without boards" ie direct negotiation between company and Union with conciliation and arbitration only at the very top. Clearly the Chairman is trying to insert a wedge between the GRWU and the other unions but there is a genuine difference of approach.

Chairman: "Would it be your view that there should be no stoppage of work until the dispute had been settled by that Tribunal". Lowth: "I should highly favour that". Mr Henderson: "You have urged in your evidence very strongly the entire abolition of the scheme of 1907. How did the men you represent take it when they became aware that you, on their behalf, had signed the scheme?" Lowth: "Rather reluctantly ... there was a discussion".

PP252-266 Alexander Walkden General Secretary RCA "we have 15,000 members out of a total number employed of 61,361 men clerks, 9,044 lad clerks and 8,684 station masters, a gross total of 79,089 in the grade I represent ... there are just a few in the ASRS but they do not at present invite them to join. They made an arrangement in 1897 under which they ceased to canvass for clerks to join their Society. Our own organisation was then formed and it is the only organisation representing that grade". Chairman: "You say you wished to join the scheme in 1907 but you were not included?" – "That is so. I think all the branches of the Association passed strong resolutions protesting against their exclusion". Chairman: "The scheme was rightly limited to the sections of employees who came within the term 'engaged in the manipulation of traffic". Walkden: "I wish to say that the clerical staff on the railways are doubly interested in this matter. Firstly because they desire fair and reasonable facilities for getting their own grievances dealt with, and secondly because they are usually called upon to perform manual labour of other grades in case of a strike , and thus to act as blacklegs. They object very strongly on principle to that and those who do comply, sometimes under intimidatory pressure from the companies, incur serious ill will from the other men over whom in the future they have to exercise supervision in a very large number of cases. That causes general ill feeling between the outdoor grades and the office staff and that friction is obviously detrimental to the satisfactory and expeditious despatch of business. Then again, clerks object strongly on the ground of public safety against being required to act as guards and signalmen or stokers in case of a strike. They prefer to be strictly neutral". This lengthy quotation sheds interesting light on the RCA's view that the Conciliation scheme could protect them from acting as scabs on strikes, and the possible compromising position of supervisors following such action.

Walkden: "In the conference of May 1910 the clerical staff registered a decision against the scheme ... The first point we wish to urge is that Trade Unions should be recognised, including our own ... for the purpose of conducting general movements ... and for dealing with local and individual grievances". Chairman: "Though you were favourable in 1908 and 1909 to this scheme, you have entirely abandoned the idea of coming into anything like the 1907 scheme?" – "Yes, we have done so partly due to the slowness of dealing with cases". Chairman: "Is Sunday work quite exceptional or is it fairly regular?" Walkden:" To enable one man to have a clear day on Sunday that involves in many cases working as long as 16 or 17 hours on a Sunday ... In some districts such as London Sunday work gives a heavier day than the average weekday ... a movement for payment for Sunday work on the Metropolitan Railway took two years and five months and is still unsettled. The allowances given are very unsatisfactory. Instead of giving the clerks a full day's pay for their Sunday work as on other lines, they give them small allowances ranging from 1/6 to 2/6 ... On the Metropolitan District Railway they started work on the subject as far back as October 12th 1906. After four years eleven months the matter is still unsettled and the men are denied access to the boardroom ... and their treatment is very unsatisfactory altogether".

PP210-218 Samuel Chorlton General Secretary United Pointsmen and Signalmen's Society (UPSS). Chairman: "You say that the Railway Conciliation Scheme gives the railway companies opportunities to insist that time wasting formalities shall be gone through before the conciliation machinery can be operated?" – "Yes". The Society has been in existence since 1882 and has 4,000 members out of a total of 35,000 signalmen, though some are members of the ASRS. Mr Henderson: "I think you were not a signatory to the 1907 scheme" – "No ... I objected to it ... on the ground that, in the first place, it was an arrangement about which the men had never been consulted; in the second place I did not consider the signatories had any real authority to sign it, and in the third place I foresaw ....that it would give the companies opportunities to place delays in the way of men's efforts to better their terms of service"

How some managers viewed the scheme:

PP 484-494 Sam Fay, General Manager of the Great Central Railway, who is often credited with being the brains behind the Conciliation scheme put forward by Lloyd George. "I think there should be some penalty for inflicting loss on the community". Under the Canadian Act "It is a penal offence to strike or advocate a strike during the consideration of the question under arbitration. If you had got that tacked on to the Conciliation scheme here ....it ought at any rate to do something to prevent a strike". "I am aware that Mr Bell of the ASRS in 1907 stated distinctively that he had no desire ... to interfere with any question affecting the management of the railway or the discipline of staff, but I am afraid it would be almost impossible to devise any recognition (of the Trade Unions) in the way in which it is asked for without inter- fering with discipline. It seems to me that in the very nature of things if the Trade Unions, if one may put it so, co-operate with the railway companies in connection with matters of discipline, it must be in the direction of relaxation of regulation and in no other way".

APPENDIX 2
EXTRACTS FROM LONDON TRANSPORT EXECUTIVE
'SCHEME FOR THE ESTABLISHMENT OF NEGOTIATING AND CONSULTATIVE MACHINERY AND PROCEDURE FOR DEALING WITH CASES OF DISCIPLINE – SALARIED AND CONCILIATION STAFF

25ᵗʰ September 1957   PD533

Known as the 'Blue Book'

2. ESTABLISHMENT AND FUNCTIONS OF SECTIONAL COUNCILS

Sectional Councils shall be established as set out in Clause 3 consisting of representatives of the Management and Staff to provide a recognised means for the discussion and where appropriate the settlement of matters arising out of the Staffs employment, such as:-

(a) the local interpretation and administration of agreements governing employment;

(b) questions relating to working hours, reliefs, timekeeping, holidays, rosters, seniority, etc

(c) questions of physical health, welfare, safety appliances and prevention of accidents;

(d) questions affecting economy and improvements in all matters relating to the operations of the Executive;

(e) publicity as to the rules and regulations, etc;

(f) questions of mutual interest affecting the well-being of the staff or of operation.

Questions which are not covered by the above provisions, with the exception of questions relating to the establishment of standard rates of pay and conditions of service, may be discussed at meetings of the Councils and referred to the Management for consideration.

A Council shall not come to a decision upon any matter which does not fall within the authority of the officials who are members of the Council.

In the event of matters of joint interest arising which concern two or more Councils, such Councils shall meet as a joint body for the purpose of considering the matters in question.

Sub-committees may be appointed from Sectional Councils as required. The number of members serving on sub-committees shall be kept to a minimum.

3. COMPOSITION OF SECTIONAL COUNCILS

The Sectional Councils shall consist of elected members of the staff as follows:

No of Council	Section	Number of Representatives
1	Clerical and Technical Staff	14–10 Clerical Classes A, B and W (Spl) and Technical Assistants 4 Senior Clerical Assistants And Engineering Assistants
2	Booking Office Staff	7–2 District 3 Tubes 2 Metropolitan

3	Train Wages Staff	11–2 District
		5 Tubes
		4 Metropolitan (1 Steam)
4	Station, etc, Wages Staff	10–2 District
		4 Tubes
		4 Metropolitan
5	Engineering Supervisory Staff	3–1 Civil
		1 Signals
		1 Mechanical
6	Traffic etc Supervisory Staff	5–1 District
		2 Tubes
		2 Metropolitan
7	Signal Engineering Wages Staff	8–4 Signal Maintenance
		2 Signal Installation and New Works
		1 Telephones
		1 Cables
8	Permanent Way Engineering Wages Staff	9–2 District
		3 Tubes (1nights)
		3 Metropolitan
		1 Miscellaneous
9	Mechanical Engineering Wages Staff	8–2 District
		4 Tubes
		1 Metropolitan
		1 Lifts and Escalators

Not more than a corresponding number of officials shall be nominated on behalf of the Management.

Only staff who are members of a Trade Union party to this Agreement shall be eligible to make nominations for or to be nominated as staff representatives of a Sectional Council.

4. CHANNELS OF COMMUNICATION

Applications with respect to any matters which, under the Scheme, are referable to a Section Council should normally first be submitted by the employee (or employees) concerned to the official immediately in charge...

Failing a reply within 7 days or a satisfactory settlement within that period, the matter may then be referred to the Staff Side Secretary of the Sectional Council concerned and it may then be raised with the official in charge of the division or section concerned...

A reply may be given in correspondence or the matter may be discussed by the Staff Side Secretary and the appropriate Staff Side representative (or representatives) concerned with the official in charge of the division or section concerned, or the appropriate official or officer at departmental headquarters. These discussions will be held with the object of facilitating consideration of matters raised and if possible resolving them without waiting for a meeting of the Sectional Council.

Failing a satisfactory settlement within 14 days from the date upon which a matter became the subject of an approach by the Staff Side Secretary the matter is automatically eligible for the agenda of the appropriate Sectional Council concerned unless otherwise agreed between the parties...

5. DECISION BY AGREEMENT
Every decision of a Sectional Council or Councils meeting as a joint body to be effective shall be by agreement of both sides.

6. FAILURE TO AGREE
If a Sectional Council or a joint meeting of Sectional Councils fails to come to a satisfactory settlement by agreement, after discussion at two or more meetings, the question at issue may be discussed between the staff representatives concerned and the Officer appointed to deal with such matters at second stage.

Failing agreement between staff representatives and the Officer appointed to deal with the matter at second stage, the matter may be referred for discussion between the headquarters officials of the Trade Union or Unions concerned and the Chief Officer. It is assumed that in all minor matters proceedings shall not be carried beyond this stage...

Subsequently, if necessary, matters other than those of a minor character, may be referred to the Negotiating Committee (hereinafter referred to)...

8. FACILITIES FOR ATTENDING MEETINGS
All members of Sectional Councils shall be given reasonable facilities for attending meetings of the Councils, and shall be given time off for this purpose without loss of pay. Free travel on the services (other than Green Line Coaches) of the Executive will be provided for all members and Secretaries of Sectional Councils for the purpose of attending meetings of Councils...

10. PROCEDURE FOR DEALING WITH CASES OF DISCIPLINE
In connection with cases of discipline, it is agreed that the principles of Clause 72 of the Report of the Royal Commission appointed to investigate and report on the working of the Railway Conciliation and Arbitration Scheme of 1907, together with the addition thereto agreed between the Railway Companies and representatives of the National Union of Railwaymen and the Associated Society of Locomotive Engineers and Firemen at meetings held in October 1915, shall be adopted.

The procedure as now amplified is as under:-

Employees charged with misconduct, neglect of duty, or other breaches of discipline, will be permitted to state their defence, to call witnesses, and to advance any extenuating circumstances, before their officers, prior to a final decision being arrived at. At such interview they may be accompanied by an advocate. In all cases an employee shall be informed in writing of the nature of the offence, and following the interview the punishment (if any) it is proposed to inflict. Where doubts arise, or where serious results to employees are likely to follow, the cases should be placed before the higher officials of the Executive. Appeals after punishment lead to a difficult position, and the necessity for them should be avoided.

If after such investigation of a charge against an employee he is adjudged guilty and is to be punished for the offence, he shall have the right of appeal to a superior officer for a reconsideration of his case, provided that that such right of appeal shall not extend to cases of a trivial character.

Any such appeal must be made in writing within seven days. If the employee so desires, he may be heard in person, and in that case also, he may be accompanied at the interview with the superior officer by a spokesman, who may either be a fellow workmate or a representative nominated by the man's Trade Union.

No member of the staff may attend as advocate or spokesman on behalf of employees over whom he has the responsibility of supervision.

NEGOTIATING COMMITTEE

1. There shall be established a Negotiating Committee which shall consist of:-
   (a) Six representatives of the London Transport Executive, appointed by the Executive, and
   (b) Six representatives of the employees of the London Transport Executive, two of whom shall be appointed by the National Union of Railwaymen, two of whom shall be appointed by the Associated Society of Locomotive Engineers and Firemen, and two of whom shall be appointed by the Transport Salaried Staffs Association (hereinafter collectively referred to as "the Unions").

2. Applications made by all or any of the Unions and/or by the London Transport Executive for the making or revision of agreements and regulations governing the rates of pay, hours of duty and other conditions of service of the employees of the London Transport Executive...shall be considered by the Negotiating Committee. The Negotiating Committee shall consider any matter referred to it in accordance with the provisions of Clause 6 of the Staff Councils Scheme...

6. In the event of the Negotiating Committee being unable to reach agreement, the question at issue shall, at the instance of the London Transport Executive or all or any of the Unions be referred to the Wages Board (hereinafter referred to)...

WAGES BOARD

8. There shall be established a Wages Board which shall consist of:-
   (a) A chairman, to be appointed by agreement between the parties, or, failing agreement, by the Minister of Labour. The appointment may be for a specified period or for the hearing of particular issues.
   (b) One representative to be appointed from time to time by the London Transport Executive
   (c) One representative to be appointed from time to time by the Unions.

No official of the London Transport Executive or official or member of the Union or Unions concerned shall be eligible for appointment as a member of the Wages Board. The Wages Board may be assisted by representatives of the parties concerned sitting as assessors...

The assessors shall be either officials of the London Transport Executive or officials or members of the three Unions concerned...

11. The findings of the Wages Board if not accepted by all parties to this scheme, shall be considered as soon as may be possible after its issue, at a joint conference of the London Transport Executive and of the Unions.

12. No withdrawal of labour or lock-out or interference with efficient operation shall take place until the cause of dispute has been dealt with under these proposals, and unless a settlement has not been reached within 28 days after the result of the deliberations of the Wages Board has been published...

BIBLIOGRAPHY

Alcock, G.W., Fifty Years of Railway Trade Unionism. Co-operative Printing Society 1922

Bagwell, Dr Philip, The Railwaymen, Allen & Unwin, Vol 1 1963, Vol 2 1982

Barker, T & Robbins, M, A History of London Transport, Allen & Unwin, Vol 1 1963, Vol 2 1976

Barman, Christian, A biography of Frank Pick, David & Charles 1979

Berlin, Mike, Never on Our Knees, Pluto Press 2006

Booth, Janine, Plundering London Underground, Merlin Press 2013

Boston, Sarah, Women Workers and the Trade Unions, Davis-Poynter 1980

Braybon, Gail, Women Workers in the First World War, Croom Helm 1981

Clegg, H.A., Labour Relations in London Transport, Basil Blackwell 1950

Cole, G.D.H., A short history of the British working class movement, Allen & Unwin 1948

Cooper, Terence, ed, The Wheels Used to Talk to Us, Tallis Publishing, 1977

Croome & Jackson, Rails Through the Clay, 2nd Edition, Capital Transport 1993

Drake, Barbara, Women in the Trade Unions, Virago 1984

Elliot, Sir John, On and Off the Rails, Allen & Unwin 1982

Fuller, Ken, Radical Aristocrats, 2nd Edition, Ishi Press 2011

Gibbon, G & Bell, R, History of the London County Council 1889-1939, MacMillan 1939

Glatter, P, London Busmen – rise and fall of a rank & file movement, in International Socialism No. 74, Jan 1975

Gordon, Alex, Unity is Strength, RMT 2012

Griffiths, Robert, Driven by Ideals – a history of ASLE&F, ASLE&F 2005

Hobsbawm, Eric, Labour's Turning Point 1880-1900, Harvester Press 1974

Minutes of Evidence before the Royal Commission on the Railway Conciliation and Arbitration Scheme of 1907, HMSO 1911

Phillips, G.A., The General Strike, Weidenfeld & Nicolson 1976

Rotondaro, Anna, Women at Work on London's Transport, Tempus 2005

Wallace, Malcolm, Single or Return, TSSA 1996

INDEX